CHILDHOOD
SOCIAL DEVELOPMENT

CHILDHOOD
SOCIAL DEVELOPMENT:
Contemporary Perspectives

edited by
Harry McGurk

Director
Thomas Coram Research Unit, Institute of Education, University of London, London, U.K.

LEA LAWRENCE ERLBAUM ASSOCIATES, PUBLISHERS LEA
Hove (UK)   Hillsdale (USA)

Reprinted 1993

Lawrence Erlbaum Associates Ltd., Publishers
27 Palmeira Mansions
Church Road
Hove
East Sussex, BN3 2FA
UK

British Library Cataloguing in Publication Data

Childhood Social Development: Contemporary perspectives
   I. McGurk, Harry
   155.4

   ISBN 0-86377-275-7 (Pbk)

Cover by Joyce Chester
Subject index by Sue Ramsey

Typeset by J&L Composition, Filey, North Yorkshire
Printed and bound by BPCC Wheatons Ltd., Exeter

Contents

Contributors

John Archer
Department of Psychology, Lancashire Polytechnic, Preston PR1 2TQ, U.K.

John Archer is Professor of Psychology at Lancashire Polytechnic, Preston. He is co-author (with Barbara Lloyd) of *Sex and Gender*, and author of *The Behavioural Biology of Aggression* (both Cambridge University Press). He had research interests in gender roles and their development, aggression and grief and loss. At the time of writing (1991–92) John Archer was a Simon Industrial & Professional Fellow at the University of Manchester, working on a book on Loss and Grief.

Jeanne Brooks-Gunn
Center for the Study of Young Children and Families, Teachers College, Columbia University, New York, NY 10027, U.S.A.

Dr Brooks-Gunn is Virginia and Leonard Marx Professor in Child Development and Director of the Center for the Study of Young Children and Families. In addition, she is the Director of the Adolescent Study Program at Teachers College and the St Luke's-Roosevelt Hospital Center of Columbia University. A developmental psychologist, she received her Master's degree from Harvard University and her PhD from the University of Pennsylvania. Her speciality is policy-oriented research focusing on familial influences upon children's development and intervention efforts aimed at ameliorating the developmental delays seen in poor children.

Charles Crook
Department of Psychology, University of Durham, South Road, Durham DH1 3LE, U.K.

Charles Crook is lecturer in Psychology at Durham University. His published research includes studies of sensory development during infancy and social development in early childhood. He is currently studying how new technology can enrich social processes inherent within educational practice.

Hans G. Furth
Life Cycle Institute, The Catholic University of America, Washington DC 20064, U.S.A.

Hans G. Furth has been Professor of Psychology at the Catholic University of America since 1960. He is author of *Thinking without Language* (Free Press, 1966), *Piaget and Knowledge* (Prentice-Hall, 1969), *Piaget for Teachers* (Prentice-Hall, 1970), *Deafness and Learning* (Wadsworth, 1973), *Thinking Goes to School* (Oxford University Press, 1975), *The World of Grown-ups: Children's Conceptions of Society* (Elsevier, 1980), and *Knowledge as Desire: An Essay on Freud and Piaget* (Columbia University Press, 1987). He is currently engaged on research on the endogenous origins of society in the development of children.

Willard W. Hartup
Institute of Child Development, University of Minnesota, 51 E. River Road, Minneapolis, MN 55108, U.S.A.

Willard W. Hartup is Professor of Child Psychology and Rodney S. Wallace Professor for the Advancement of Teaching and Learning, University of Minnesota. He has been interested in childhood social development for 40 years, especially the development significance of peer relations. He is former Editor of *Child Development* and is currently (1992) President-elect of the Society for Research in Child Development.

Robert A. Hinde
St John's College, Cambridge CB2 1TP, U.K.

Robert A. Hinde was formerly a Royal Society Research Professor and Honorary Director of the Medical Research Council Unit on the Development and Integration of Behaviour, Madingley, Cambridge, and is currently Master of St John's College, Cambridge. He has carried out research in the fields of ethology, child development and interpersonal relationships. Among his books are *Towards Understanding Relationships* (1979), and *Individuals, Relationships and Culture* (1987).

Steven R. Kane
Life Cycle Institute, The Catholic University of America, Washington DC 20064, U.S.A.

Steven Kane is a doctoral candidate in the Human Development program of the Psychology Department at the Catholic University of America. He is currently conducting a longitudinal, ethnographic investigation of the development of peer culture through pretend play in a preschool classroom. He is also interested in the social development of children with autism and other communication handicaps.

Harry McGurk
Thomas Coram Research Unit, Institute of Education, University of London, 27/28 Woburn Square, London WC1H 0AA, U.K.

Harry McGurk is Director of the Thomas Coram Research Unit at the Institute of Education, University of London. He is the author of an introductory text on child development and has edited three volumes on various aspects of childhood social development. At the Thomas Coram Research Unit he has responsibility for a major, multidisciplinary programme of fundamental and applied research on a range of topics concerned with the development of children and their families.

Roberta L. Paikoff
Institute for Juvenile Research, Department of Psychiatry, University of Illinois at Chicago, 95th St. at King's Drive, Chicago, IL 60628, U.S.A.

Roberta L. Paikoff is Assistant Professor of Psychology at the Institute for Juvenile Research in the Department of Psychiatry, University of Illinois at Chicago. She completed her PhD in Child Psychology at the Institute of Child Development, University of Minnesota, and was a postdoctoral fellow at Hebrew University and at the Educational Testing Service. She has recently edited a volume on family relationships during adolescence in the *New Directions for Child Development* series, and co-authored, with Jeanne Brooks-Gunn, a review of the literature on parent–child relationships at puberty. Her major research interests involve studying the interplay among developmental processes during the transitions into and out of adolescence, with a particular emphasis on family relationships, constructions of the self, future planning and risk-taking behaviour.

H. Rudolph Schaffer
Department of Psychology, University of Strathclyde, Turnbull Building, George Street, Glasgow G1 1RD, U.K.

Rudolph Schaffer is Professor of Psychology at the University of Strathclyde. He is the author of a number of books dealing with early social development, including *The Growth of Sociability* (Penguin), *Mothering* (Fontana and Harvard University

Press), *The Child's Entry into a Social World* (Academic Press) and *Making Decisions About Children* (Blackwell). His research interests focus on development in the early years, with particular reference to socialisation processes, the development of interpersonal relationships and infant behaviour. He is founding editor of the journal *Social Development*.

James Youniss
Life Cycle Institute, The Catholic University of America, Washington DC 20064, U.S.A.

James Youniss is Professor of Psychology and Director of the Life Cycle Institute at the Catholic University of America. He has devoted the past decade of research to children's understanding of interpersonal relationships and published two books on this topic: *Parents and Peers in Social Development* (University of Chicago Press, 1980) and, with Jacqueline Smollar, *Adolescent Relations with Mothers, Fathers and Friends* (University of Chicago Press, 1985). He is currently working on the socialisation of knowledge, including the social formation of the discipline of child studies.

Editor's Introduction

Almost a decade and a half ago I had the pleasure of working with a group of colleagues to produce a book on childhood social development that provided an account of some of the important issues engaging researchers in the field at that time (McGurk, 1978). The book was well received and is still to be found on reading lists in many colleges and universities. However, the field has progressed considerably since its publication. It seemed appropriate, therefore, to reflect this progress in a new volume on social development, and I contacted all the contributors to the earlier book, inviting them to join me in a new endeavour. Almost all of them agreed to do so. One of the original contributors, Anthony Ambrose, is no longer active in research in the field; the biological-evolutionary perspective about which he wrote in the 1978 book is reflected in the present volume in a chapter by Robert Hinde. Sadly, Corrinne Hutt, who contributed an important chapter on sex differences in social development to the earlier volume, died unexpectedly a year or so after its publication; a chapter on contemporary perspectives on sex differences in social development has been contributed by John Archer.

This volume comprises a collection of original essays on contemporary perspectives on social development, from infancy to adolescence, by prominent British and American scholars each of whom is actively engaged in research in this field. The aim of the book is not to provide a definitive account of all aspects of childhood social development. Accordingly, many topics are omitted that would commonly appear in a comprehensive textbook. Moreover, the present volume is not merely a revision or update of the 1978 book. Rather, the contributors were invited to reflect upon the current scene in social development research and to develop their own distinctive viewpoint and contribution to the field. What emerges is an account of research in action, and debate in progress, in this important area of contemporary developmental psychology.

The first three chapters of this volume are concerned with aspects of the interplay between biological and psycho-social processes in social development during infancy, childhood and adolescence. Chapters 4, 5 and 6 are each devoted to consideration of the development of social understanding, and the acquisition of social skills, as products of social processes. Chapter 7 examines the development of friendship between children and its contribution to their social growth. The final chapter highlights the cultural embeddedness of social development and discusses how our understanding of social development can be enhanced by taking account of cultural context.

Although each chapter is concerned with a different aspect of social development, there are a number of themes that recur throughout the volume. Two of these are worthy of particular comment, for they feature large in much contemporary thinking about social development. The first concerns the nature of social development. The acquisition of social understanding and the development of social skill are not individual achievements of children reared in isolation. Rather, they are the outcome of social processes in which the developing child engages, sometimes in unequal partnership with experienced adults, at other times in more equal partnership with peers and playmates; in both cases developmental change is a co-constructive outcome.

A second recurrent theme is a concern for developmental researchers to take fuller account than they may traditionally have done of the nature of the cultural settings in which social development occurs. Different cultures have different customs and artefacts, and these can constrain development in different ways. Although this issue is the specific focus of the final chapter of the volume, it is one that is also rehearsed from time to time in earlier chapters.

These two themes are reflected in several chapters, both in empirical and in theoretical contexts. Until relatively recently Piagetian cognitive-developmental theory overshadowed all other conceptualisations of developmental processes. Over the past decade or so, however, increasing dissatisfaction with Piaget's theoretical conceptualisations has been ex-pressed. With respect to the topic that is the focus of the present volume—social development—Piagetian theory and research have come under attack on two counts. First, even as a theorist of cognitive development, Piaget stands accused of ignoring a major aspect of such development, namely, the acquisition of social knowledge and understanding. In fact, during recent years, numerous studies of the development of societal understanding have been conducted from a Piagetian perspective (for example, Berti & Bombi, 1988; Furth, 1978).

These studies, however, have been carried out and interpreted within the standard individualistic-constructivist account of development originally advanced by Piaget, and so are vulnerable to the second general criticism of Piagetian theory and method. This concerns Piaget's failure to take into account the social context of development. Piaget's child is a social isolate embarked on an individual odyssey of scientific discovery on the basis of which individual conceptions of the world are constructed and internalised. There are no partners in this constructivist enterprise. Occasionally there may be encounters with other travellers engaged in their own journey of cognitive construction. Such encounters may even result in modification of pre-existing cognitive structures. However, even this reconstruction is conceptualised, in Piagetian theory, as neither shared nor socially distributed; cognitive change may be the outcome of social exchange, but the process of change itself is individual, not social.

During the past decade disaffection with the asocial nature of orthodox Piagetian theory has had its most salient manifestation in the growth of interest in the theory of the social construction of mind and cognition advanced by Lev Vygotsky (see Rogoff, 1990; Wertsch, 1985). As Schaffer (this volume) points out, Vygotsky has now overtaken Piaget in the citation stakes. Vygotsky's perspective on the nature of development is not directly represented in any of the chapters of the present volume, but the influence of Vygotsky's thought and theory is indirectly evident in a number of contributions, particularly those by Schaffer and by Youniss.

Like human morphology and human behaviour, human sociability has an evolutionary history. It is appropriate, therefore, that the first chapter of this volume, by Robert Hinde, should be devoted to a consideration of the extent to which ethological principles—derived largely from the study of animals in their natural habitats—can contribute to the psychological understanding of human social development. Two points need to be borne in mind, however. First, readers will search in vain in Hinde's chapter for advocacy of "nature" over "nurture"; fortunately, that arid debate features little, if at all, in this volume. Second, by corollary, although Hinde draws on data from studies of animals in their natural environments, there is no argument either that evidence from animal studies can demonstrate what is "natural" for humans, or that there is any biological or evolutionary imperative that whatever may be "natural" in any given situation is necessarily best. By contrast, Hinde argues for integration between different conceptual approaches to human development. Rather than comparing and contrasting rival approaches and assessing the validity of competing hypotheses, Hinde suggests that we should be seeking to understand the contributions that different perspectives have made to understanding human behaviour and development in all its complexity. He argues that integration should take place at the level of abstracting principles and concepts that have yielded insights in one domain and determining how they might be applicable to others. Employing this approach he explores how principles and concepts developed from the study of animal ethology can fruitfully be applied to the study of human social development.

Two further aspects of Hinde's chapter are also noteworthy. First, he points out that it is becoming increasingly recognised that many aspects of child development, social development in particular, can be fully understood only when the child is viewed as a contributing member of a network of relationships. It is within the context of relationships that development takes place. One of the most significant shifts of research focus over the past decade has been away from studying development as something that happens to, or is achieved by, *individuals* towards a view of development as a *co-constructive process*; a recurrent theme throughout this volume. Second, Hinde highlights how such an orientation entails conceptualising measures—whether derived from children or from adults—that are taken in social situations as being characteristics of *relationships* rather than of individuals. The implications of this perspective for theories of social development are considerable. For example, with respect to attachment theory (Ainsworth, 1982) it shifts the focus away from the concept of the insecurely attached *child* towards the notion of insecurity as a characteristic of the *relationship* between the child and a specific other. This, in turn, would imply a more differentiated concept of attachment than perhaps is entertained at present, and would also have implications for how the concept of attachment is utilised in the context of, for example, the contemporary debate over the influence of the experience of day care on young children's social and emotional development (cf. Belsky, 1988; Clarke-Stewart, 1988).

The theme of the complex interplay between biological and social influences on human development is also reflected in the second chapter of this volume, by John Archer, on the origins and development of sex and gender differentiation. Archer considers and rejects the argument that the behaviour and attitude stereotypes of gender roles have their origins in pre-existing bio-genetic characteristics such as temperament. Temperament and other similar characteristics are continuously distributed, with about equal variability, within both sexes. Gender stereotypic characteristics, such as aggression and assertiveness, are more dimorphic.

Archer also rejects the argument that gender role differences are wholly socially transmitted and maintained through, for example, child rearing and socialisation practices. While social transmission processes have a part to play in the maintenance of power and status differentials between the sexes and in the manner of expression of such differentials, such processes are held by Archer to be insufficient to account for the origins and universality of gender differentiation.

The account of the origin and development of gender roles that Archer does espouse takes as its starting point the acknowledged behavioural differences between male and female infants with respect to physical interaction and rough-and-tumble play. From the earliest months of life onwards boys manifest greater engagement in such activities than girls. Archer argues that girls find such patterns of interaction unattractive and unrewarding and that they are inclined, therefore, to avoid them. This initial, biologically determined, difference between the sexes is taken by Archer to provide a sufficient condition to facilitate segregation of the sexes as distinct groups. Thereafter, social and psychological processes can operate to produce gender role differentiation and stereotypy.

The primary social and psychological processes that Archer perceives as operating on initial sex segregation are those postulated by the social identity theory of intergroup relations. Thus Archer integrates a biological account of the origins of sex differentiation and segregation with a social psychological account of the development and maintenance of gender role differences. This account of the development of gender roles is one that, like the arguments advanced by Hinde, stresses the extent to which social development must be understood in the context of relationships. Throughout his chapter, Archer draws attention to the differences that emerge in the ways in which boys and girls relate to their peers. For example, from middle childhood boys tend to interact in large groups with other boys, girls in small groups with other girls; boys show more concern than girls for role conformity, while girls show a greater concern for intimacy; correspondingly, boys tend to have extensive, and girls intensive, relationships, and so on. Archer typifies boys and girls as essentially growing up in different cultures with different cultural styles. Thus, when, after puberty, heterosexual interactions increase, young men and young women both have to learn new ways of dealing with relationships although the culture from which young women emerge may provide a more adapted preparation for this transition than that afforded to young men. Certainly, differences in cultural style, to continue the metaphor, can contribute to difficulties and misunderstandings in cross-sex interactions during adolescence and adulthood.

It should be noted that, as with Hinde's chapter, Archer's contains no suggestion that natural is best. Archer locates the origins of sex segregation in a biological context. However, gender roles are not dictated by biological imperatives, but emerge as cultural products.

Chapter 3, by Jeanne Brooks-Gunn and Roberta Paikoff, also addresses the interplay between biological, social and psychological influences on social development. The focus of their chapter is on social development during adolescence. Brooks-Gunn and Paikoff argue cogently that the hormonal, physiological and associated physical changes that occur in boys and girls around puberty and immediately afterwards are the most significant biological events in the life of the individual since the prenatal period and the earliest years of life. These changes influence the ways in which boys and girls think and feel about themselves. They also affect how they are evaluated and responded to by peers, parents and society at large. Around adolescence significant changes are also occurring in cognitive ability. Accordingly, Brooks-Gunn and Paikoff argue, understanding social development during adolescence requires an integrative approach that takes account of mutual influences and interactions between biological, affective, cognitive and social processes. Brooks-Gunn and Paikoff present a model of how these complex, multi-dimensional interactions might be conceptualised, and proceed to present an interpretative account of relevant contemporary research in terms of their model. The chapter provides a valuable integrative perspective from which the complex processes of social development during adolescence can be viewed.

The chapter by Rudolph Schaffer, Chapter 4, and the succeeding chapters by Youniss and by Furth, illustrate how, over the past decade or so, psychological research on social development has increasingly reflected recognition of the extent to which social development itself involves the operation of social processes. Understanding social development requires that these processes are studied directly, not merely speculated upon.

Schaffer's particular concern is with what he refers to as "joint interaction episodes". These are social exchanges during which the individuals involved pay joint attention to and act jointly on an external object or event. Thus defined, joint interaction episodes can involve participants at any level of development. In Schaffer's chapter, however, the primary focus is on episodes involving an adult and a child.

For the student of social development, joint interaction episodes are of interest from at least two perspectives. First, they are developmental phenomena in their own right, subject to rapid change from the beginning of post-natal life. For example, although joint interaction episodes can be observed to occur betwen caretaker and child from early infancy, their structure initially is quite asymmetrical in terms of the relative contributions by the participants. The infant's contributions are initially spontaneous and relatively random; it requires a sensitive, skilled interlocutor to manage the episode and to transform the infant's behaviour into an action, thus integrating it into a meaningful social exchange. For example, the infant's momentary visual attention to a salient object can serve to specify a topic on which the adult caretaker may comment. With increasing age the infant's contribution to joint interaction episodes becomes less spontaneous and more intentional, and the structure of the episodes becomes more symmetrical.

There is a further structural aspect to the developmental character of joint interaction episodes. Initially each episode is relatively brief, involving only a few turns before a new episode begins. Along with increasing age, not only do episodes become more symmetrical; they also become more extended.

The second perspective from which joint interaction episodes are of concern to social developmentalists is more processual and functional. Now the focus shifts from interaction episodes as interesting objects of study to interaction episodes as contributors to the very process of development. The concern becomes one of understanding the contribution that participation in joint interaction episodes makes to development across a variety of domains—social, cognitive and societal. From this perspective, participation in joint interaction episodes not only enhances the child's social competence but also provides the context within which the child acquires new knowledge and arrives at new understandings about the physical, social and psychological worlds. Here there is a clear analogy between the functional status of Vygotsky's "zone of proximal development" (see Rogoff, 1990; Wertsch, 1985) and joint interaction episodes. Schaffer touches on this analogy but it is not a primary focus of the chapter.

Although Schaffer's chapter encompasses the status of joint interaction episodes from both the perspectives described, his primary concern is with their functional status—with the developmental functions served by the young child's participation in joint interaction episodes. Two questions are addressed: "Do joint interactions work?" and, if so, "How do they work?".

To the first question, Schaffer offers a cautious but affirmative response. There is good evidence to suggest that, for example, in the short term at least, participation in joint interaction episodes enhances children's cognitive development. However, if we are to achieve anything approximating to a full understanding of the contribution of these episodes to the developmental process in the medium-to-long term, then evidence from carefully designed longitudinal studies will be required. Such evidence is lacking at the moment.

To the "how" question, Schaffer identifies the cognitive conflict induced by the necessity for the child to come to grips with the perspective of the interactive partner as the ingredient of joint interaction episodes most likely to be implicated in bringing about developmental change. Here Schaffer espouses the arguments originally advanced by Willem Doise and his colleagues (Mugny & Doise, 1978) but generalises them beyond Doise's peer conflict model.

In addition to providing a stimulating and provocative overview of a new and rapidly developing area of social development research, Schaffer's chapter also offers an agenda for future research. The need for more longitudinal research on the functional effectiveness of joint interaction episodes has already been identified. However, there is also a need for more research on the "how?" question. Although the cognitive conflict model is a productive and challenging one, there are many joint interactions in which the developing child participates that involve no conflict of any kind. We need to understand how they, too, make their contribution to the developmental process.

In his chapter on parent and peer relations and the emergence of cultural consciousness, Chapter 5 of this volume, Youniss is critical of theories of social development that fail to locate development in its cultural context. He is critical, too, of theoretical accounts that, while appropriately contextualising development in culture, speak of developmental processes exclusively in terms of cultural transmission or socialisation. Youniss acknowledges Piaget's failure to recognise that developmental processes are rooted in culture. He also argues, however, that to attribute social development solely to processes of social and cultural transmission is to leave the child with too passive a role to play. The challenge, as perceived by Youniss, is to create a theoretical account of development that integrates analyses of processes of cultural transmission and socialisation with proper attention to what is known of children's own active constructions.

Youniss offers a model that potentially meets these criteria by combining aspects of Piaget's epistemology with insights gained from research on children's relationships and interactions with peers and parents. Although he does not compare his model of development with that offered by Vygotsky, there are many points of contact between them. Youniss's model could serve as a much needed bridge between cultural and cognitive approaches to the study of social development and the development of social understanding.

In the integrated account of developmental processes offered by Youniss a significant role is identified for children's participation in discourse—both with peers and parents—as a context within which social knowledge is constructed, reconstructed, and, importantly, shared. This theme is reflected also in the succeeding chapter by Furth and Kane.

Furth is a Piagetian and a radical constructivist. He pioneered the early attempts to provide a cognitive-developmental account of children's acquisition of societal understanding (Furth, 1978). Along with Kane, he takes as the starting point for their chapter the marked discrepancy, or décalage, revealed in Furth's earlier work, between children's understanding of the physical and the social world; the former has a much more logically consistent quality before corresponding consistency is evident in the latter.

Furth's earlier work on children's understanding of society focused on their conceptualisations of the workings of such societal phenomena as the bank, work and the economy. These are all aspects of the social world of grown ups to which children have relatively little direct access. In the present chapter Furth and Kane assess young children's social understanding as it is reflected in a world with which they are much more familiar; the world of pretence and fantasy play. This assessment, based on detailed analysis of the discourse that takes place during an extended "dressing-up" play session by three children aged between 4 and 6 years, unveils a level of complexity and sophistication in their social understanding undreamt of in the earlier work. When acting out their own social world these young girls reveal relatively precocious understanding of complex social rules and mores. Moreover, in their negotiations with each other, they manifest clear differentiation between pretend and reality, and skilfully move between the two domains. On these bases they are able to enter into elaborate plays and shared, complementary fantasies involving a complex web of rules and procedures.

Furth and Kane make the strong claim that it is within such imaginative constructions that much societal learning takes place; as is implied in the title of their chapter—"Children constructing society". There is no question of the sophistication of the level of social understanding revealed by these young children in their play. There is still room for debate, however, as to whether such sophistication is founded on exogenous or endogenous learning. While acknowledging the significance of the former, Furth and Kane, consistent with their Piagetian orientation, emphasise more the latter. The analysis presented in the present chapter, together with that offered in the preceding one by Youniss, holds forth promise for a productive integration of cognitive-developmental and cultural perspectives in research and theory on social development.

Chapter 7 of this volume, by Willard Hartup, is devoted to consideration of the origins and development of friendships among children from infancy to adolescence. From toddlerhood onwards children spend increasing amounts of time with others of their own age. Moreover, even quite young children show preferences for the company of some of their peers over others; children become friends with each other as well as playmates. In addition to presenting an account of research on childhood friendship as an important phenomenon in its own right, Hartup also discusses the developmental significance of friendships and assesses the extent to which experience of and participation in friendships are prerequisites for adequate psycho-social adjustment in later life. From this perspective, Hartup identifies four significant functions of childhood friendships.

First, interactions between friends provide the developing child with opportunities for acquiring, practising and elaborating basic social skills;

the extended accounts of the exchanges between the three play actors provided in the chapter by Furth bear eloquent testimony to the extent to which this is the case. Second, friends and playmates are sources of information about self and other and about the world. The earlier chapters by Schaffer and by Youniss contain illustrative examples of this function of friendship and peer relations. Third, friendships provide children with intimacy and with sources of emotional support. Fourth and relatedly, friendships afford learning opportunities for the mutual regulation and management of close relationships between equals and may therefore serve as templates for the development of intimate relationships in later life.

Hartup evaluates the evidence from contemporary research on children's friendships for the light it casts on our understanding of its functions. There is considerable evidence to indicate, for example, that children with emotional difficulties and children referred for child guidance are more likely to be friendless or to experience difficulty in peer relationships. Also, there is evidence to indicate that youngsters who are disliked by their peers are at greater risk of school drop-out and mental health difficulties in adolescence and later life. At the same time, some children who are relatively lacking in friendships are still able to make satisfactory later adjustments. Hartup concludes, cautiously, that the experience of friendship provides children with a developmental advantage, but that such experience is not an essential prerequisite for adequate social functioning in later life.

As well as providing an overview of what contemporary research contributes to our understanding of children's friendships, Hartup's chapter also identifies areas of ignorance and provides an agenda for future research in the field. In particular, we lack solid information on processes of friendship formation and management in children. Also, there is little good prospective research on the influence of children's friendships on their later development. Both kinds of deficiency can be made good only be well designed, carefully executed longitudinal research. Here, Hartup echoes a plea made by Schaffer earlier in the volume.

In the final chapter of this volume, Charles Crook argues that in much traditional research on social development there has been a tendency to dissociate the study of social development from the cultural context in which it is taking place. Social development occurs in the context of the culture in which children are growing up and into which they are being integrated. Acquiring familiarity with the meaning and significance of the artefacts of one's culture is an important aspect of the enculturation process. Crook argues that as developmentalists we should start our research in full recognition of the organising role of cultural context. He suggests that we will thus gain a fuller appreciation of the complex texture of social experience and of the relationships of that experience to the artefacts of contemporary society.

Ours is an information technology society, of which the computer is the most salient and ubiquitous symbol. There is a great deal of contemporary research on the influence of computers on children's learning and cognitive development. However, much less attention has been given to computers as cultural artefacts that serve to organise, promote and constrain social experience. This is the perspective that Crook develops, and in his chapter he examines the various ways in which children's interactions with computers may influence social development. In particular he examines the notion of computers as convivial tools that can stimulate socially organised problem-solving in contexts where a group of children interact with each other around their interaction with a computer; such group use is the common mode of experience of computers that children have in British primary schools.

As with several of the other authors in this volume, Crook identifies a research agenda whereby knowledge and understanding of the processes of social development can be enhanced. For example, he argues that analysis of children's interactions with each other around computers in the classroom could facilitate understanding of the role of conflict and co-construction in bringing about cognitive change, an issue already raised in Schaffer's chapter. However, Crook goes beyond the cognitive conflict model to argue that problem-solving interactions around computers provide children with direct, practical experience of the extent to which knowledge is socially constructed and negotiated. Approached from this perspective, the deployment of computer technology affords opportunities for children to develop representations of problem solving as a socially coordinated activity and of knowledge and understanding as processes that are themselves socially distributed. Crook acknowledges that his perspective represents a radical departure from the prevailing ethos of formal education, but argues that the issues involved represent challenges for the attention of a research community concerned to understand the social and cultural nature of social development processes.

My task in editing this volume was greatly facilitated by the level of cooperation I received from all the contributors. The responsibility for the final form and contents of the book is, of course, my own, but I would like to express my grateful thanks to the colleagues whose work is presented here. I am indebted also to Michael Forster of Lawrence Erlbaum Associates Ltd. for his encouragement and support in the preparation of the volume. Finally, I wish to record my gratitude to Maria Harrison for her assistance with preparing the manuscript for publication.

REFERENCES

Ainsworth, M. D. S. (1982). Attachment: Retrospect and prospect. In C. M. Parkes & J. Stevenson-Hinde, (Eds.) *The Place of Attachment in Human Behaviour.* New York: Basic Books.

Belsky, J. (1988). The "effects" of infant day care reconsidered. *Early Childhood Research Quarterly, 3,* 235–272.

Berti, A. E., & Bombi, A. S. (1988). *The Child's Construction of Economics.* Cambridge: Cambridge University Press.

Clarke-Stewart, A. (1988). The "effects" of infant day care reconsidered reconsidered: Risks for parents, children and researchers. *Early Childhood Research Quarterly, 3,* 293–318.

Furth, H. G. (1978). Young children's understanding of society. In H. McGurk, (Ed.) *Issues in Childhood Social Development.* London: Methuen.

McGurk, H. (1978). (Ed.) *Issues in Childhood Social Development.* London: Methuen.

Mugny, G., & Doise, W. (1978). Socio-cognitive conflict and structure of individual and collective performances. *European Journal of Social Psychology, 8,* 181–192.

Rogoff, B. (1990). *Apprenticeship in Thinking: Cognitive development in social context.* New York: Oxford University Press.

Wertsch, J. V. (1985). (Ed.) *Culture, Communication and Cognition: Vygotskian perspectives.* Cambridge: Cambridge University Press.

1 Human Social Development: An Ethological/Relationship Perspective

Robert A. Hinde

M.R.C. Development and Integration of Behaviour Group, Madingley and St. John's College, Cambridge, U.K.

INTRODUCTION

Direct parallels between animals and humans are dangerous because of the differences in cognitive abilities; because of the importance of cultural factors in the human case; because the diversity of animal species and human cultures make it too easy to find superficial parallels; and because there are difficulties in finding the appropriate level of analysis at which to make comparisons (Hinde, 1987). Nevertheless the orienting attitudes of ethology can prompt new perspectives on human development, and animal data can suggest principles whose applicability to the human case can subsequently be assessed.

In this chapter I am not concerned with the methodological contributions made by students of animal behaviour, which have been well reviewed elsewhere (e.g. Martin & Bateson, 1986). In focusing on the conceptual orientation that an ethological approach can bring to studies of child development, I have not attempted a complete review, but rather to sketch some areas, selected in part by my own predilections, where a biological approach has been valuable. Limitations of space preclude discussion of a number of other areas where biological concepts have been used by child developmentalists, such as sensitive periods (see Bateson, 1988, & Hinde, 1987), or where biological and psychological approaches are proceeding in tandem, such as the issue of continuity/discontinuity (Hinde & Bateson, 1984; Rutter, 1987) and the study of non-verbal communication (e.g. van Hooff, 1972).

We have, I believe, passed the stage in which biologists and developmental psychologists glowered at each other from opposite sides of an apparently unbridgeable crevasse. Few developmental psychologists still think that our evolutionary history is irrelevant to our current nature, and few biologists still think that principles sufficient for understanding the behaviour of animals are also likely to be adequate for our own. My current aim, therefore, is to attempt to specify just what sort of bridges can be built. In order to avoid going over old ground, I shall assume that certain issues are now generally agreed:

(a) Items or aspects of behaviour cannot be divided into those that are genetically determined and those that are the products of experience (see e.g. Oyama, 1985). Rather, individuals and their behaviour are to be seen as the result of continuing transactions between the individual at each point in time and the environment and, tracing this backwards, between the genes and their environment. This does not mean that characteristics of the individual or of behaviour are direct reflections of the genes, or indeed of the environment. However, there are some aspects of human behaviour that are so developmentally stable that they appear in all or virtually all environments experienced by human individuals.

(b) Natural selection operates through the reproductive success of individuals or their close relations. Selection operating to favour one species or group over another is unlikely to be effective, because it would pay individuals to cheat when a rule operated to disadvantage them with respect to their group companions, even though adherence to that rule could benefit the group as a whole. However, it has been suggested that group selection may operate in certain special contexts—for instance to promote cooperation leading to success in inter-group warfare (Alexander & Borgia, 1978; Bateson, 1988).

(c) Natural selection has operated to produce not only more or less fixed patterns of behaviour, but also alternative strategies to meet varying circumstances. For instance, while it may be best to be at the top of a dominance hierarchy, when not at the top a variety of alternative behavioural styles may be preferable to challenging the leadership (Lack, 1954; 1966).

(d) Individuals do not learn all things with equal ease: rather there are constraints on what can be learned and predispositions to learn some things rather than others. A classic example is song-learning in some birds: the chaffinch only sings the species-characteristic song if it has heard others singing it, but can learn only chaffinch song (Thorpe, 1961; Seligman & Hager, 1972; Hinde & Stevenson-Hinde, 1973). Similar principles are likely to operate in our own species. The constraints and predispositions may, of course, result from experience.

(e) Humans are unique in many respects, but humans are also one of a vast number of species, each with its own repertoire of behaviour and behavioural alternatives. That repertoire has been evolved to develop in and to suit a limited range of environmental circumstances. This basic orientation underlies all that follows.

Since misunderstandings are so frequent, it must quickly be said that this does not mean genetic determinism, nor does it mean that what is natural is necessarily best. These issues will be discussed later.

PHYSIOLOGICAL CONSIDERATIONS

During the period in which my own children were growing up, the debate in the country between schedule and on-demand feeding was gradually resolved in favour of the latter. Part of the evidence was comparative. Across mammals in general, suckling frequency is inversely related to the protein content of the milk. Those mammals that suckle their young very infrequently (e.g. once every two days), have very concentrated milk, and vice versa (Table 1.1). Human milk is dilute, suggesting that they are adapted to being suckled frequently. In harmony with this view, mammalian babies that are suckled infrequently suck faster and for a shorter period than those that are suckled frequently: human babies suck very slowly, suggesting that they are adapted to being suckled frequently (Blurton Jones, 1972).

Because milk concentration and sucking frequency can be measured relatively objectively, this is evidence that is fairly easy to accept. Much of what follows is similarly concerned with the desirability of recognising the nature of children (and parents), though behavioural characteristics are less tangible than physiological ones. But to prevent misunderstanding from the start, it is wise to repeat that there is no implication that what is "natural" is always right.

TABLE 1.1
Relation Between Milk Concentration and Suckling
Interval (After Blurton Jones, 1972).

Species	Milk Concentration	Suckling Interval (approx.)
Tree shrews	Very High	48 hours
Rabbits	High	24 hours
Ungulates (cached young)	High/moderate	4 hours
Ungulates (following young)	Moderate	2–3 hours
Apes	Low	1 hour
Humans	Low	?

INTEGRATION OF DIVERSE FACTS

A biological perspective can help to integrate facts about development that otherwise seem diverse and unrelated. It is apparent that, in animals, the various characters of anatomy, physiology and behaviour form an harmonious whole adapted to the species way of life. To take a crude example, birds have wings adapted for flying, they have skeletal, muscular, vascular and respiratory systems efficient for flying, and they use flight. In the same way the composition of milk, the physiology of suckling, babies' demands, and one could add the milk ejection reflex and so on, all fit together.

But it does not end there: the system of co-adaptation can be followed almost indefinitely. Thus newborn primates are relatively helpless, but their mothers must move about to find food. With few exceptions, most of them carry their babies with them, and it is probable that this was also the case in early humans. A number of facts support this hypothesis. First, the Moro reflex (Prechtl & Lenard, 1968) and vestigial grasping reflex of the human newborn indicate that they originally held onto their mothers. Second, unlike the young of those mammals that cache their infants in a nest or hiding place, human newborns do not have to be stimulated by the mother to urinate or defaecate. And third, the poor thermoregulatory ability of human newborns is more compatible with their being carried than with their being cached or following their mothers (Blurton Jones, 1972). With the reduction of maternal body hair it must have become difficult for babies to grasp their mothers, especially as, by analogy with modern hunter gatherers, mothers were probably responsible for much of the food gathering. Presumably the establishment of home bases ameliorated this issue (Isaac, 1979). The continuous maternal availability that this implies would have been associated with maternal protection and with infant dependence on that protection. Hence the "irrational fears of childhood" mentioned later.

It would have been in a mother's evolutionary interests to direct her maternal care to her own infant, or of those of close relatives. Indeed in mammals in general, female animals unrelated to the mother may be potential competitors to her own, so that a female will do better not to aid them and even to harm them. Hence fear of strangers, emerging around the age when the infant becomes capable of independent locomotion, must have been adaptive in our environment of evolutionary adaptiveness (and may still be so).

Furthermore a mammalian infant must learn to seek protection and comfort from its own parent. Thus a close mother–infant relationship is in the interests of both. It is from this perspective one must view the smile, the games that parents and infants play, affect attunement (Stern, 1985), the importance of social referencing, and other issues that contribute to attachment. Infants thrive better with parents who are sensitively responsive, not only because such parents provide for their needs in the short-term, but also because sensitive responsiveness promotes a better long-term relationship.

However, we must beware of the implication that mothers who behave in an ideally sensitive way will raise an ideally well-adapted infant in all circumstances. Animals acquire alternative strategies, which they exploit to meet the prevailing circumstances. The data seem to show that sensitive parenting and a secure parent–child relationship leads to a socially well-adjusted personality, while a more unpredictable and tensionful attachment relationship leads to a more aggressive and competitive individual. A biologist might ask, why is it this way round? Why does not sensitive mothering lead to a spoiled child, a stricter regime to gentleness and consideration for others? One possible answer is that natural selection has shaped offspring to use parental styles as "cues" to the environmental conditions they will have to face when they reach reproductive age. The only evidence about later conditions available to the infant are those current at the time, and if they involve a competitive social situation for the parent, leading to less sensitive parenting, it may pay the offspring to develop a competitive temperament (see Hinde, 1984; 1986).

LEVELS OF SOCIAL COMPLEXITY

Some issues, so well known to the developmental psychologist and to the person-in-the-street that they are easily neglected, have an importance that is more apparent in studies of animals in relatively simple situations. For example, it is impossible to work long with monkeys without recognising that the behaviour of individuals is crucially influenced by the presence of group companions (e.g. Rowell & Hinde, 1963), and that the relationships within a group differ from each other and affect each other (e.g. Hinde, 1972). These are issues that were long neglected by many developmentalists. It is now becoming recognised that many aspects of child development can be understood fully only when the child is seen as a contributing member of a network of relationships (Ainsworth, Blehar, Waters, & Wall, 1978; Bowlby, 1969; Dunn & Kendrick, 1982; Sullivan, 1938); that childrens' behaviour is affected by the social situation (e.g. Donaldson, 1978; Samuel & Bryant, 1984; Light & Perret-Clermont, 1986); that even the cognitive operations an individual uses to solve a problem may vary with the social context (Carraher, Carraher & Schliemann, 1985); and that aspects of social (Bowlby, 1969; Ainsworth et al., 1978) and cognitive (Vygotsky, 1934; Doise & Mugny, 1984; Perret-Clermont & Brossard, 1985) development depend on early relationships.

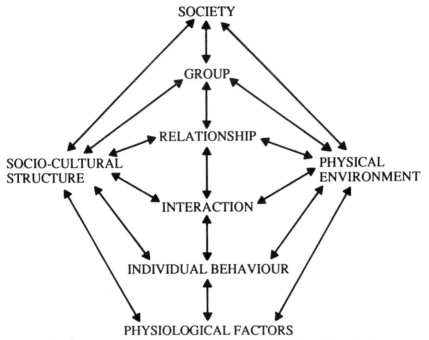

FIG. 1.1   Dialectic relations between successive levels of social complexity.

Furthermore, the extent to which relationships affect relationships is a matter of much current concern (Minuchin, 1985; Hinde & Stevenson-Hinde 1988; Hinde, 1989).

This has led to an emphasis on the need to distinguish successive levels of social complexity—ranging from individuals through interactions (of relatively short duration), relationships (involving sequences of interactions between two individuals such that each interaction is affected by past and by expectations of future ones), and groups to societies. Each of these levels of social complexity has properties not relevant to the preceding ones, and each has dialectical relations with the others (Fig. 1.1). For instance relationships differ according to whether they consist of one or many types of interaction: this is a property irrelevant to particular interactions. And the nature of a relationship affects, and is affected by, both the interactions from which it is constituted and the group or family within which it is embedded. Thus, each of these levels must be thought of not as an entity but as a process in continuous creation through the agency of the dialectics. Furthermore, each level influences and is influenced by the system of ideas, values, myths, institutions etc. current in the social group (the sociocultural structure) and by the physical environment (see Hinde 1987 for a further discussion).

Two issues important for developmentalists may be emphasised. First, measures of children taken in (or with implicit reference to) a social situation are liable to be measures of relationships and not of the characteristics of individuals. For instance, on the basis of their behaviour in the Ainsworth strange situation, children were classified as securely, anxiously or avoidantly attached to their parents. This was previously often referred to as if it were a characteristic of the child, but in fact the attachment classification may differ between child–mother and child–father relationships (Grossmann, Grossmann, Huber, & Wartner, 1981; Main & Weston, 1981) and is a characteristic of the relationship. Stevenson-Hinde (1986) has pointed out that measures can be arranged along a continuum from individual measures to relationship measures. Height and weight, but very few psychological characteristics, are at the individual end. The various temperament dimensions are also near, but at varying distances from the individual end. The attachment categories are near the relationship end.

Second, generalisations about relationships cannot be obtained from generalisations about interactions. Such a course would lose some of the most important properties of relationships—namely those that depend on the relative frequencies and patterning of the constituent interactions. For instance, a given number of commands from a mother who also often expresses affection will have a different meaning for a child than will the

TABLE 1.2

Steps Involved in Generalising About Interactions Across Dyads and Generalising About Relationships

Interactions approach	
Dyad	*Interaction type*
A – B	X ⎫
C – D	X ⎬ ----> Generalization
E – F	X ⎭
A – B	Y ⎫
C – D	Y ⎬ ----> Generalization
E – F	Y ⎭
Relationships approach	
Dyad	*Interaction type*
A – B	X ⎫
A – B	Y ⎬ ----> Generalization ⎫
A – B	Z ⎭ ⎬ ---->
C – D	X ⎫ ⎪
C – D	Y ⎬ ----> Generalization ⎭
C – D	Z ⎭

same number of commands from an affectionless mother. (See Hinde & Stevenson-Hinde, 1987, for further discussion.) Generalisations about relationships must be based on data about relationships, not data about interactions (Table 1.2).

This poses a difficulty, because relationships can be assessed along an almost infinite number of dimensions. Of course, though the issue is often neglected, the same is true of interactions; thus aggression can be assessed in terms of intensity, duration, frequency, context dependence and so on. But the problem is much more acute with relationships. Not only are they measurable along many dimensions, but some of their most important properties may be revealed only by ratio measures: the proportion of occasions on which a baby cries in which the mother picks it up tells us something about their relationship apart from the frequencies of picking up or of crying. Some suggestions for categorising the dimensions of human relationships are given in Hinde (1979).

The importance of ratio measures has a further implication, namely that comparisons must be made at the relationship rather than at the interaction level. For instance, the home correlates of the aggression of young children in preschool concern the relations between (at least) two dimensions of parental behaviour—maternal control and maternal warmth (Baumrind, 1971).

DIALECTICS

We have seen that the several levels of social complexity and the socio-cultural structure exert mutual influences upon each other. An example of such mutual influences is provided by the development of some fears and phobias.

Fears of being alone, of darkness and so on used to be called the "irrational fears of childhood". Darwin (1872) and Bowlby (1969; 1973) have pointed out that such fears would have made very good sense in our environment of evolutionary adaptedness, when infants depended on the proximity of their mothers for survival, and strange individuals or situations were dangerous.

Although fear responses to stimuli of different sorts are only moderately correlated (e.g. Stevenson-Hinde, 1989) and develop at different ages (Marks, 1987), evidence from twin studies shows that a considerable proportion of the variance between individuals is related to genetic factors (e.g. Plomin & Rowe, 1977; 1979). The influence of past selection pressures is indicated by the fact that marked fears and phobias are usually concerned with stimuli that might have signified danger in our environment of evolutionary adaptedness, such as snakes, and not with cigarettes, atomic bombs or cars, which actually kill many people today (Darwin,

1872; Marks, 1987). Indeed young children who have never previously seen a snake start to show fear of a snake moving over the ground when about 3 years old (Prechtl, 1950).

However responses to potentially dangerous stimuli are crucially influenced by social referencing in both monkeys (Seyfarth & Cheney, 1986) and humans (Klinnert et al., 1983): the child observes the behaviour of the caregiver, and this influences its own subsequent behaviour. The importance of concomitant social stimuli probably accounts in large part for the ethnic and class differences in fear responses (Kagan, Kearsley, & Zelazo, 1978).

Although experience thus plays an important role in fear behaviour, fear responses to some objects (e.g. snakes, spiders) are learned more readily and extinguish more slowly than those to "neutral" stimuli such as flowers (Ohman, Dimberg, & Ost, 1984). The issue is beautifully illustrated in a series of experiments by Mineka (1987).

1. Wild-caught rhesus monkeys are usually afraid of snakes.
2. Lab-reared rhesus monkeys show little fear of snakes.
3. Lab-reared rhesus monkeys exposed to a videotape of a wild-reared rhesus monkey being afraid of a snake usually become afraid of snakes thereafter.
4. Lab-reared rhesus monkeys shown a similar videotape of a wild-reared rhesus monkey being afraid of a flower do not become afraid of flowers (or snakes).

In brief, rhesus monkeys have a propensity to be afraid of snakes, which is enhanced by social referencing.

However, in humans that is not all. Snakes play a very important part in our mythology. Sometimes, though rarely, their salience has enabled them to become positive symbols. More usually, (and this is nowhere more clearly illustrated than in the Rubens paintings of the lost souls being cast down into Hell with snakes gnawing at their genitals), they have become symbols of evil. It is reasonable to suggest that this is not just coincidental, but a consequence of dialectic relations between the levels of social complexity, as illustrated in Fig. 1.2. Thus development of snake phobias seems to depend on dialectic relations between an initial propensity, relationships with the caregiver, and the sociocultural structure.

Another fear, that of being left alone, resembles fear of snakes in a number of ways, and is also likely to have been adaptive in our environment of evolutionary adaptedness (Bowlby, 1969). It appears early on, peaking around the end of the first year. It is markedly influenced by experience, and its incidence differs between cultures (Kagan et al., 1978). There is no need here to elaborate on the way in which studies of

Fear of Snakes

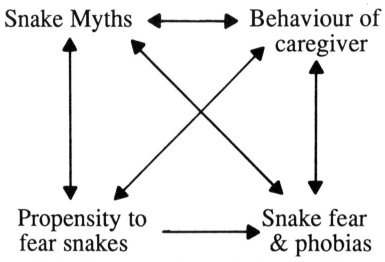

FIG. 1.2   Dialectic relations in the genesis of snake fears and phobias.

separation became one of the cornerstones of attachment theory (Bowlby, 1969; Ainsworth et al., 1978).

CONFLICTS OF INTERESTS

We take it for granted that parents should, at least to some extent, sacrifice their own interests for the sake of their children. In biological terms, however, this is the most general case of kin selection—parents secure the survival of their own genes by looking after their offspring.

However the biological interests of parent and offspring do not always run parallel, because it is also necessary to consider the effects of the costs incurred by the parent in rearing the current offspring on the parent's likely success in rearing future offspring. For example, the survival chances of an infant are greater the later it is weaned, but at the same time continued nursing both reduces the mother's chances of conceiving again and drains her resources so as to make her less able to rear any future infant she might conceive. There will come a point when it will be in the first child's interests to continue to suckle and in the mother's biological interests to discontinue so that she can rear another infant successfully (Trivers, 1972). Although a number of other issues complicate the matter, there is much evidence that infants are selected to attempt to elicit more parental investment than the parent is selected to give. This suggests that weaning conflict has evolutionary origins, and gives a certain perspective to the manner in which mothers may push children on from breast to solid food, from cot to bed, or from home to school before the children would make the moves on their own.

However, we must not stop the evolutionary argument there. First, the point of balance between the interests of parent and offspring will vary according to circumstances. Second, if the conflict of interest between parent and offspring results in the parent rejecting the infant earlier than it would otherwise leave, natural selection may have acted to adapt infants to that situation. Thus, while infants may be adapted to get as much parental care as they reasonably can, their development may be "optimal" when they do not get as much as they strive to get, or if their parents treat them as more mature than they are (optimal is of course a slippery concept—see page 17). This evolutionary view is compatible with the empirical findings that cognitive development depends in part on parents treating children as if their capacities were slightly greater than those currently developed (Bruner, 1978), and that healthy development depends both on parental sensitivity to infants' needs and parental encouragement of independence.

An extreme case of a conflict of interests between parent and offspring arises when the chances of infant survival are small, so that any parental investment is likely to be wasted. Daly & Wilson (1984) showed that a high proportion of the cases of infanticide occur when (a) the infants' fitness potential was poor because of deformity, sickness or circumstances and (b) the parental resources were inadequate. In addition, (c) in many cases the infant was not the putative parents' own. Similarly, in a study of 300 middle class Los Angeles women Essock-Vitale & McGuire (1985a & 1985b) found that pregnancies were more likely to be terminated voluntarily if the woman was unmarried or uncertain of the paternity of her child. Of course, it must be emphasised that this compatibility between empirical data on infanticide or abortion and evolutionary considerations must be seen in the context of the known diversity of proximate factors affecting such issues (see eg Engfer & Schneewind, 1982; Engfer, 1986, on child abuse).

There are other contexts in which an evolutionary perspective provides another level of understanding about the nature of human relationships. For example, it might be predicted that as a mothers' chances of conceiving and rearing another infant decrease with her age, she would be more self-sacrificing with the current one, and especially so with an infant she believed to be the last born. Again, siblings are as closely genetically related to each other as parents to children, so individuals are likely to be willing to incur costs in order to help their siblings. At the same time, siblings are rivals for parental attention: ambivalence in the sibling relationship is thus to be expected.

DIRECTION OF EFFECTS

It is now generally accepted that the nature of the parent–child relationship is affected by both parent and child. What is less well appreciated is that the answers to questions about the direction of effects are critically affected by the precise way in which the questions are framed. The principle is well illustrated by a relatively simply biological example, namely the relations between the time that young rhesus monkeys spend on their mothers' backs and the frequency with which their attempts to gain contact are rejected. First, a straightforward measure of whether infant or mother is *primarily responsible* for time on the mother over a given time interval can be obtained as follows. The proportion of contact-makes due to the infant less the proportion of contact-breaks due to the infant will be positive if the infant is primarily responsible for contact, and negative if the mother is. The difference is usually negative in the early weeks, and becomes positive later.

Second, we may ask whether *changes* in mothers or *changes* in infants are primarily responsible for the age-related *decrease* in the time the infant spends on the mother. The data show that the frequency of maternal rejections increases as the time spent on the mother decreases: this is compatible with the view that it is primarily changes in the mother that are responsible for the age-changes in time on the mother, increased frequency of maternal rejections increasing the time the infant spends off the mother (Table 1.3).

Third, we may ask whether the *differences* between mother-infant dyads in time on the mother are due more to *differences* between infants or to *differences* between mothers. Using a similar argument the correlation between frequency of rejections and time on the mother at each age are consistently negative in the early weeks and positive later, indicating that

TABLE 1.3
Causality of Changes in Behaviour of an Infant Rhesus

Type of change	Time on mother	Frequency of maternal rejections
Mother–Infant $\longrightarrow$	+	−
Mother–Infant $\longleftarrow$	−	+
Mother–Infant $\longleftarrow$	+	+
Mother–Infant $\longrightarrow$	−	−

Assessing the extent to which changes in time spent on the mother by an infant rhesus are due to changes in the mother or changes in the infant.

The four rows concern four possible types of change (mother more possessive, mother more rejecting, infant more dependent, infant less dependent). The symbols indicate the resultant direction of change in two measures. With changes in the infant/mother, the measures change in the same/opposite directions.

with young infants inter-mother differences are more important than inter-infant differences, while later the reverse is the case.

The point to be emphasised here is that the three questions yield different answers. In the early weeks it is the mothers who are primarily responsible for contact, but changes in mothers that are primarily responsible for the decrease in contact. However the relative importance of differences between mothers or differences between infants changes with age, the former being more important early, and the latter later (Hinde, 1979).

ESTABLISHMENT OF PRINCIPLES

The last two sections in this paper concern the need for caution. I emphasised from the start that the value of a biological perspective did not lie in direct parallels between animals and humans, but in the enunciation of principles likely also to be applicable in the human case. Beyond that, however, there may be need for caution in the level at which those principles are applied. We may consider one example. If an infant is separated from its mother for a while, the infant is likely to be disturbed for some time after reunion, and long-term personality development may be affected. In monkeys, the effects are more severe, the less harmonious the mother–child relationship. In so far as the effects seem to be more severe in humans in underprivileged families (Rutter, 1972), the animal and human data seem to be compatible. But now we may ask, under which circumstances is the infant likely to be most upset—when the mother is removed and the infant is left in its home situation, or when the infant is removed to a strange place (eg hospital) and the mother stays at home? In the human case there seems little doubt that the former would involve less trauma. In monkeys, the opposite appears to be the case. One reason is that the mother, on being returned to the home cage, has to re-establish her relationships with the other adults in the group as well as cope with the demands of her infant. This would be much less the case with a human mother returning to her family (Hinde & McGinnis, 1977). Thus the level at which the principles abstracted from the monkey data are applied to the human case is crucial.

DESIDERATA

The second type of caution concerns the view that what is natural is best. Evolutionary arguments about human behaviour concern ways in which human behaviour was adaptive in our environment of evolutionary adaptedness. Adaptive, in that context, implies an effect on reproductive success, but in promoting human health and happiness today reproductive success is not always the first concern. Furthermore the genes that were then selected for may interact in a very different way with the environmental factors that developing humans encounter nowadays, and what is desirable in a modern environment may be very different from what was once desirable.

We must in fact consider three types of desiderata. First, the biological desideratum of reproductive success. How far are our child-care and socialisation practices compatible with an organism whose ancestors were adapted in a different environment for reproductive success. In some cases, at least, the sociocultural structure seems to have imposed practices that are contrary to the biological interests of those concerned. Schedule feeding was one such example. The stark nature of most delivery rooms and the practice of delivering the mother while she is lying on her back, seem to be others. In most societies a sympathetic woman, usually well known to the mother, is present to comfort and help her, and delivery usually occurs with the mother sitting, standing, squatting, kneeling or leaning back with support. Kennell & Klaus (Kennell, 1986) have shown that the presence of a sympathetic woman and a squatting or sitting position can reduce the length of labour and the risk of complications. This raises the question of what human behavioural tendencies and/or what power group within a society give rise to practices that are not in the best interests of the individual mother.

Second is the cultural desiderata of fitting in with the cultural ideals and values in which the child develops. There could, for instance, be incompatibility between socialisation practices aimed at raising a cooperative boy and macho ideals in the society at large. Or there may be incompatibility between parenting practices involving maternal sensitivity and care and the mother's social goals: furthermore frustration of the latter may induce a decrease in sensitivity.

Finally, there is the individual desideratum of psychological well-being. This desideratum is not easy to define, but is usually taken to imply a capacity to cope with adverse circumstances—perhaps especially over attachment related issues. How far it is synonymous with or compatible with biological and cultural desiderata is at present a matter of controversy (Hinde & Stevenson Hinde, 1990).

CONCLUSION

The conventional scientific dogma requires that rival theories be pitted against each other and one chosen on the basis of a crucial experiment. Given the complexity of human behaviour, such an approach can be counter-productive. Rather than choosing one or the other, we must attempt to marry them, or to assess where each is relevant or valid. In this chapter a number of issues in which an ethological approach has helped or can help in understanding human development have been mentioned. None involves direct comparisons between animals and humans. Rather the emphasis is on abstracting principles or concepts from the relatively simple animal case; principles or concepts whose utility in the human case can then be assessed.

REFERENCES

Ainsworth, M. D. S., Blehar, M. C., Waters, E., & Wall, S. (1978). *Patterns of attachment*, Hillsdale, N.J.: Lawrence Erlbaum Associates Inc.

Alexander, R. D. & Borgia, G. (1978). Group selection, altruism and the levels of hierarchical organisation of life. *Annual Review of Education and Systems, 9*, 449–74.

Bateson, P. (1988), and Hinde, R. A. (1987). Developmental changes in sensitivity to experience. In M. H. Bornstein (Ed.), *Sensitive periods in development*, (pp. 13–34). Hillsdale, N.J.: Lawrence Erlbaum Associates Inc.

Baumrind, D. (1971). Current patterns of parental authority. *Developmental Psychology Monographs 4*, (1, Pt. 2).

Blurton Jones, N. (1972). Comparative studies of mother–child contact. In N. Blurton Jones (Ed.), *Ethological studies of child behaviour*. Cambridge: Cambridge University Press.

Bowlby, J. (1969). *Attachment and loss, 1. Attachment*. London: Hogarth.

Bowlby, J. (1973). *Attachment and loss. 2. Separation*. London: Hogarth.

Bruner, J. S. (1978). Learning how to do things with words. In J. S. Bruner & A. Gartlan (Eds.), *Human growth and development*. Oxford: Clarendon Press.

Carraher, T. N., Carraher, T. W., & Schliemann, A. D. (1985). Mathematics in the streets and in the schools. *British Journal of Developmental Psychology, 3*, 21–29.

Daly, M., & Wilson, M. (1984). A sociobiological analysis of human infanticide. In G. Hausfater, & S. B. Hrdy, (Eds.), *Infanticide: Comparative and evolutionary perspectives*. New York: Aldine.

Darwin, C. (1872). *The Expression of the emotion in man and the animals*. London: John Murray.

Doise, W., & Mugny, G. (1984). *The social development of intellect*. Oxford: Pergamon.

Donaldson, M. (1978). *Children's minds*. London: Fontana.

Dunn, J., & Kendrick, C. (1982). *Siblings: Love, envy and understanding*. Cambridge, Mass.: Harvard University Press.

Engfer, A. (1986). *Kindesmisshandlung: Ursachen, Auswirkungen, Hilfen*. Stuttgart: Enke.

Engfer, A., & Schneewind, K. A. (1982). Causes and consequences of harsh parental treatment. *Child Abuse and Neglect, 6*, 129–39.

Essock-Vitale, S. M., & McGuire, M. T. (1985a). Women's lives viewed from an evolutionary perspective. 1. Sexual histories, reproductive success and demographic characteristics of a random sample of American women. *Ethology and Sociobiology, 1*, 233–43.

Essock-Vitale, S. M., & McGuire. M. T. (1985b). Women's lives viewed from an evolutionary perspective. 2. Patterns of helping. *Ethology and Sociobiology, 6*, 155–73.

Grossmann, K. E., Grossmann, K., Huber, F., & Wartner, U. (1981). German children's behaviour towards their mothers at 12 months and their fathers at 18 months in Ainsworth's strange situation. *International Journal of Behavioral Development, 4*, 157–81.

Hinde, R. A. (1972). Social behaviour in sub-human primates, *Condon Lectures*. Oregon System of Higher Education.

Hinde, R. A. (1979). *Towards understanding relationships*. London: Academic Press.

Hinde, R. A. (1984). Biological bases of the mother–child relationship. In J. D. Call, E. Galenson, & R. L. Tyson, (Eds.), *Frontiers of Infant Psychiatry, vol. 2* (pp. 284–294). New York: Basic Books.

Hinde, R. A. (1986). Some implications of evolutionary theory and comparative data for the study of human prosocial and aggressive behaviour. In D. Olweus, J. Block, & M. Radke-Yarrow, (Eds.), *Development of antisocial and prosocial behaviour* (pp. 13–22). Orlando: Academic Press.

Hinde, R. A. (1987). *Individuals, relationships and culture*. Cambridge: Cambridge University Press.

Hinde, R. A. (1989). Reconciling the family systems and the relationships approaches to child development. In K. Kreppner, & R. Lerner, (Eds.), *Family systems and life-span development* (pp. 149–164). Hillsdale, N.J.: Lawrence Erlbaum Associates Inc.

Hinde, R. A., & Bateson, P. (1984). Discontinuities versus continuities in behavioural development and the neglect of process. *International Journal of Behavioural Development, 7*, 129–143.

Hinde, R. A., & McGinnis, L. (1977). Some factors influencing the effects of temporary mother–infant separation—some experiments with rhesus monkeys. *Psychological Medicine, 7*, 197–222.

Hinde, R. A., & Stevenson-Hinde, J. (1973). *Constraints on learning*. London: Academic Press.

Hinde, R. A., & Stevenson-Hinde, J. (1987). Interpersonal relationships and child development. *Developmental Review, 7*, 1–21.

Hinde, R. A., & Stevenson-Hinde, J. (Eds.) (1988). *Relationships within families*. Oxford: Oxford University Press.

Hinde, R. A., & Stevenson-Hinde, J. (1990). Attachment. Biological, cultural and individual desiderata. *Human Development, 33*, 62–72.

van Hooff, J. A. R. A. M. (1972). A comparative approach to the phylogeny of smiling and laughter. In R. A. Hinde (Ed.), *Non-verbal communication* (pp. 209–237). Cambridge: Cambridge University Press.

Isaac, G. L. (1979). Casting the net wide: A review of archaeological evidence for early hominid land-use & ecological relations. In *Nobel symposium, current argument on early man*. Oxford: Pergamon.

Kagan, J., Kearsley, R. B., & Zelazo, P. R. (1978). *Infancy: Its place in human development*. Cambridge, Mass: Harvard University Press.

Kennell, J. (1986). *John Lind Memorial Lecture*. World Congress of Infant Psychiatry, Stockholm.

Klinnert, R. D., Campos, J. J., Sorce, J. F., Emde, R. N., & Sredja, R. (1983). Emotions as behaviour regulators. In R. Phitchik, and H. Kellerman, (Eds.), *The emotions (vol. 2)*. New York: Academic Press.

Lack, D. (1954). *The natural regulation of animal numbers*. Oxford: Clarendon Press.

Lack, D. (1966). *Population studies of birds*. Oxford: Clarendon Press.

Light, P., & Perret-Clermont, A-N. (1986). Social construction of logical structures and social construction of meaning. *Dossiers de Psychologie, 27*. Université de Neuchatel.

Main, M., & Weston, D. (1981). The quality of the toddler's relationship to mother and father: Related to conflict behaviour and the readiness to establish new relationships. *Child Development, 52*, 932–40.

Marks, I. (1987). *Fear, phobias and rituals*. Oxford: Oxford University Press.

Martin, P., & Bateson, P. (1986). *Measuring behaviour*. Cambridge: Cambridge University Press.

Mineka, S. (1987). A primate model of phobic fears. In H. Eysenck, & I. Martin, (Eds.), *Theoretical foundations of behaviour therapy*. New York: Plenum.

Minuchin, P. (1985). Families and individual development: Provocations from the field of family therapy. *Child Development, 56*, 289–301.

Ohman, A., Dimberg, U., & Ost, L-G. (1984). Animal and social phobias. In S. Reiss, & R. R. Bootzin, (Eds.) *Theoretical issues in behaviour therapy.* New York: Academic Press.

Oyama, S. (1985). *The ontogeny of information.* Cambridge: Cambridge University Press.

Perret-Clermont, A.-N., & Brossard, A. (1985). On the interdigitation of social and cognitive processes. In R. A. Hinde, A.-N. Perret-Clement, & J. Stevenson-Hinde, (Eds.), *Social relationships and cognitive development* (pp. 309–327). Oxford: Oxford University Press.

Plomin, R., & Rowe, D. C. (1977). A twin study of temperament in young children. *Journal of Psychology, 97*, 107–113.

Plomin, R., & Rowe, D. C. (1979). Genetic and environmental aetiology of social behaviour in infancy. *Developmental Psychology, 15*, 62–72.

Prechtl, H. F. R. (1950). Das Verhalten von Kleinkindern gegenuber Schlangen. *Wiener Zeitschrift für Philosophie, Psychologie und Paedagogie, 2*, 68–70.

Prechtl, H. F. R., & Lenard, H. G. (1968). Verhaltensphysiologie des Neugeborenen. In *Forschritte de Paedologie.* Berlin: Springer Verlag.

Rowell, T. E., & Hinde, R. A. (1963). Responses of rhesus monkeys to mildly stressful situations. *Animal Behaviour, 11*, 235–243.

Rutter, M. (1972). *Maternal deprivation reassessed.* Harmondsworth: Penguin.

Rutter, M. (1987). Continuities & discontinuities from infancy. In J. Osofsky (Ed.), *Handbook of infant development* (pp. 1256–98). New York: Wiley.

Samuel, J., & Bryant, P. (1984). Asking only one question in the conservation experiment. *Journal of Child Psychology and Psychiatry, 25*, 315–18.

Seligman, M. E. P., & Hager, J. L. (Eds.). (1972). *Biological boundaries of learning.* New York: Appleton-Century-Crofts.

Seyfarth, R., & Cheney, D. L. (1986). Vocal development in vervet monkeys. *Animal Behaviour, 34*, 1640–58.

Stern, D. (1985). *The interpersonal world of the infant.* New York: Basic Books.

Stevenson-Hinde, J. (1986). Towards a more open construct. In G. A. Kohnstamm (Ed.), *Temperament discussed* (pp. 97–106). Lisse: Swets & Zeitlinger.

Stevenson-Hinde, J. (1989). Behavioural inhibition: Issues of context. In J. S. Reznick (Ed.), *Perspectives on Behavioral Inhibition* (pp. 125–38). Chicago: University of Chicago Press.

Sullivan, H. S. (1938). The data of psychiatry. *Psychiatry, 1*, 121–34.

Thorpe, W. H. (1961). *Bird song*: Cambridge: Cambridge University Press.

Trivers, R. L. (1972). Parental investment and sexual selection. In B. Campbell (Ed.), *Sexual selection and the descent of man, 1871–1971.* Chicago: Aldine.

Vygotsky, L. S. (1934). *Thought and language.* Cambridge, Mass.: M.I.T. Press.

2 Childhood Gender Roles: Social Context and Organisation

John Archer
Lancashire Polytechnic, Preston, U.K.

INTRODUCTION

This chapter concerns the childhood gender roles of the two sexes. As this first sentence indicates, I shall use the term sex to refer to the binary categories of male and female, and gender to refer to the "fuzzy" categories of masculine and feminine, attributes associated to a greater or lesser extent with one of these. This follows the distinction made by Maccoby (1988), and used by Bem (1989).

Studies of childhood gender roles have tended to concentrate on the contrasting activities and interests of the two sexes. Role differentiation during childhood extends beyond these differences in content, involving different rules, organisational patterns and developmental pathways, which operate within two very different social contexts.

Boys and girls interact mainly with their own sex, and their patterns of social relations are very different, boys interacting in larger groups where status and reputation are important, and girls showing more intimate interactions and friendships. Role conformity is emphasised more for boys, and the few cross-sex interactions initiated by boys are such that they serve to emphasise the boundary between their social world and that of girls. The internal structure of masculine and feminine roles is also different. The feminine role shows inconsistency between traditional and modern features; that is between the role of women as wives and mothers and their partial acceptance into the world of work outside the home. The masculine role shows three different aspects that are related to developmental changes. These are avoidance of femininity, the physically-based role of boyhood, and the achievement-based role of adults. The principal developmental change for girls is an increase in the rigidity of the feminine role at puberty.

Three broad types of explanation have been applied to gender roles. Biological explanations involve the control of sex-typical behaviour through maturational processes, resulting from genetic inheritance and, in the long-term, evolutionary history. Socialisation or cultural explanations involve the impact and internalisation of cultural values during development: in psychology, such explanations have concentrated on how the content of gender roles is acquired by the next generation, within a social learning or a cognitive developmental framework. A large body of research has been concerned with this broad process. Structural explanations involve the direct influence of the structure of society on people's behaviour and dispositions. The distinction between this and a cultural explanation depends on whether internal dispositions or situational contingencies control behaviour (House, 1981). In a way, this distinction parallels the person-situation debate in psychology.

Structural explanations have been applied to sex differences in some social psychological characteristics by writers such as Henley (1977), Spender (1980) and Eagley (1983; 1987). For example, Eagley (1983) showed that in naturally-occurring settings men tend to be more influential and women more readily influenced, and that these differences stem from formal status inequalities in the roles of men and women. In laboratory settings, and in small groups, sex differences of small magnitudes are also found in leadership and influenceability, although in these specific instances formal status inequalities are absent. Eagley argued that these sex differences nevertheless stem from experience with hierarchical social structures where men have higher status, and that this experience creates expectancies about men's and women's behaviour that affect informal social interactions in ways that confirm these expectancies. This type of explanation, which can be applied to a number of other sex differences in social behaviour (Eagley, 1987), explains characteristics of the interaction of men and women as a direct manifestation of their position in the wider social structure. In so doing, it constitutes a radical departure from the socialisation explanations that had previously been offered for sex differences (cf. Maccoby & Jacklin, 1974).

Structural explanations of this sort have not been systematically applied to the development of gender roles, since most previous discussions have concentrated on the content of roles and how these are acquired (but cf. Archer, 1984; Maccoby, 1986; Thorne, 1986). In this chapter I shall consider the extent to which a structural role perspective can be applied to the organisation of childhood gender roles: specifically, I shall ask whether there are features that can be understood as the direct manifestation of the status inequalities of men and women in society.

Crucial to this approach is the concept of power, which has been defined in different ways and used at different levels of analysis (e.g., Ragins & Sundstrom, 1989). When applied at the level of the whole society, power refers to the higher status that accrues to men as a result of their access to more influential and higher-paid occupations outside the home, and the lower status that is associated with women's occupations, domestic work and child-care (e.g., Polatnick, 1973). Other levels of analysis are embedded within, and dependent on, this wider societal view of power relations. These include the level of the organisation, interpersonal interactions, and the individual.

Since structural explanations focus on the overall social system, they may be limited in accounting for findings at the individual or small group level because they do not specify the mechanisms affecting individual behaviour. One body of research that may potentially be helpful in bridging this gap is the social identity theory of intergroup relations (Tajfel, 1982). This has been concerned in general terms with the derivation of an individual's self-concept from membership of a wider social category. Of particular relevance for the present chapter is research on the consequences for individuals of comparisons between the wider social categories to which they belong and those of higher or lower status (Breakwell, 1979; Williams, 1984; Williams & Giles, 1978). Consideration is therefore given to contributions from intergroup relations research that might explain how status inequalities of men and women at the societal level can produce features that are like those which have been found in research on the social behaviour of boys and girls.

Although a major aim of this chapter is to determine the extent to which a structural explanation in terms of power can account for the rules, organisational patterns and social context of childhood gender roles, the limits of this explanatory framework will be recognised, and alternative explanations will be put forward where appropriate.

SEX SEGREGATION

During childhood, boys and girls tend to form groups that are exclusively of their own sex. This generalisation is based on considerable cross-cultural as well as North American research evidence (Hartup, 1983; Maccoby, 1986, 1988; Maccoby & Jacklin, 1987).

Sex segregation has its origins in the early preschool years, becoming more pronounced throughout elementary school (Maccoby, 1988). Although same-sex interactions are more common in preschool children, opposite-sex ones still occur, for example in the form of cooperative social play or offering mutual help (McGrew, 1972; Strayer, 1980; Hold-Cavell, Attili, & Schleidt, 1986).

Studies involving social preferences or friendship patterns have revealed a stronger pattern of sex segregation than those concentrating on the pattern of interactions. Pre-school boys and girls show clear preferences for their own sex (Maccoby & Jacklin, 1974, p. 211; 1987; Maccoby, 1986). For example, Hold-Cavell et al. (1986) found that same-sex peers were chosen more often for parallel play (involving play with objects and shared interests). At school ages, studies of preferences and friendships also reveal stronger sex segregation than is apparent in interaction patterns.

Same-sex preferences have been found as early as 2 years of age. LaFreniere, Strayer and Gauthier (1984) studied the affiliative behaviour of 1–6 year old children in a Canadian urban day-centre, and found that 2 year old girls initiated more positive social behaviour towards other girls than towards boys. Boys began to show preferences at a later age, but subsequently surpassed girls in the extent of their preferences.

At school ages, although sex segregation is generally more exclusive, there are certain contexts in which there is more opposite-sex interaction. Thorne (1986), in a study of two elementary schools in the U.S. identified several circumstances in which sex segregation appeared to be relaxed: where the children's activity was engaged in an absorbing task that encouraged cooperation and lessened attention to sex; in games where teams were not involved, and when adults organised mixed-sex encounters; when the children were grouped according to other criteria than sex; and outside school, in less public settings. Thorne emphasised these examples as counters to the generalisation of sex segregation, which he viewed as arising to some extent from the organisation of children in the school.

Studies of children's friendships and interactions outside school are consistent with Thorne's viewpoint. Abrams (1989) asked 5, 8 and 11 year old British children about their opposite-sex friendships. The 5 year olds said that they had fewer than before starting school, because of physical separation. The opposite-sex friendships of the 8 year olds most often involved relatives, or friends from pre-school days. The 11 year olds reflected on their small number of opposite-sex friends, but saw their social relationships as changing in the near future, as romantic attachments began.

Ellis, Rogoff and Cromer (1981) observed the social interactions of children aged from 1 to 12 years at home or outdoors, in a middle income neighbourhood of Salt Lake City. They found that although same-sex companions were observed in 33% of interactions overall, and this increased with age, nevertheless opposite-sex companions were found in 28% of all observations.

A different view of context-induced variations was taken by Maccoby and Jacklin (1987). They concluded that increased cross-sex interactions occur when the children's natural inclinations are constrained in some way, for example when adults intervene, or when limited playmates are available.

They argued that when children are left to themselves, segregation becomes more pronounced.

Several researchers have concluded that sex segregation occurs in widely different cultures. Whiting and Edwards (1988) presented data from six cultures (in India, Okinawa, The Philipines, Mexico, Kenya and the U.S.) showing that children aged 4 to 10 years are found in sex-segregated groups for much of the time, and that this is more pronounced with children of the same age, and when adults are not present. Observing children from the Efe and Lase groups of the rain forests of Zaire, Morelli (cited in Whiting & Edwards, 1988) found that children aged 3 years or less showed a preference for playing with same-sex peers. Freedman (1980) also reviewed evidence that sex segregation occurred in a range of non-Western cultures (e.g., Chinese, Japanese, Balinese, Kenyan, Indian and Kalahari !Kung).

There is, however, other evidence to indicate that both the degree of sex segregation and its age of onset may vary in different cultures. Maccoby (1986) suggested, on the basis of informal observations of kibbutz-reared children, that the experience of long-lasting mixed-sex social groups of similar ages may serve to break down sex segregation. In a study of children in rural Kenya, Harkness & Super (1985) found that, despite marked sex segregation in adulthood, the sex composition of childhood groups was approximately equal in the two youngest groups studied (up to 6 years), and although unequal in the 6–9 year old group, sex segregation was still not complete. The researchers remarked that the pattern of development did not appear to fit the model derived from U.S. culture, and they emphasised the impact of the setting on behaviour. Maccoby and Jacklin (1987), on the other hand, viewed this finding as a result of the situation constraining the children's behaviour through limitations on the available playmates.

THE SUBCULTURES OF BOYS AND GIRLS

Boys and girls gradually develop different subcultures within their segregated groups. This process serves to separate the sexes further, and becomes an important reason for segregation during the school years.

Based on a comprehensive review of the evidence at that time, Maccoby and Jacklin (1974, p. 207) concluded that the difference between boys' and girls' play could best be described as follows: girls play intensively with one or two "best friends", whereas boys play in larger groups. Studies of a wide range of ages have since confirmed this conclusion (Maccoby & Jacklin, 1987), and extended it to identify a general difference in the social relations of boys and girls. For example, Waldrop and Halverson (1975) found that the meaning of "sociability" was different in the two sexes at 7½ years of age. The most social boys tended to have extensive relations with their peers, whereas the most social girls had intensive relations, generally centered around one other girl. Adolescent girls and boys show similar contrasting patterns. Young women either have one best friend or a small number of close friends (Griffin, 1986), whereas boys are more likely to form a gang or a group (Willis, 1977), a pattern that is perpetuated in adulthood in male activities such as drinking and sports.

The differences in cultural styles between boys' and girls' groups go beyond their types of social relations (Maccoby, 1986; Maccoby & Jacklin, 1987). Boys engage in rougher games, they fight more, and show more overt dominance-related interactions. Boys' play also tends to occur in more public places, with less surveillance than is given to girls (Newson & Newson, 1986). Girls' play is characteristically more co-operative, emphasising a strong convention of turn-taking. Self-disclosure, for example telling secrets, is important and break-ups are emotional, with new friendships forming at the expense of old ones (Lagerspetz, Bjorkqvist & Peltonen, 1988).

Maltz and Borker (1982) analysed the content of social speech used in boys' and girls' groups. They concluded that girls use speech mainly to maintain friendly interactions, and to create and maintain close relationships based on equality and fairness. Girls frequently express agreement with others' ideas, let others have their turn, and acknowledge what they have to say when they speak. As a result, girls experience difficulties with unfriendly interactions.

In contrast, boys use speech to assert their status, to attract and maintain an audience, and to assert themselves when others are speaking. Boys play in larger, more hierarchically arranged groups, with status a major feature. A boy who is able to use speech to serve this end will be more successful than one who simply uses physical aggression. Observational studies of groups of boys support this conclusion by showing that dominance rank is positively correlated with more affiliative aspects of social behaviour, such as measures of sociability (McGrew, 1972), having more play partners (Jones, 1984) and receiving help (Strayer, 1980).

When a girl or boy begins heterosexual interactions after puberty, they encounter someone from a different subculture. Maltz and Borker (1982) argued that the different cultural styles of boys and girls form the basis for difficulties and misunderstandings in adolescent and adult cross-sex conversations.

EXPLAINING SEX SEGREGATION

In seeking to explain sex segregation, I will first address the main issue of its origin in early development, and second consider how it is maintained and strengthened during childhood. As indicated in the previous section, the second of these is associated with the impact of the contrasting subcultures.

Freedman (1980, p. 267) proposed the following biological explanation of sex segregation: "Probably as a result of basic temperamental differences, boys and girls, like monkey and baboon youngsters, tend to play with others of the same sex from the first moment when such a choice is possible". Freedman viewed the following differences as being important: boys are more active (covering more space in their play), show more rough-and-tumble play, and are louder, more chaotic and more disorganised in their play; girls, on the other hand, play in smaller groups and engage in closer, quieter and more orderly games. These differences are regarded as a consequence of a different neural organisation in boys and girls, and were seen as directly causing sex segregation. However, most of them have been observed in segregated groups, so that it is difficult to specify which aspect might have caused the segregation in the first place.

Maccoby and Jacklin (1987) identified a crucial weakness in any type of argument that seeks to explain sex segregation on the basis of pre-existing "sex differences", for example in temperament, namely that these show a wide variation within each sex. Yet the preference for same-sex interactions is a more or less categorical difference. It is therefore difficult to account for one in terms of the other. In their own longitudinal study, Maccoby and Jacklin (1987) were unable to find any relationship between individual temperamental and behavioural differences and the degree to which children played with the same or opposite sex.

Maccoby and Jacklin also found that individual differences in the extent of gender-stereotyping in play at 4½ years were unrelated to preferences for playing with the same or opposite sex at that time. The level of gender-stereotyped play in all-boy or all-girl groups at this age was generally low. The degree to which children were gender-stereotyped in their activities at 45 months was also unrelated to whether they showed a preference for same-sex play a year later. In fact it was those girls with the more masculine assertive behaviour who most preferred to play with girls. These findings are clearly inconsistent with the socialisation explanation that previous learning of gender-stereotyped play preferences become generalised to preferring children who share these preferences. Other findings by Maccoby and Jacklin (1987) are also inconsistent with an explanation based on learning gender-stereotyped activities: same-sex preferences are greater in the absence of adults (who are seen as promoting gender-stereotyping); bringing boys and girls together increases rather than decreases same-sex preferences; 4½ year old boys and girls played separately even when the play equipment was the same for each sex (Maccoby, 1988).

Maccoby and Jacklin (1987) argued that since the degree of participation in same-sex play is not related to individual temperamental or gender stereotyping measures, and is unstable among individuals from one week to the next, it is best approached as a group phenomenon. By this they mean that it is based on recognition that another child is either a member of one's own group or of another group, rather than on individually varying characteristics. This enables some of the basic findings of intergroup relations research (see Introduction) to be applied to the process. It is known, for example, that clear distinctions are made between ingroup and outgroup members, that the extent of such distinctions, and identification with the ingroup, depends on the salience of category membership; members behave so as to enhance the distinctiveness and positive evaluation of their group; members of the outgroup are seen as homogeneous; and between-group cooperation on specific tasks does not prevent ingroup bias continuing.

Nevertheless, these principles do not account for the formation of the ingroup and outgroup in the first place, except in showing that category membership must be salient. The crucial question is what initial difference between boys and girls is both salient and general enough to be used as a basis for group categorisation. Maccoby (1986; 1988) has suggested that interaction styles differ between the sexes from an early age. Furthermore, the less physically assertive female style is ineffective in influencing a male partner, and hence girls find interacting with this category of child aversive. Studies of pre-school children show that the techniques used by girls in dominance disputes consist mainly of verbal persuasion, which works well with other girls but is ignored by boys (Powlishta & Maccoby, 1990). This would explain the finding that girls initially avoid interacting with boys, and only later does the reverse process occur (LaFreniere et al., 1984). It still leaves the subsequent avoidance of girls by boys to be explained: presumably, this can be viewed as part of the general tendency to avoid femininity that boys develop from an early age.

Several studies support Maccoby's view that sex differences in interaction styles are present early in life. Jacklin and Maccoby (1978) found that 33 month old boys and girls played more actively and engaged in more social interaction in same-sex than in opposite-sex pairs: in mixed pairs, girls became passive and watched their male partner. These results have been replicated for 19–42 month and 3–3½ year old children in the U.K. (Lloyd & Smith, 1986; Duveen, Lloyd & Smith, 1988), although Duveen et al. did find that in 3½–4 year old children social behaviour was greater in mixed-sex than same-sex pairs (who had been constrained to play together). Powlishta and Maccoby (1990) found that boys aged 42–60 months dominated girls in a competitive (but not a cooperative) task when no adult was present.

Play and activity differences have been found between boys and girls at even earlier ages when they are observed individually with their mothers. Goldberg and Lewis (1969) found that 13 month old boys spent more time with "active" toys and girls played more with blocks, a pegboard and a toy dog and cat. Jacklin, Maccoby and Dick (1973), in a similar investigation using different toys, found comparable (but not entirely consistent) results. Smith and Daglish (1977) found that 12–24 month old boys engaged in more active play, and play with transportation toys, whereas girls of the same age played more with soft toys and dolls. Lloyd and Smith (1985) also found that boys engaged in more vigorous play than girls in the second year of life. Studies of gender-stereotypic toy choice have usually located this at a later age than these activity differences (exceptions being LaFreniere et al., 1984; O'Brien & Huston, 1985; Caldera, Huston & O'Brien, 1989). This would seem to indicate that early differences in play result from different activity-levels and interaction styles by boys and girls, rather than prior gender-stereotypic learning of toy preferences. Although there may be some room for argument with regard to these particular findings, when they are considered along with the other studies reviewed previously, the evidence converges on this conclusion.

Maccoby's explanation would appear to involve the following stages: the interaction styles of males and females differ from early in life; these differences have negative consequences for girls in most of their interactions with boys; girls can distinguish between the categories girl and boy; the ability to categorise, along with the salience of these categories owing to their negative consequences, leads to the elaboration of a categorical distinction between the female ingroup and the male outgroup. It is important to realise that this explanation is not a wholly biological one, like that of Freedman (1980). It is interactive in the sense that the initial difference is the first step in a process that subsequently involves, first, incompatible or unrewarding interactions, and second, group categorisation.

The question of the developmental origin of the sex differences in interaction styles does concern biological processes. Maccoby (1988) referred to prenatal hormonal influences as their possible source, but there is little definite evidence, except to note that same-sex peer groups are characteristic of the young in many primate species (Nakamichi, 1989). In the rhesus monkey, preferences develop even in the absence of social interactions with peers (Suomi, Hackett & Harlow, 1970).

On the basis of cross-species comparisons of primates, S. G. Brown (1988) suggested that the choice of play partners by juveniles and adolescents reflects the type of individuals they will interact with during adulthood. In many primate species, such as the rhesus monkey, the males move out from their natal group at puberty, and form single-sex groups, whereas females tend to remain in their group of origin (Crook, 1980; Savin-Williams, 1980a). In these cases, Brown argued, males mainly play with other males. Species where both sexes move from their natal group, such as the gorilla, are, Brown suggested, characterised by mixed-sex play. Surveys of human societies indicate that the most common pattern of inheritence of land and property is through the male offspring, so that in this case it will be the females who are most likely to move away from the natal group (Crook, 1980). Yet there is pronounced sex segregation in the young of humans.

Nevertheless, the general idea that social behaviour during childhood might be related to the likely social conditions during adulthood is an important one, which has been elaborated in the sociobiological concept of the alternative reproductive tactic. This refers to adjustments animals make, which enhance lifetime reproductive fitness (Archer, 1991): these may be achieved through short-term behavioural changes or through developmental processes. Developmental flexibility may be based on responding to cues indicative of the likely environmental conditions to be encountered during adulthood. Draper and Harpending (1982; 1987) have suggested that in societies where father absence is the custom, this provides a developmental cue indicating features such as male machismo and rivalry, pronounced female subordination, and lack of parental care. In these societies, the mother cares for the child in the early years, and then there is intense peer-group contact, accentuating those aspects of male groups that are associated with segregation, such as competition, aggressive displays, and antagonism to females. Negative attitudes to males are also pronounced among females in father-absent societies.

There are also circumstances under which the extent of sex segregation and the development of subcultures are lessened. Earlier I described research by Harkness and Super (1986) and Thorne (1986), who both argued that context was important for initiating and maintaining sex segregation. They referred to cultural variations in the degree and age of onset of segregation, the lesser degree of segregation of boys and girls outside school and in pre-school groups, and the importance of mechanisms such as ridicule for maintaining segregation. Nevertheless, they neglected the considerable evidence of cross-cultural regularities in sex segregation, as well as findings that the children themselves initiate segregation.

Having said this, context *is* important—not for the origin of sex segregation but for its development and maintenance. This was shown by a range of findings reviewed in the section on sex segregation. These enable us to cónclude that the *extent* of segregation depends on structural influences, reflecting the dominant institutions of the society, for example whether children help adults with tasks or go to school, and whether they are reared in a small nuclear family or more communally as in a kibbutz.

There is also variation within a culture; for example, in western cultures, whether the social context is within or outside the school.

The intergroup processes outlined earlier influence the degree to which sex segregation develops and is maintained. Processes involving enhancing the distinctiveness and positive evaluation of one's own group at the expense of the other, can be seen to operate in single-sex groups. Carter and McCloskey (1983/4) found that children aged 5–12 years would react negatively to cross-sex friendship choices by their peers, and that this reaction was more pronounced at older ages. Maccoby (1988) referred to teasing by other children when a school-age child is interested in the other sex. These results can be viewed in terms of socialisation pressures for conformity to gender-stereotypes, but the intergroup relations perspective allows the processes generating such pressures to be understood at a group level.

The evidence discussed in this section suggests that early preferences for same-sex interactions arise independently of gender-stereotyping, and cannot be accounted for by individually-varying attributes, which differ on average between boys and girls. A sex difference that is both salient and widespread probably forms the basis for the operation of the intergroup processes that gradually produce separate groups with different cultural styles. The extent to which these outcomes are more or less pronounced in a given case further depends on cultural cues encountered during development, such as father-absence, and the impact of the context, which may accentuate or attentuate segregation. This account provides a complex picture, in which biological, group and contextual processes all play a part.

Status inequalities in society play only a limited part in this explanation. They could only exert an influence after sex segregation has begun. It is the girls who first seek to avoid contact with boys. This is the reverse of what is found later on, when avoidance of feminine activities by boys is pronounced. The outcome of these initial encounters between boys and girls can be viewed in terms of power relations, but only power enacted at an individual level, rather than societal sources of power. It results from the physical characteristics of the actors rather than from their membership of categories endowed with power in the wider society: it is what Lukes (1974) referred to as "one-dimensional power" (see Archer & Lloyd, 1985, pp. 148–159).

RIGIDITY IN MALE DEVELOPMENT

Sex segregation and the different subcultures of boys and girls provide the social context for the development of distinct gender roles during childhood. Those of boys and girls differ in some general organisational features, and in their development. These topics form the remainder of this chapter.

Rigidity refers to the degree to which cross-gender activities are avoided (Archer, 1984). It corresponds to the opposite of what role theorists referred to as latitude (e.g., Levinson, 1959). Their studies showed that the bounds of acceptable behaviour may be wide or narrow according to whether the activity is seen as central or peripheral to group membership, and the individual's status within the group. Here we are concerned with the relative latitude shown in boys' and girls' roles.

In an earlier article (Archer, 1984), three types of evidence supporting the view that there is greater rigidity in boys' than girls' roles was reviewed: role related activities; perceptions of gender-appropriate activities; and adults' reactions to gender-appropriate and cross-gender activities. In each case, there is further evidence.

Studies of play show that, at 1½–3½ and 3–4 years, both sexes use masculine toys to a similar extent in pretend play, whereas feminine toys were used much less by boys than girls (Lloyd & Smith, 1985; Lloyd, Duveen & Smith, 1988). Edelbrock and Sugawara (1978) found that 3–5 year old boys showed greater preferences for masculine figures, activities and objects, than girls did for feminine ones. Hartup, Moore and Sager (1963) found that when 3–8 year old boys or girls were left with a neutral or cross-gender toy, girls spent more time with the cross-gender toy than boys did, a difference that increased with age. When 9–16 year old children were asked to choose whether (gender-stereotyped) activities were appropriate for a boy or a girl or both, girls rated some masculine activities as appropriate for their own sex, but boys did not rate any feminine activities as appropriate for their sex.

More pronounced gender-stereotyping by boys than girls has been shown in studies of 11 year old children's self-ratings (Kelly & Smail, 1986), and 11–17 year olds' preferences for school subjects (Davies & Fossey, 1985). When children and adolescents evaluated a hypothetical boy's or girl's preference for a variety of interests, gender-stereotyped preferences were stronger for boys than for girls (Emmerich & Shepard, 1982).

The reactions of children to peers who show gender-inappropriate activities are again more pronounced for a boy than a girl. When 3–5½ year olds were shown line drawings of children crossing gender role boundaries, such as a boy wearing nail varnish, or a girl with a crew-cut, they showed stronger reactions to masculine than feminine role transgressions (Smetana, 1986). Carter and McCloskey (1983/4) interviewed children aged 5–12 years about a hypothetical peer who violated their own ideas about gender-typed traits, toy choice, activities and friend choice. They reacted more negatively to cross-gender toy and friend choice by a boy than by a girl.

In a study of two U.S. elementary schools, Thorne (1986) found that boys who did not conform to the criteria for masculinity, or who played with girls, were teased, ridiculed or shunned by other boys, and were openly referred to as "girls". These boys were also found sitting closest to the girls. Best (1983) also found that boys with feminine characteristics were rejected by other boys. In a study of status in groups of adolescent boys at summer camp, Savin-Williams (1980b) found that the lowest-ranking boys were viewed as the most feminine, and also as the most religious, submissive and quiet, which are feminine stereotypic traits (Bem, 1974; Spence, Helmreich & Stapp, 1975).

Adults' reactions to children's cross-gender behaviour is demonstrated in studies of student samples, and in concern shown by parents over cross-gender behaviour by boys. Martin (1990) asked college students to evaluate their own and society's acceptance of cross-gender behaviour by boys and girls, and to make judgements about these children's expected behaviour as adults. Cross-gender behaviour was rated as less acceptable for boys than for girls, and feminine boys were rated as less well-adjusted and more likely to grow up to be homosexual. The raters expected that girls would be much more likely to "grow out" of cross-gender behaviour when they were older.

Feminine boys tend to attract parental concern or even alarm, and (in the U.S.) be referred to professionals for treatment. Previously (Archer, 1984), I have described a study of feminine boys referred for treatment from the U.C.L.A. Gender Clinic Program as manifesting "childhood gender disturbances". The reason for parental (and especially paternal) concern in these cases stemmed from worries that the child would grow up to be homosexual (cf. previous paragraph). Recent evidence indicates that this was in fact a correct forecast of their future sexual orientation. Green et al. (1987) followed up a sample of boys originally referred to the clinic in 1969–74, before the age of 12, and compared them with a matched control group. Most of the "feminine boys" developed homosexual or bisexual orientations (assessed at 13 to 23 years), whereas the majority of the comparison group were heterosexual or had not yet developed sufficiently clear signs of sexual interest. Doll play and feminine role-play during childhood were most closely associated with later homosexual orientation, but it was not associated with cross-dressing, absence of rough-and-tumble play, lack of sports participation, or frequency of reporting the desire to be a girl.

Concern over behaviourally feminine boys can be contrasted with the partially legitimised label "tomboy". Studies of school playgrounds (Thorne, 1986; Luria & Herzog, 1985, cited in Maccoby, 1986) show that there are usually several girls who can be classed as "tomboys". They are found to have enhanced status with other girls as a result of mixing with boys. They are skilled at activities central to the world of boys, especially games such as soccer, baseball, and basketball.

Thorne found that being a tomboy was a matter of degree: some girls sought access to boys' groups but were excluded, and others limited their interactions with boys to specific sports. Yet interview studies show that a large proportion of girls and women regard themselves as a tomboy or as having been one (Plumb & Cowan, 1984; Hyde, Rosenberg, & Behrman, 1977), suggesting that it is viewed as a positive characteristic. In a rating-scale study of 11 year olds' attitudes to school subjects (Archer & Macrae, 1991), girls were found to view masculine subjects as difficult and feminine ones as easy. This was also supported by a qualitative analysis of interview answers from a sample of 13–15 year old girls (Archer & McDonald, unpublished), who applied "difficult" to masculine, but not feminine, school subjects. These findings are also consistent with the view that the masculine subculture excludes or limits girls' entry to it.

Although there is a clear contrast between attitudes to feminine boys and to tomboys, this is in a sense a misleading comparison. When Plumb and Cowan (1984) asked girls to choose activities they liked from a gender-stereotyped list, those who described themselves as tomboys chose masculine *and* feminine activities to a similar extent, whereas those who did not fit this label preferred feminine activities. This contrasts with the choices of the feminine boys in Green's studies, which represent a substitution of the feminine for the masculine, rather than a preference for both.

The imbalance in role latitude discussed in this section would appear to persist into adulthood. For example, historical studies have documented the greater acceptability of individual women adopting the masculine role in a religious context, and the discouragement of male transvestitism (Bullough, 1974); those few documented cases of men successfully passing as women (Ellis, 1928) mostly occurred in the aristocracy.

EXPLANATIONS OF MASCULINE ROLE RIGIDITY

A number of sources have suggested that the greater rigidity of the masculine role can be attributed to status inequalities between men and women at the societal level. These inequalities are so widely recognised that they permeate most social interactions, including those of children. Feminine behaviour entails a loss of status for a boy whereas masculine behaviour entails an increase in status for a girl (Thorne, 1986). In their historical accounts of women who passed as men, Bullough (1974) and Wheelwright (1989) advanced a similar view. Commenting on the toler-ance of female cross-dressers in Christian myths and legends, Bullough (1974, p. 1382) wrote that they were accepted because "they were striving to become more male-like and therefore better persons". Male transvestites, on the other hand, were discouraged because they lost status. For men, status loss was seen as threatening, except when carried out in a playful manner.

Feinman (1981) offered a very similar explanation for his findings that college students approved of cross-gender behaviour to a greater extent when it was performed by a girl than by a boy. He suggested that any high status person performing behaviour associated with a low status group will evoke more disapproval than the reverse case. This study only concerned gender, and merely confirmed data on which the hypothesis was based. In another study, Feinman (1984) did manipulate the age as well as the sex of the actor, by describing him or her as an adult or a child. He replicated the previous finding, and also found (as predicted) that cross age-appropriate behaviour was more disapproved of for adults (where status was lowered) than for children (where it was increased). To test the hypothesis more fully, studies involving manipulation of other status-related distinctions, such as social class, or formal rank, are required.

Cross-cultural evidence provides additional support for the importance of status in determining boys' avoidance of femininity. Commenting on their study of 12 communities in Africa, Asia and America, Whiting and Edwards (1988) found that where there was most status inequality in the society, there was a more active and obvious struggle by young boys to dissociate themselves from women. For example, they sought to avoid settings where their mothers were present to a greater extent than was the case for boys from more egalitarian societies.

Research carried out in the social identity theory framework (Turner, 1987; Brown, 1988) suggests that the greater masculine role rigidity can be understood in terms of the relationship between social identification and group status. In studies involving artificially-formed laboratory groups differing in status, members of high-status groups showed greater identification with their own groups than those from low-status groups. The group identification of low-status group members was lowered further if they viewed themselves as possessing high task-ability, and the boundary between the groups was seen as "permeable", i.e. upward mobility was possible (Ellemers, van Knippenberg, de Vries, & Wilke, 1988).

Social identity research is also relevant to the observation that some girls seek access to boys' groups by becoming tomboys. Social identity depends on intergroup comparisons. For girls, the lower status group, the outcome of these comparisons will be negative, and will produce lower self-esteem (R. Brown, 1988). One response to this situation is for members of the lower status group to seek to gain access to the higher status one. This has been found in research on ethnic minority groups (R. Brown, 1988, p.250), and is consistent with the historical evidence that individual women have achieved enhanced status in this way (see previous paragraph; also Wheelright, 1989; Williams & Giles, 1978). In the study by

Ellemers et al. (1988), described earlier, when group boundaries were seen as "permeable", as opposed to impermeable, high-ability members of the low-status group identified less with their own group. This would seem to correspond to the position of tomboys in Thorne's study, and to women who strive to become male-like in historical accounts. It is also summed up by the following comment from a feminist researcher on language: "Women can only aspire to be as good as a man; there is no point in trying to be as good as a woman" (Spender, 1984, p. 201).

In summary, it is suggested that the greater rigidity of the masculine role results from the higher status of men at a societal level. Although there is no evidence on this point, awareness of the status inequality between men and women probably develops early in life, since it pervades a wide range of interactions between the sexes. There is some evidence that the acceptability of crossing group boundaries varies with status when sex is not involved, and there are also cross-cultural comparisons that are consistent with the status explanation. Both the rigidity of the masculine role and why some girls seek to adopt cross-gender roles can be understood in terms of intergroup relations research on groups differing in status.

ENHANCING GENDER BOUNDARIES

When viewed in terms of group relations theory, the boundaries between the social worlds of boys and girls can be regarded as to some extent "permeable", i.e. some movement between them is possible—but it is asymmetrical in direction. In this section I consider the processes that limit this permeability, and produce its asymmetrical pattern.

As discussed earlier, Thorne (1986) was particularly interested in the nature of cross-sex interactions in U.S. elementary school children. Some interactions (referred to as "borderwork"), were viewed as serving the function of enhancing gender boundaries. Examples included contests or games where teams of each sex competed, cross-sex rituals of chasing and pollution, and group invasions. Although each sex had its own chasing games, cross-sex games were identified by special names, such as chase and kiss. Pollution rituals involved the other sex being viewed as having germs, or "cooties".

These activities were asymmetrical. Although boys occupied much more space in the playground, it was nearly always they who disrupted girls' games, often by first asking to join in. Girls developed ritualised responses, such as guarding their play activities, chasing boys away and telling adults. Pollution rituals were similarly asymmetrical, girls nearly always being the ones who were viewed as contaminated, again serving to strengthen the taboo against boys playing with girls.

Many features of Thorne's borderwork can also be identified at older ages. Studies of classroom interactions between teenage boys and girls, involving a masculine activity such as science or computing, show boys monopolising resources at the expense of the girls (Kelly, 1985; Whyte, 1984). In some cases, they denigrate girls' abilities and make sexual comments (Archer & McDonald, unpublished). In his ethnographic study of working-class boys in the U.K., Willis (1977) described the interaction between "the lads" and girls as involving domination by the boys who take the initiative and continually make suggestive comments.

Interaction between the sexes during adulthood, particularly in the workplace—which is usually male-dominated—shows some features of borderwork, although in modified forms. Since sexual harassment was identified as a problem for working women (Silverman, 1976/7), it has received considerable publicity and study. It consists of a variety of activities such as comments about a woman colleague's appearance, sexual advances, open display of soft pornography, and even the showing of sex films and videos, all resulting in the characterisation of women as sex objects, and by implication as non-competitors in the world of men.

There are also features of men's comments about women that are similar to the pollution rituals described by Thorne. In addition to the obvious parallels with cultural attitudes viewing menstruating women in this light, there are male comments about the smell of female genitals that have the effect of "putting women down", of defining them as inferior. In a study of the experiences of Dutch policewomen who were working with a majority of male colleagues, 90% said they had experienced coarse remarks from the men. One of the most offensive was a comparison of a female colleague's vaginal odour to that of "a rotten fish" (Ott, 1989, p. 50). Such remarks are common in macho male cultures. They can also be made by aggressively assertive homosexual men, again as a way of denigrating women: in his autobiographical novel, Edmund White described one gay man as habitually referring to women as "Fish". When two women entered a gay coffee shop, he stared aggressively at them, and said: "There's such a strong smell of Fish in here tonight, wouldn't you say?" (White, 1988, p. 43).

Thorne used the term "borderwork" to denote the function these activities have in strengthening the boundaries between boys' and girls' groups, and he argued that most of them will come from boys, in accordance with their higher status. In anthropological research, activities that define the boundaries of a group have been recognised as being important for maintaining group identity (Barth, 1969).

Intergroup relations research can help to identify the nature of activities that serve to make group membership more salient. Intergroup competition, rather than cooperation, and collective rather than individual group encounters, are both known to increase group identification (Oakes, 1987). These broadly parallel the sorts of activities described as "borderwork" by Thorne. Intergroup relations research can also help to identify the likely consequences of increasing the salience of gender. In a study where sex was made salient for participants in a group discussion, by the presence of two males and two females, they defined themselves as more typical members of their sex, and in terms of more stereotypic attributes (Hogg & Turner, 1987). Women, but not men, showed ingroup bias, and tended to describe themselves in terms of more positive stereotypic attributes. Self-esteem was also affected by increasing gender salience, that of males being increased whereas that of females was decreased, a finding predicted for groups showing unequal status (Hogg & Turner, 1987). These findings suggest that one consequence of enhancing gender boundaries through borderwork will be to increase self-esteem in boys and lower it in girls, and another will be to increase ingroup bias among the girls. Cronin (1980) found that 10 year old girls would compete in all-female groups in an academic competition, but would defer to boys and show lowered performance in mixed-sex competitive groups. Such findings are consistent with a lowering of self-esteem shown by girls when gender is made salient.

ROLE INCONSISTENCIES

So far, I have covered issues connected with sex segregation. I now turn to a different topic, that of role inconsistencies. These are shown by both sexes, but in different forms. For girls, the main source of inconsistency is between beliefs and actions based on traditional conceptions of the feminine role, and those based on the roles of apparently successful and emancipated women in western societies. This is obviously associated with the changes in women's roles that have occurred throughout this century, particularly since the Women's Movement of the 1960s. For boys, inconsistency in role requirements may also be traced to historical change, but of less recent origin. In their case, on the one hand there is a boyhood masculine role which emphasises action and adventure, with an emphasis on toughness and athleticism, and involves games based on fictional television or film characters, or on sporting heroes. On the other hand, the adult roles of real men whom they know will generally involve more mundane activities (Archer, 1984; 1989).

Feminine role inconsistency has been investigated in adults mainly in terms of the perceived role conflict experienced by women who work outside the home (e.g., Fisher & Gitelson, 1983; Ilyas, 1990). This topic has been little investigated in children, but the following two studies do indicate an awareness of female role inconsistencies, reflecting the process of social change, in children of different ages.

In one study (Duveen & Shields, cited in Duveen & Lloyd, 1986), children aged 3, 4 and 5 years, were shown photographs of men and women engaged in various work roles, and were asked if they could also occupy parental and domestic roles. Although many of the children (and especially the girls) recognised that women could have different roles, they did not recognise that men could occupy both work and domestic roles.

In a British interview study of 10–15 year old girls' participation in, and perceptions of, sports (Archer & McDonald, 1990), many girls said that they played particular sports that had previously been regarded as "masculine". In relation to soccer, a third of the sample of 43 girls said that other girls of their age played soccer, and 16% played it themselves. Yet over half referred to soccer in response to a question about which sports girls are not expected to play: ambivalence was evident in many of the answers, with qualifying remarks like "but a lot do now". Such findings illustrate gender role content in the process of changing.

For boys there are two parallel masculine roles, the boyhood role of sports, rough games and adventures, whose requirements have been investigated in studies such as Hartley (1959) and Best (1983), and the adult role of men they know (Archer, 1984). This topic is discussed further in the next section, in relation to developmental change, and an explanation is considered there.

DISCONTINUITY IN MALE ROLE DEVELOPMENT

Developmental discontinuity refers to changes in underlying psychological processes controlling actions (Archer, 1984). Here I am concerned with the suggestion of David and Brannon (1976) that there are three stages in male role development: avoidance of femininity; the physical role of boyhood (outlined in the previous section); and the adult male role based on achievemnt (Archer, 1984).

Avoidance of femininity is seen by Hartley (1959) and David and Brannon (1976) as learned at an early age by boys. The study of O'Brien and Huston (1985) supports this suggestion. From 15 months onwards, boys chose toys stereotyped (by parents) for their own sex, whereas for girls there was a gradual increase with age in the use of toys stereotyped for their own sex. This is in the reverse direction to the development of opposite-sex interactions, discussed earlier.

The long-term consequences of these early prohibitions may include "homophobia" (e.g., Walker & Antaki, 1986) and difficulties shown by men in expressing or acknowledging feelings (e.g., Brearley, 1986). Studies measuring the content of the role prescribed for adult men reveal avoidance of femininity as one of three factorially-distinct aspects (Thompson & Pleck, 1986).

David and Brannon suggested that during childhood, until the midteens, positive guides based on the boyhood physical role are superimposed on the avoidance of femininity. Again there is evidence consistent with this suggestion. In an ethnographic study of children in a U.S. elementary school, Best (1983) found that there were clear prescriptions for masculinity, emphasising physical toughness, strength and bravery, and striving for status. These were combined with rejection of feminine attributes, and of girls.

Omark and co-workers also found that both Swiss and U.S. boys aged 3–10 years showed great concern over being tough, and that the rank order of toughness was stable over time from 6 to 11 years of age (Weisfeld, Omark & Cronin, 1980). Dominance, assessed by a questionnaire measure, was strongly related to physical appearance and to athletic ability throughout school ages, until 15 years old. Weisfeld et al. (1980) noted that these results were found in a school that emphasised academic success. A similar relationship between dominance and athletic ability was found in a study of groups of 12–14 year old boys in summer camps by Savin-Williams (1980b), and in a larger-scale study by Weisfeld, Bloch and Ivers (1983) and Weisfeld et al. (1987), covering the ages 6 to 18 years. Features described as "toughness" formed the second factor identified in Thompson and Pleck's (1986) study of the adult masculine role.

David and Brannon's third stage in masculine role development, again superimposed on the previous ones, is based on achievement in a range of possible activities, but not generally emphasising physical prowess. This is held to begin in the midteens. There is also evidence consistent with this view from the longitudinal studies referred to above. Weisfeld et al. (1980) found that intelligence (as perceived by others) showed a substantial correlation with dominance and leadership at 16–18 years, but not at earlier ages. Weisfeld, Muczenski, Weisfeld, and Omark (1987) found that social success was substantially related to perceived intelligence at 17–18 years. The third factor identified in Thompson and Pleck's (1986) study was concerned with achievement in the world of work.

The first phase in masculine role development can be explained as an early consequence of the greater rigidity of the masculine role, which is attributable to the societal power relations of men and women. The other two result from historical changes (Archer, 1984; 1989). The emphasis on physical strength and athletic skills in boyhood represents, in historical terms, preparation for the possible fighting and combat role. This is superseded by the achievement-based role because it is more important for the skills needed in an industrialised western society. This type of explanation views childhood gender roles in terms of their function as preparation for adulthood roles, and is similar to the sorts of explanation that have been offered for differences in play between boys and girls and in different cultures (Smith, 1982).

Viewed in this way, it is apparent that the achievement-based masculine role is a fairly recent historical addition. For most men, at most times during human history and prehistory, the adult masculine role will have required physical strength, fitness and fighting ability. For example, in ancient Greece, every boy was given athletic and combat training from an early age, and athletic competitions grew out of this preparedness, with events often reflecting different skills associated with the warrior role.

DISCONTINUITY IN FEMININE ROLE DEVELOPMENT

Several writers have remarked on a discontinuity in feminine role development at puberty (Katz, 1979; Hill & Lynch, 1982; Archer, 1984), consisting of increased role rigidity. Katz described a drastic decrease in the tolerance of tomboyish activity, and a lessening in the value of sporting activities and academic achievement. Instead, interest becomes focused on dating, attractiveness, and future marriage plans. Hill and Lynch (1982) put forward a similar view, which they termed the "gender intensification hypothesis": they reviewed evidence supporting the following conclusions about changes in girls' role-related behaviour at adolescence: (1) there is greater anxiety and self-consciousness; (2) achievement is sharply delineated into feminine (artistic, social) and masculine (mathematical, mechanical and physical) spheres of interest; (3) there is greater concern about disruption of self-esteem; and (4) personal relationships with other girls become more sophisticated and intimate.

Different aspects of the feminine role may potentially be dissociable from one another. It is particularly important to bear this in mind when assessing the research evidence for increased role rigidity at puberty, which will be discussed under the following headings: (1) tolerance of tomboyish activities; (2) interest in stereotypically masculine academic subjects, careers and sports; (3) interest in boys, dating and fashion; (4) friendship patterns.

Considering the first area, Thorne (1986) observed more pressure being brought to bear on tomboyish activities at the time leading up to puberty. Heterosexual rituals were found to suppress other types of interactions between the sexes (see Abrams, 1989), so that one 11 year old tomboy had to work hard to maintain her "buddy" relationship with the boys. Thorne also reported that adult women who were tomboys found early adolescence to be a painful time when they were pushed away from boys' activities.

Evidence for a decrease in masculine interests, such as sports, mathematics, science, and scholastic achievement, is mixed. Two studies cited in an earlier review of this topic (Archer, 1984) showed decreased academic performance and spatial ability after adolescence. A large-scale U.S. longitudinal study carried out in the 1960s and 1970s (Hilton & Berglund, 1974) found no sex difference in mathematical achievement in the 5th grade (age 11 years), but after this boys pulled ahead of girls. These differences were paralleled by the numbers of each sex perceiving mathematics as interesting. A longitudinal study in the U.K. (Doherty & Dawe, 1985) found a decline in positive attitudes to school science from 12 to 15 years for both sexes, but the decline was much more marked for girls. One interesting aspect of these results was the finding that early maturing girls developed particularly unfavourable attitudes to school science in years one and two of secondary school (ages 11–13 years). Doherty and Dawe suggested that achievement of femininity becomes an overriding priority in a girl's life following puberty, so that early maturers become aware of this sooner than later maturers. This explanation parallels the gender intensification hypothesis.

Davies and Fossey (1985) interviewed children from a London secondary school about their favourite subjects, and whether they thought particular school subjects were suitable for boys or girls or both. They found that girls aged 14–15 and 16–17 years showed significantly more feminine choices for their favourite subjects than those aged 11–12 years (data analysis carried out on Davies & Fossey's figures by the author: 11–12yr vs. 14–15yr, $\chi^2=4.9$, $1df$, P<0.05; 11–12yr vs. 16–17yr, $\chi^2=17.90$, $1df$, P<0.001).

A cross-sectional interview study of 10–15 year old girls carried out in the U.K. in 1986–7 (Archer & McDonald, 1991) found no indication that stereotypically masculine school subjects, such as science or maths, were less preferred by post-menarchal girls than pre-menarchal girls. It therefore provided no support for the hypothesis that girls lose interest in such subjects following puberty. However, 14–15 year olds did show fewer masculine favourite subjects than at younger ages, indicating a possible decline in masculine interests at a slightly later age, in accordance with Davies and Fossey's findings. There is, therefore, some consistency with a broader hypothesis that locates the intensification of some gender-related activities later than puberty. These results are, therefore, consistent with those of Hilton and Berglund (1974) that interest in maths falls off in secondary school, but not with those locating the decline in positive attitudes to science at the onset of menarche (Doherty & Dawe, 1985).

Sport is generally regarded as a masculine area of interest. Tyler (1973) and Katz (1979) suggested that girls play fewer sports after puberty, and those that are played will be feminine. Emmerich and Shepard (1982) asked boys and girls to rate whether various activities would be preferred by a boy or a girl. Girls but not boys showed increased stereotyping of masculine activities, such as sport, from late childhood (10.9 years) through early and later adolescence (13.8 and 16.8 years). However, the interview study of Archer and McDonald (1990) found no evidence to support the predicted decreased interest in masculine sports, and in sport overall, following puberty. Since some recent studies suggest that sports participation and a feminine self-concept are now more compatible, and a range of sports are acceptable for women (Weisfeld, Bloch & Ivers, 1984; Hoferek & Hanick, 1985), this finding probably reflects social change in the types of activities that can be reconciled with a feminine identity.

A similar explanation might be offered for the findings on mathematics, referred to earlier, since there has been particular emphasis on trying to break down gender-stereotypes in this area. Bearing in mind the potential dissociation of role-related components, it is likely that social change has occurred in areas such as sports and school subjects, but much less (if at all) in avoidance of masculinity, and interpersonal concerns.

Obviously increased interest in boys and dating is to be expected after puberty. What is less expected is a finding by Schofield (1981) that 12–13 year old girls' popularity with other girls was positively related to their popularity with boys, but boys' status with other boys did not depend on their relations with girls. This asymmetry echoes that found in interactions between the sexes, discussed earlier.

There is evidence that the friendship patterns found between younger girls become more intense after puberty. Cross-cultural studies (reviewed by Savin-Williams, 1980a) show that pubescent girls leave their childhood play groups either to join the household or to develop predominantly dyadic friendships with other girls. Studies carried out in the U.S. and U.K. also indicate that intense same-sex friendships consisting of pairs or threes are the typical pattern for girls from around the ages of 12–16 years, contrasting with the larger friendship groups formed by boys at these ages (Griffin, 1986; Savin-Williams, 1980a; Willis, 1977).

Overall there is evidence for a decline in tomboyish behaviour and an increase in activities concerned with attractiveness and dating after puberty. The evidence for decreased interest in achievement, masculine school subjects and sports activities is more mixed.

EXPLAINING CHANGES IN THE FEMININE ROLE AT ADOLESCENCE

At a societal level, the various changes in the feminine role at adolescence can be viewed as reflecting men's definition of females in terms of their relations to men and their importance as potential wives and mothers. This interpretation combines both the sociobiological prediction that there will be a conflict of interests between the sexes, and the structural power

analysis that men—the higher status group—will seek control over reproduction. Sociobiological theory predicts that where possible, males will
seek to control access to females as reproductive resources: it follows from
natural selection theory that it is generally females who limit sexual access,
and males who seek to ·mate as widely as possible (Trivers, 1972).
Nevertheless, females show a tendency to mate outside of their established
pairs (Hrdy, 1981; Small, 1989). If males have the power to maximise their
own reproductive interests at the expense of those of females, they will do
so, for example by controlling the activity of females to whom they are
related, or with whom they are paired. Sexually mature girls become a
valuable commodity in a male-dominated society, and it is seen as
important that they behave appropriately.

   This analysis leads to the conclusion that it is male power at a societal
and family level that is crucial for the restriction of girls' activities from the
time when their value as a potential wife, mother and child-rearer can be
fulfilled. This process would be expected to occur to a greater extent in
traditional cultures, where the impact of male power is more absolute
(Archer, 1984). Here, there is greater emphasis on preserving virginity and
controlling the girl's future so that it follows a traditional path. Throughout
human history, males have sought to control female sexual activities in
various ways (Hrdy, 1981).

   This sort of control of female reproduction by males is less in modern
secular societies. Even here, there are still many pressures, from families
and the wider culture, on girls to conform to traditional patterns. The
emphasis on preserving virginity may not be as strict as in traditional
societies, but there is still much evidence of the operation of the double-
standard and the importance of not being seen as "easy" for a girl's social
position and reputation (e.g., Lees, 1986).

   This analysis concentrates on the control of women's reproductive lives
by male interests, and views restrictions of interests after puberty as
following from this control. A rather more subtle explanation has been
offered in terms of the intergroup relations perspective. Abrams (1989)
suggested that before puberty boys and girls form "psychological groups"
who are in competition with one another (as indicated in earlier sections).
For girls, puberty acts as a social signal for this to change, so that instead of
positive identity being gained from continued competition with boys, it is
gained by achieving stereotypically feminine characteristics that are valued
by the higher status older boys, with whom the girls are able to associate.
This enables them to gain a positive sense of identity compared with that of
boys of their own age. This analysis focuses on the girl being able to use her
emergent sexuality to enhance her status in a world where it is defined in
terms of male interests. At a societal level, it would still constitute a
manifestation of gender-based power relations.

CONCLUSIONS

The social context of childhood gender roles is that they develop in sex-segregated groups that show contrasting interaction styles and subcultures. Evidence suggests that the formation of these groups is initially based on same-sex preferences that cannot be attributed to gender-stereotyping or sex differences in temperament. Instead, they appear to be the result of the establishment of group categorisation based on the unsatisfactory outcome of early cross-sex interactions for girls. In this process, the power relations of men and women at a societal level play little or no part, although the interactions can be viewed in terms of power at an interpersonal or dyadic level.

The greater rigidity of the masculine role can be attributed to the wider power imbalance in society, and intergroup relations research indicates that stronger group identification is characteristic of higher status groups. It also demonstrates that high-ability members of a lower-status group show particularly low group identification where upward mobility is possible. These findings may explain why individual girls seek to enter the social world of boys but not vice versa.

"Borderwork" refers to forms of cross-sex interactions initiated by males, which are usually carried out collectively and are disruptive or assertive in nature. Intergroup relations research indicates that such interactions will enhance the salience of group membership, the function that has been ascribed to borderwork. Intergroup relations research also indicates that one consequence of this process will be to increase the self-esteem of the higher status group, i.e. boys, and lower that of the lower status one, i.e. girls. Again, the power imbalance at a societal level can explain the asymmetrical nature, and consequences of, borderwork.

Sources of role inconsistency are attributable to historical changes, involving the emancipation of women, and the replacement of male status based on physical prowess by achievement in various socially-valued areas.

Three aspects of the masculine role were identified as emerging in development, first avoidance of femininity, second the physical role of boyhood, and third an achievement-based masculine role. These are superimposed on one another. The first is part of the early manifestation of the greater rigidity of the masculine role, and the other two represent the processes of historical change referred to above.

Evidence for increased role rigidity and emphasis on femininity at adolescence in girls is mixed, but there does appear to be some decline in masculine activities and an increase in feminine concerns such as physical attractiveness. This developmental change was attributed to a combination of societal power relations—males controlling the reproduction of females—and an evolutionarily-based conflict of interest between the sexes. However, an alternative explanation from intergroup relations research stresses the use of emerging sexuality to gain power from alliances with older boys.

In conclusion, many but not all aspects of the rules, organisational patterns and social context of childhood gender roles can be understood in terms of greater male power at a societal level. Examination of intergroup processes can illuminate the ways in which sex segregated groups are formed, and how status inequalities influence individual and group characteristics of boys and girls.

REFERENCES

Abrams, D. (1989). Differential association: Social developments in gender identity and intergroup relations during adolescence. In S. Skevington, & D. Baker (Eds.), *The social identity of women* (pp.59–83). London & Newbury Park: Sage.

Archer, J. (1984). Gender roles as developmental pathways. *British Journal of Social Psychology, 23,* 245–256.

Archer, J. (1989). Childhood gender roles: Structure and development. *The Psychologist, 2,* 367–370.

Archer, J. (1991). Sociobiology and psychology: Problems and prospects. *Journal of Social Issues. 47,* 11–26.

Archer, J., & Lloyd, B. B. (1985). *Sex and gender.* New York: Cambridge University Press.

Archer, J., & McDonald, M. (1990). Gender roles and sports in adolescent girls. *Leisure Studies, 9,* 225–240.

Archer, J., & McDonald, M. (1991). Gender roles and school subjects in adolescent girls. *Educational Research, 33,* 55–64.

Archer, J., & McDonald, M. (unpublished). *A qualitative analysis of interviews about school subjects with adolescent girls.*

Archer, J., & Macrae, M. (1991). Gender-perceptions of school subjects among 10–11 year olds. *British Journal of Educational Psychology, 61,* 99–103.

Barth, F. (1969). Introduction. In F. Barth (Ed.), *Ethnic groups and boundaries: The social organization of culture difference* (pp.9–38). Oslo: Universitetsforlaget.

Bem, S. L. (1974). The measurement of psychological androgyny. *Journal of Consulting and Clinical Psychology, 42,* 155–162.

Bem, S. L. (1989). Genital knowledge and gender constancy in preschool children. *Child Development, 60,* 649–662.

Best, R. (1983). *We've all got scars: What boys and girls learn in elementary school.* Bloomington: Indiana University Press.

Breakwell, G. (1979). Women: Group and identity? *Women's Studies International Quarterly, 2,* 9–17.

Brearley, M. (1986). Counsellors and clients: Men or women. *Marriage Guidance, 22,* 3–9.

Brown, R. (1988). *Group processes: Dynamics within and between groups.* Oxford: Blackwell.

Brown, S. G. (1988). Play behaviour in lowland gorillas: Age differences, sex differences and possible functions. *Primates, 29,* 219–228.

Bullough, V. L. (1974). Transvestites in the middle ages. *American Journal of Sociology, 79,* 1381–1394.

Caldera, Y. M., Huston, A. C., & O'Brien, M. (1989). Social interaction and play patterns of parents and toddlers with feminine, masculine, and neutral toys. *Child Development*, *60*, 70–76.

Carter, D. B., & McCloskey, L. A. (1983/4). Peers and the maintenance of sex-typed behavior: The development of children's conceptions of cross-gender behavior in their peers. *Social Cognition*, *2*, 194–314.

Cronin, C. L. (1980). Dominance relations and females. In D. R. Omark, F. F. Strayer, and D. G. Freedman (Eds.), *Dominance relations: An ethological view of human conflict and social interaction* (pp.299–318). New York & London: Garland S.T.P.M. Press.

Crook, J. H. (1980). *The evolution of human consciousness*. Oxford & New York: Oxford University Press.

David, D. S., & Brannon, R. (1976). The male sex role: Our culture's blueprint for manhood, and what it's done for us lately. In D. S. David, & R. Brannon (Eds.), *The forty-nine percent majority: The male sex-role*. Reading, Mass.: Addison-Wesley.

Davies, D., & Fossey, J. (1985). Gender-roles and children's views of school subjects and vocational choice. Paper presented at the BPS London Conference, 1985. (*Bulletin of the British Psychological Society Abstracts*, *39*, A38.)

Doherty, J., & Dawe, J. (1985). The relationship between developmental maturity and attitude to school science: An exploratory study. *Educational Studies*, *11*, 93–107.

Draper, P., & Harpending, H. (1982). Father absence and reproductive strategy: An evolutionary perspective. *Journal of Anthropological Research*, *38*, 255–273.

Draper, P., & Harpending, H. (1987). A sociobiological perspective on the development of human reproductive strategies. In K. B. McDonald (Ed.), *Sociobiological perspectives on human development* (pp.340–372). New York & Berlin: Springer.

Duveen, G., & Lloyd, B. (1986). The significance of social identities. *British Journal of Social Psychology*, *25*, 219–230.

Duveen, G., Lloyd, B., & Smith, C. (1988). A note on the effects of age and gender on children's social behaviour. *British Journal of Social Psychology*, *27*, 275–278.

Eagley, A. H. (1983). Gender and social influence: A social psychological analysis. *American Psychologist*, *38*, 971–981.

Eagley, A. H. (1987). *Sex differences in social behavior: A social role interpretation*. Hillsdale, N.J.: Lawrence Erlbaum Associates Inc.

Edelbrock, C., & Sugawara, A. I. (1978). Acquisition of sex-typed preferences in preschool-aged children. *Developmental Psychology*, *14*, 614–623.

Ellemers, N., van Knippenberg, A., de Vries, N., & Wilke, H. (1988). Social identification and permeability of group boundaries. *European Journal of Social Psychology*, *18*, 497–513.

Ellis, H. (1928). *Studies in the psychology of sex. vol. VII. Eonism and other supplementary studies*. Philadelphia, Penn.: F. A. Davis.

Ellis, S., Rogoff, B., & Cromer, C. C. (1981). Age segregation in children's social interactions. *Developmental Psychology*, *17*, 399–407.

Emmerich, W., & Shepard, K. (1982). Development of sex-differentiated preferences during late childhood and adolescence. *Developmental Psychology*, *18*, 406–417.

Feinman, S. (1981). Why is cross-sex-role behavior more approved for girls than for boys? A status characteristic approach. *Sex Roles*, *7*, 289–300.

Feinman, S. (1984). A status theory of the evaluation of sex-role and age-role behavior. *Sex Roles*, *10*, 445–456.

Fisher, C. D., & Gitelson, R. (1983). A meta-analysis of the correlates of role conflict and ambiguity. *Journal of Applied Psychology*, *68*, 320–333.

Freedman, D. G. (1980). Sexual dimorphism and the status hierarchy. In D. R. Omark, F. F. Strayer, & D. G. Freedman (Eds.), *Dominance relations: An ethological view of human conflict and social interaction* (pp.261–271). New York & London: Garland S.T.P.M. Press.

58   ARCHER

Goldberg, S., & Lewis, M. (1969). Play behavior in the year-old infant: Early sex difference. *Child Development*, *40*, 21–31.
Green, R., Roberts, C. W., Williams, K., Goodman, M., & Mixon, A. (1987). Specific cross-gender behaviour in boyhood and later homosexual orientation. *British Journal of Psychiatry*, *151*, 84–88.
Griffin, C. (1986). Qualitative methods and female experience. Young women from school to the job market. In S. Wilkinson (Ed.), *Feminist social psychology* (pp.173–191). Milton Keynes & Philadelphia, Penn.: Open University Press.
Harkness, S., & Super, C. M. (1985). The cultural context of gender segregation in children's peer groups. *Child Development*, *56*, 219–224.
Hartley, R. E. (1959). Sex-role pressures and the socialization of the male child. *Psychological Reports*, *5*, 457–468.
Hartup, W. W. (1983). Peer relations. In P. H. Mussen (Ed.), *Handbook of child psychology*, Vol. 4, 4th edn. (pp.103–196). New York: Wiley.
Hartup, W. W., Moore, S. G., & Sager, G. (1963). Avoidance of inappropriate sex-typing by young children. *Journal of Consulting Psychology*, *27*, 467–473.
Henley, N. M. (1977). *Body politics: Power, sex and nonverbal communication*. Englewood Cliffs, NJ: Prentice Hall.
Hill, J. P., & Lynch, M. E. (1982). The intensification of gender-related role expectations during early adolescence. In J. Brooks-Gunn, & A. C. Petersen (Eds.), *Girls at puberty: Biological and psychological perspectives* (pp.201–229). New York & London: Plenum.
Hilton, T. L., & Berglund, G. W. (1974). Sex differences in mathematics achievement—A longitudinal study. *Journal of Educational Research*, *67*, 231–237.
Hoferek, M. J., & Hanick, P. L. (1985). Woman and athlete: Toward role consistency. *Sex Roles*, *12*, 687–695.
Hogg, M. A., & Turner, J. C. (1987). Intergroup behaviour, self-stereotyping and the salience of social categories. *British Journal of Social Psychology*, *26*, 325–340.
Hold-Cavell, B. C. L., Attili, G., & Schleidt, M. (1986). A cross-cultural comparison of children's behaviour during their first year in a preschool. *International Journal of Behavioural Development*, *9*, 471–483.
House, J. (1981). Social structure and personality. In M. Rosenberg, & R. H. Turner (Eds.), *Social psychology: Sociological perspectives* (pp.525–561). New York: Basic Books.
Hrdy, S. B. (1981). *The woman that never evolved*. Cambridge, Mass.: Harvard University Press.
Hyde, J. S., Rosenberg, B. G., & Behrman, J. A. (1977). Tomboyism. *Psychology of Women Quarterly*, *2*, 73–75.
Ilyas, Q. S. M. (1990). Determinants of perceived role conflict among women in Bangladesh. *Sex Roles*, *22*, 237–248.
Jacklin, C. N., & Maccoby, E. E. (1978). Social behavior at thirty-three months in same-sex and mixed-sex dyads. *Child Development*, *49*, 557–569.
Jacklin, C. N., Maccoby, E. E., & Dick, A. E., (1973). Barrier behavior and toy preference: Sex differences (and their absence) in the year-old child. *Child Development*, *44*, 196–200.
Jones, D. C. (1984). Dominance and affiliation as factors in the social organization of same-sex groups of elementary school children. *Ethology and Sociobiology*, *5*, 193–202.
Katz, P. A. (1979). Development of female identity. In C. P. Kopp (Ed.), *Becoming female* (pp.3–28). New York: Plenum.
Kelly, A. (1985). The construction of masculine science. *British Journal of Sociology of Education*, *6*, 133–154.
Kelly, A., & Smail, B. (1986). Sex stereotypes and attitudes to science among eleven-year-old children. *British Journal of Educational Psychology*, *56*, 158–168.

LaFreniere, P., Strayer, F. F., & Gauthier, R. (1984). The emergence of same-sex affiliative preferences among preschool peers: A developmental/ethological perspective. *Child Development*, *55*, 1958–1965.

Lagerspetz, K. M. J., Bjorkqvist, K., & Peltonen, T. (1988). Is indirect aggression typical of females? Gender differences in aggressiveness in 11- to 12-year-old children. *Aggressive Behavior*, *14*, 403–414.

Lees, P. (1986). *Losing out*. London: Hutchinson.

Levinson, D. J. (1959). Role, personality and social structure in the organizational setting. *Journal of Abnormal and Social Psychology*, *58*, 170–180.

Lloyd, B. B., Duveen, G., & Smith, C. (1988). Social representations of gender and young children's play: A replication. *British Journal of Developmental Psychology*, *6*, 83–88.

Lloyd, B., & Smith, C. (1985). The social representation of gender and young children's play. *British Journal of Developmental Psychology*, *3*, 65–73.

Lloyd, B., & Smith, C. (1986). The effects of age and gender on social behaviour in very young children. *British Journal of Social Psychology*, *25*, 33–41.

Lukes, S. (1974). *Power: A radical view*. London: Macmillan.

Maccoby, E. E. (1986). Social groupings in childhood: Their relationship to prosocial and antisocial behavior in boys and girls. In D. Olweus, J. Block, & M. Radke-Yarrow (Eds.), *Development of antisocial and prosocial behavior: Research, theories and issues* (pp.263–284). New York & London: Academic Press.

Maccoby, E. E. (1988). Gender as a social category. *Developmental Psychology*, *24*, 755–765.

Maccoby, E. E., & Jacklin, C. N. (1974). *The psychology of sex differences*. Stanford, Cal.: Stanford University Press.

Maccoby, E. E., & Jacklin, C. N. (1987). Gender segregation in childhood. In H. W. Reese (Ed.), *Advances in child development and behavior*, Vol. 20 (pp.239–287). New York & London: Academic Press.

McGrew, W. C. (1972). *An ethological study of children's behavior*. New York: Academic Press.

Maltz, D. N., & Borker, R. A. (1982). A cultural approach to male-female miscommunication. In J. J. Gumperz (Ed.), *Language and social identity* (pp.196–216). New York: Cambridge University Press.

Martin, C. L. (1990). Attitudes and expectations about children with nontraditional and traditional gender roles. *Sex Roles*, *22*, 151–165.

Nakamichi, M. (1989). Sex differences in social development during the first 4 years in a free-ranging group of Japanese monkeys, *Macaca fuscata*. *Animal Behaviour*, *38*, 737–748.

Newson, J., & Newson, E. (1986). Family and sex roles in middle childhood. In D. J. Hargreaves, & A. M. Colley (Eds.), *The psychology of sex roles* (pp.142–158). London & New York: Harper & Row.

Oakes, P. (1987). The salience of social categories. In J. C. Turner (Ed.), *Rediscovering the social group: A self-categorization theory* (pp.117–141). Oxford: Blackwell.

O'Brien, M., & Huston, A. C. (1985). Development of sex-typed play in toddlers. *Developmental Psychology*, *21*, 866–871.

Ott, E. M. (1989). Effects of the male-female ratio at work: Police women and male nurses. *Psychology of Women Quarterly*, *13*, 41–57.

Plumb, P., & Cowan, G. (1984). A developmental study of destereotyping and androgynous activity preferences of tomboys, nontomboys, and males. *Sex Roles*, *10*, 703–712.

Polatnick, M. (1973). Why men don't rear children: A power analysis. *Berkeley Journal of Sociology*, *18*, 45–86.

Powlishta, K. K., & Maccoby, E. E. (1990). Resource utilization in mixed-sex dyads: The influence of adult presence and task type. *Sex Roles*, *23*, 223–240.

Ragins, B. R., & Sundstrom, E. (1989). Gender and power in organizations: A longitudinal perspective. *Psychological Bulletin*, *105*, 51–88.

Savin-Williams, R. C. (1980a). Social interactions of adolescent females in natural groups. In H. C. Foot, A. J. Chapman, & J. R. Smith (Eds.), *Friendship and social relations in children* (pp.343–364). Chichester & New York: Wiley.

Savin-Williams, R. C. (1980b). Dominance and submission among early adolescent boys. In D. R. Omark, F. F. Strayer, & D. G. Freedman (Eds.), *Dominance relations: An ethological view of human conflict and social interaction* (pp.217–229). New York & London: Garland S.T.P.M. Press.

Schofield, J. W. (1981). Complementary and conflicting identities: Images and interaction in an interracial school. In S. R. Asher, & J. M. Gottman (Eds.), *The development of children's friendships* (pp.53–90). New York: Cambridge University Press.

Silverman, D. (1976/7). Sexual harassment: Working women's dilemma. *Quest, 3*, 15–24.

Small, M. (1989). Aberrant sperm and the evolution of human mating patterns. *Animal Behaviour, 38*, 544–545.

Smetana, J. (1986). Preschool children's conceptions of sex-role transgressions. *Child Development, 57*, 862–871.

Smith, P. K. (1982). Does play matter? Functional and evolutionary costs of animal and human play. *The Behavioral and Brain Sciences, 5*, 139–184 (with commentaries).

Smith, P. K., & Daglish, L. (1977). Sex differences in parent and infant behavior in the home. *Child Development, 48*, 1250–1254.

Spence, J. T., Helmreich, R., & Stapp, J. (1975). Ratings of self and peers on sex role attributes and their relation to self-esteem and conceptions of masculinity and femininity. *Journal of Personality and Social Psychology, 32*, 29–39.

Spender, D. (1980). *Man made language*. London: Routledge & Kegan Paul.

Spender, D. (1984). Defining reality: A powerful tool. In C. Kramarae, M. Schulz, & W. M. O'Barr (Eds.), *Language and power* (pp.194–205). Beverley Hills, Cal.: Sage.

Strayer, F. F. (1980). Child ethology and the study of preschool social relations. In H. C. Foot, A. J., Chapman, & J. R. Smith (Eds.), *Friendship and social relations in children* (pp.235–265). Chichester & New York: Wiley.

Suomi, S. J., Hackett, G. P., & Harlow, H. F. (1970). Development of sex preferences in rhesus monkeys. *Developmental Psychology, 3*, 326–336.

Tajfel, H. (1982). Social psychology of intergroup relations. *Annual Review of Psychology, 33*, 1–39.

Thompson, E. H. Jr., & Pleck, J. H. (1986). The structure of male role norms. *American Behavioral Scientist, 29*, 531–543.

Thorne, B. (1986). Boys and girls together. . . . But mostly apart: Gender arrangements in elementary schools. In W. W. Hartup, & Z. Rubin (Eds.), *Relationships and development* (pp.167–184). Hillsdale, N.J.: Lawrence Erlbaum Associates Inc.

Trivers, R. L. (1972). Parental investment and sexual selection. In B. Campbell (Ed.), *Sexual selection and the descent of man* (pp.136–179). Chicago: Aldine.

Turner, J. C. (1987). *Rediscovering the social group: A self-categorization theory*. Oxford: Blackwell.

Tyler, S. (1973). Adolescent crisis: Sport participation for the female. *DGWS Research Reports: Women in Sports, 2*, 27–33. Washington, D.C.: American Alliance for Health, Physical Education and Recreation.

Waldrop, M. F., & Halverson, C. F., Jr. (1975). Intensive and extensive peer behavior: Longitudinal and cross-sectional analyses. *Child Development, 46*, 19–26.

Walker, P., & Antaki, C. (1986). Sexual orientation as a basis for categorization in recall. *British Journal of Social Psychology, 25*, 337–339.

Weisfeld, G. E., Bloch, S. A., & Ivers, J. W. (1983). A factor analytic study of peer-perceived dominance in adolescent boys. *Adolescence, 18*, 229–243.

Weisfeld, G. E., Bloch, S. A., & Ivers, J. W. (1984). Possible determinants of social dominance among adolescent girls. *Journal of Genetic Psychology, 144*, 115–129.

Weisfeld, G. E., Muczenski, D. M., Weisfeld, C. C., & Omark, D. R. (1987). Stability of boys' social success among peers over an eleven-year period. In J. A. Meacham (Ed.), *Interpersonal relations: Family, peers, friends* (pp.58–80). Basel: Karger.

Weisfeld, G. E., Omark, D. R., & Cronin, C. L. (1980). A longitudinal and cross-sectional study of dominance in boys. In D. R. Omark, F. F. Strayer, & D. G. Freedman (Eds.), *Dominance relations: An ethological view of human conflict and social interaction* (pp.205–216). New York & London: Garland S.T.P.M. Press.

Wheelright, J. (1989). *Amazons and military maids: Women who dressed as men in the pursuit of life, liberty and happiness.* Boston & London: Pandora.

White, E. (1988). *The beautiful room is empty.* London: Picador (Pan Books).

Whiting, B. B., & Edwards, C. P. (1988). *Children of different worlds: The formation of social behavior.* Cambridge, Mass. & London: Harvard University Press.

Whyte, J. (1984). Observing sex stereotypes and interactions in the school lab and workshop. *Educational Review, 36,* 75–86.

Williams, J. A. (1984). Gender and intergroup behaviour: Towards an integration. *British Journal of Social Psychology, 23,* 311–316.

Williams, J. A., & Giles, H. (1978). The changing status of women in society: An intergroup perspective. In H. Tajfel (Ed.), *Differentiation between social groups.* New York: Academic Press.

Willis, P. E. (1977). *Learning to labour: How working class kids get working class jobs.* Farnborough, U.K.: Saxon House.

3 Changes in Self-Feelings During the Transition Towards Adolescence

Jeanne Brooks-Gunn
Columbia University, New York, U.S.A.

Roberta L. Paikoff
University of Illinois at Chicago, U.S.A.

INTRODUCTION

The transition from childhood into adolescence no longer only captures the popular imagination, but has become a major field of scholarly endeavour in its own right (see Brooks-Gunn & Petersen, 1983; 1991; Brooks-Gunn, Petersen, & Eichorn, 1985; Feldman & Elliott, 1990; Gunnar & Collins, 1988; Lerner, Petersen, & Brooks-Gunn, 1991; Levine & McAnarney, 1988; Montemayor, Adams, & Gullotta, 1990). The adolescent years constitute a unique developmental phase when rapid biological changes are occurring in an organism that is relatively mature cognitively and socially, and is capable of reflecting upon these changes (Brooks-Gunn, 1986). However, in addition to these biological events, cognitive and social-cognitive abilities are undergoing change as well, becoming more differentiated and multidimensional (Keating, 1990). At the same time as these biological and cognitive transformations are occurring, the young adolescent is confronted with a plethora of social events, larger in number and in variety than before (Compas, 1987a, b; Simmons, Burgeson, & Reef, 1988). These include moves to more demanding school environments; increases in unsupervised time (and hence more opportunities for engagement in

The writing of this chapter, and the research reported here, were supported by a grant from the National Institutes of Child Health and Human Development. The authors were at the Educational Testing Service, whose support is appreciated. We wish to thank M. Warren and N. Baydar as well as H. McGurk for their comments, and R. Deibler and J. Traeger for manuscript preparation.

63

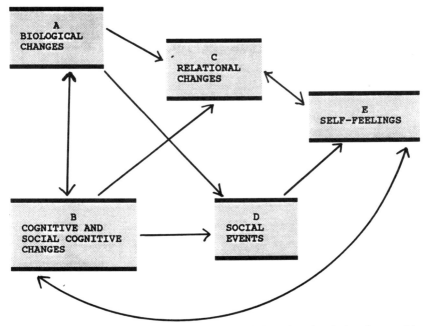

FIG. 3.1 An heuristic model focusing on changes in four domains during the transition towards adolescence as they influence self-feelings.

so-called adult behaviours such as smoking and alcohol use); and changes in peer and family relationships, and, in some cases, initiation of sexual behaviour (Entwisle, 1990; Feldman & Elliott, 1990; Hill, 1981, 1983; Katchadourian, 1990; Lipsitz, 1977; Savin-Williams & Berndt, 1990). A great deal of research in the last decade has attempted to examine and describe these changes. In addition, many scholarly and literary accounts of young adolescents focus on whether and in what ways conceptions of the self are altered, due to the changes mentioned above. The well-worn phrase *"Sturm und Drang"* captures the stereotypically accepted characterisation of adolescents with their sense of a self in flux. It also portrays adolescents as having struggles on intrapsychic and relational levels.

In this chapter, we consider how the adolescent's sense of self might be influenced by changes occurring in four domains—pubertal growth, social-cognitive processes, social events, and relationships. An heuristic model, presented in Fig. 3.1, presents possible associations between the adolescents' self-feelings/and changes in these four domains.

It is hypothesised that pubertal changes (A in Fig. 3.1) may have direct effects upon self-feelings (E in Fig. 3.1), via hormonal level increases and the acquisition of secondary sexual characteristics. Pubertal changes also may affect self-feelings indirectly, via their influence on relationships (C in Fig. 3.1) and social events (D in Fig. 3.1). Cognitive and social-cognitive changes (B in Fig. 3.1) could influence self-feelings directly as well as indirectly via influences upon relationships and social events. Self-feelings might also alter social cognitions, as indicated by the bi-directional arrow between B and E. Relationship changes are likely to influence self-feelings, and self-feelings are also likely to alter relationships, as indicated by the bi-directional arrow between C and E. Finally, social events are hypothesised to influence self-feelings, with the potential bi-directionality of this association indicated in Fig. 3.1.

We wish to emphasise several limitations of our model. The first is that the possible contributors to self-feelings are restricted. Only changes that clearly occur during the transition from childhood to adolescence are included in the model. Other factors no doubt contribute to self-feelings during this transition; these include predisposing individual characteristics and childhood experiences in the family, peer group, and school. These factors are salient at other life stages as well. Our focus is on those factors that are subject to change during the transition towards adolescence and that are somewhat unique to this transition (Brooks-Gunn, 1988), not on those factors that are likely to be operating across life stages. Consequently, the heuristic model is incomplete as it excludes potential contributors to self-feelings for earlier life phases.

A second limitation is the fact that all the changes associated with the transition towards adolescence occur within a particular socio-cultural context. Contextual factors may affect self-feelings directly or indirectly, via the types of social events experienced, and relationships with parents and peers. While clearly important, contextual variation is not a prime focus of this chapter, in part because most of the research to be reviewed has not taken such variations into account. The vast majority of process-oriented studies have looked at American, white youth. Notable exceptions include the work of Simmons and her colleagues, who studied black and white children making the transition towards adolescence (Simmons & Blyth, 1987); Magnusson and his colleagues, who have followed a sample of Swedish girls (Stattin & Magnusson, 1990); and Olweus and his colleagues, who have seen several cohorts of Finnish boys (Olweus, Mattsson, Schalling, & Low, 1988). Research including minority youth and youth from a range of socio-economic backgrounds has not tended to focus on mechanisms underlying self-feelings (Spencer & Dornbusch, 1990).

In this chapter, we review what is known about changes during the transition towards adolescence, focusing on the domains listed in Fig. 3.1. First, evidence about changes in self-feelings during this life phase is reviewed, after defining what is meant by self-feelings. Second, research documenting changes in biology, social cognition, relationships, and social events during the first half of adolescence is considered. Third, we explore links between increases in negative self-feelings on the one hand and biology, social cognition, relationships, and social events on the other. We consider both direct and indirect influences of the four domains of changes upon self-feelings, even though most research is not designed to consider changes in all four domains simultaneously, so that indirect pathways are rarely elucidated. The chapter concludes with a discussion of the implications of the findings and our conceptual model for the study of the transition towards adolescence.

SELF-FEELINGS AT THE TRANSITION TOWARDS ADOLESCENCE

Research on the self has focused on dimensions of reasoning about the self, as well as on the affective valence of beliefs regarding the self (Harter, 1983, 1990; Wylie, 1979). Multiple terms exist to describe each of these aspects; we use the terms "self-definitions" and "self-beliefs" to refer to cognitions about the self (B in Fig. 3.1) and "self-feelings" to refer to the affective valence attributed to self-definitions and beliefs (E in Fig. 3.1). Both aspects are discussed in this chapter. Self-feelings are considered an outcome variable, while reasoning abilities, definitions and beliefs about the self are considered as social-cognitive process variables.

While dimensions of content and structure of thinking with regard to the self are most appropriately considered as social-cognitive factors, dimensions of *feelings* with regard to the self are clearly more socio-emotional in nature (although it is often quite difficult to separate issues of affect and cognition with regard to self conceptions; see Isen, 1985; Lapsley, 1990). Self-esteem, self-worth, and negative affect are the major aspects of self-feelings studied in adolescents to date. The premise of much of this research is that the transition towards adolescence, given the concatenation of physical, social, and cognitive events co-occurring at this time, results in an increase in negative self-feelings.

Current research tends to support this premise, as negative self-feelings increase during the first half of adolescence. When negative self-feelings are assessed vis-a-vis depressive affect or symptomatology, most (but not all) studies document increases in negative self-evaluations. This is true for diagnosed clinical depression as well as for depressive symptoms (Cantwell & Baker, 1991; Puig-Antich & Gittelman, 1982; Rutter, Izard, & Read, 1986). These changes seem to occur between the ages of 10 to 11 and 14 to 15, although few studies chart year-by-year prevalence during this period. In a notable exception, the Isle of Wight study, the prevalence of clinical severe depression was 0.015% in children aged 10 to 11, while it was 1.5% at age 14 (Rutter, Graham, Chadwick, & Yule, 1976). Depressive

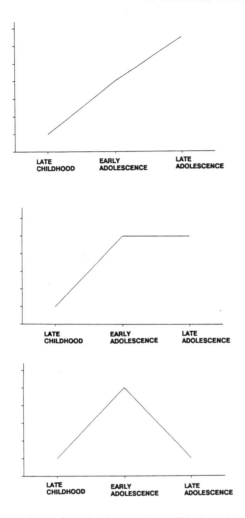

FIG. 3.2   Three possible trajectories for negative self-feelings during late childhood and adolescence.

symptoms also increased in this sample: 11% of the 10-year-olds reported symptoms such as moodiness, misery, depression, and feelings of self-deprecation while half of the 14- to 15-year-olds did so. The increase in depressive symptoms and clinical depression is more pronounced in girls than boys (Kandel & Davies, 1982; Cantwell & Baker, 1991; Radloff, 1991; Petersen, Sarigiani, & Kennedy, 1991; Rutter et al., 1976; Nolen-Hoeksema, 1987).

A related question is whether negative self-feelings in the second half of adolescence continue to rise, fall back to childhood levels, or maintain the levels seen in the first half of adolescence (Fig. 3.2). Available evidence suggests that mean levels of depressive symptoms do not return to pre-adolescent levels. Additionally, at least for girls, mean levels of depressive symptoms tend to continue to increase throughout the adolescent years (Baydar, Brooks-Gunn, & Warren, 1991; Brooks-Gunn & Petersen, 1991; Petersen et al., 1991). A lc ngitudinal comparison from the middle adolescent years through the middle 20s suggests that mean levels of depressive symptoms rise during this time period as well (Kandel & Davies, 1982). Finally, a within-family study indicates that mothers have higher mean levels of depressive symptoms than do their adolescent daughters (Paikoff, Brooks-Gunn, & Carlton-Ford, 1991).

Much of this research relies on cross-sectional examination of mean levels of a particular dimension of self-feelings, comparing different-aged individuals. A more useful approach is longitudinal in nature, which allows for assessment of stability and continuity as well as prevalence. Depressive symptomatology scores are moderately stable from year to year (Baydar et al., 1991), while continuity is even seen over a 10-year period (Kandel & Davies, 1982). Thus, even while mean levels of depressive symptomatology are increasing over the first half of adolescence, the relative rank order is relatively stable. Put another way, the mean increases are not due to a few individuals reporting negative self-feelings, but to a rise across most adolescents.

Other aspects of self-feelings have not been as extensively studied as depressive symptoms. While emotional lability (or mood swings) has received much theoretical interest, few studies have directly addressed the degree of mood lability found in young adolescents, or changes in mood lability from childhood to adolescence or from adolescence to adulthood. In a novel series of studies, Csikszentmihalyi, Larson and their colleagues (Csikszentmihalyi & Larson, 1984; Larson, Csikszentmihalyi, & Graef, 1980; Larson & Lampman-Petraitis, 1989) have examined mood lability by providing adolescents with beepers and having the adolescents report mood at a series of random times over a day or week. These studies suggest important individual variations in mood swings (with most adolescents experiencing relatively minor mood changes, while some experience extreme mood shifts and others experience few, if any, mood shifts).

Another aspect of self-feelings involves the attribution of value to the self, most commonly labelled as self-esteem. While results of studies assessing changes in self-esteem over time are not wholly consistent (Harter, 1983; Savin-Williams & Demo, 1984; Wylie, 1979), the largest longitudinal study of the transition towards adolescence has reported a dip in children's self-esteem during the middle school years compared to the late elementary school and high school years (Simmons & Blyth, 1987). This dip, however, appears to be short-term in nature, especially for boys

(Simmons & Blyth, 1987). In a beeper study of self-esteem (similar to the mood lability work discussed earlier), the majority of adolescents were found to have relatively stable levels of self-esteem, with few experiencing wide variation in self-feelings (Savin-Williams & Demo, 1984).

From this discussion, it should be clear that not all adolescents experience extremely negative self-feelings. Only a few become clinically depressed. Several intensive longitudinal studies suggest that about 20% of all adolescents have particular difficulties during this time period (Offer, 1987; Hauser & Bowlds, 1990). These findings have led to more refined models for explaining the increases in negative self-feelings. All take an individual difference approach, and all consider, in various degrees of detail, the influence of biological growth, cognitive and social-cognitive development, increase in the frequency of social events, and relational realignments taking place from the ages of 10 to 15. However, few take into account all of these changes simultaneously. This has led to a fragmentation in our ability to specify the mechanisms that result in increased negative self-feelings. Such a shortcoming is not surprising in that these more differentiated models are relatively new in the field of adolescence (until a decade ago, most research focused on documenting the existence of negative self-feelings, not on their underlying factors). More serious, however, is the lack of attention paid to modelling *changes* in negative self-feelings over time. The question is, why do some individuals experience a change in self-feelings while others do not? Are these changes the result of changes in physical growth, cognitive and social cognitive development, social events, or relationships with others? In this chapter, we pay particular attention to those studies that have attempted to address these issues.

While beyond the scope of this chapter to discuss methodological issues in detail, it is important to note, at least in passing, that measurement issues plague the study of self-feelings (as is true of other functional domains). Particular concerns include individual differences in the time-frame used by adolescents when asked about emotional functioning; the domains tapped by different measures; the comparability of constructs over the childhood and adolescent years; and other similarities and differences between different respondents (Brooks-Gunn & Paikoff, 1991; Brooks-Gunn, Rock, & Warren, 1989; Cantwell & Baker, 1991; Harter, 1990; Kandel & Davies, 1986; Radloff, 1991; Weissman et al., 1987). Also, it is unclear whether self-feelings differ as a function of age and cognitive functioning. A final measurement concern is how different aspects of self-feelings are intertwined. Measures vary with respect to domain generality and specificity (Wylie, 1979). Additionally, some measures are highly interrelated. For example, self-worth and depressive symptomatology are highly associated: overlapping domains may be tapped by self-worth and depressive symptomatology measures or low self-worth may result in depressive symptoms (Brooks-Gunn, Rock, & Warren, 1989).

CHANGES DURING THE ADOLESCENT TRANSITION

Biological Changes of Puberty

The biological changes of puberty constitute the most significant physiological and physical changes since the first year of life, leaving very few cells in the body unchanged. The biological changes have been extensively studied. We discuss here three aspects of puberty—hormonal changes, physical growth, and the timing of pubertal development.

Hormonal Changes

Pubertal maturation is controlled by the reproductive endocrine system, which first operates during the fetal period. Events are controlled largely by complex interactions among the brain, the pituitary gland, and the gonads (ovaries in women and testes in males). The pituitary is a small organ at the base of the brain, which receives signals from the brain and releases hormones into the bloodstream. These hormones, in turn, influence organs throughout the body, regulating growth and many other aspects of normal body functioning. Signals back to the brain, either through nerve pathways or via hormones in the blood, complete the circuit. Two systems of particular importance in adolescent development are the hypothalamus/pituitary/gonadal axis that regulates sexual maturation and reproduction, and the hypothalamus/pituitary/adrenal axis that controls many aspects of the body's response to stress.

Before birth, gonads develop in males and begin to secrete hormones called androgens. Androgens set in motion a series of events that result in the development of male internal and external sex organs and in specific changes in the hypothalamus-pituitary-gonadal axis. This process results in the birth of a boy; if it does not occur, the result is a girl. After what appears to be a short burst of sex steroid activity in the first few months of life, this hormonal system then operates at a fairly low level until middle childhood (Brooks-Gunn & Reiter, 1990; Reiter, 1987; Reiter & Grumbach, 1982).

Two independent processes, controlled by different mechanisms but closely linked temporally, are involved in the increase of sex-steroid secretion in the prepubertal and pubertal periods. One process, adrenarche, involves production of androgens by the adrenal gland; this precedes by about two years the second event, gonadarche, which involves reactivation of the quiescent hypothalamic-pituitary-gonadotropin-gonadal system.

Hormonal changes may have direct effects on self-feelings, via alterations in arousal or affective states. Links between specific neuroendocrine alterations and self-feelings have not been made for the pubertal child, although relevant work is being done for adults with affective disorders. Another path of influence might be via secondary sexual characteristic development, which is dependent on hormonal increases for its activation (Miller-Buchanan, Eccles, & Becker, 1992; Paikoff & Brooks-Gunn, 1990b).

Physical Changes

Growth during childhood and adolescence occurs because of a complicated, harmonious interaction of multiple and diverse factors. Genetic influence, nutritional status, hormonal changes and the presence or absence of diseases modulate, both qualitatively and quantitatively, the growth process during adolescent years. The physical changes of puberty, extending from pre-teenage to the end of the second decade, have been carefully described (Marshall & Tanner, 1969; 1970). The key changes that occur in a continuous process are often described as occurring in stages (Figs. 3.3 and 3.4). In girls, breast development is divided into five stages and in boys, genital development is also divided into five stages. Additionally, five pubic hair stages have been described for girls and for boys.

Breast budding, typically the first sexual characteristic to appear in girls, occurs at approximately 10.5 years. In one-fifth of girls, the appearance of pubic hair occurs prior to breast buds. The interval between breast budding and adult breast configuration is about 4.5 years and is similar for girls who mature at younger or older ages. Menarche (the first menses) occurs at about 12.5 years in the United States, about 2.5 years after breast buds appear. Menarche follows the peak height velocity, the age at which the most rapid growth occurs; in fact, the time of maximum deceleration of height growth is most closely associated with menarche. The peak height velocity occurs before development of pubic hair in one-fourth of girls and in the initial stage of, or probably before, breast development in one-fourth of girls. The growth spurt begins approximately 6 to 12 months before breast budding, at a mean age of 9.6 years (see Fig. 3.3). A wide variation exists in the sequence of events involving breast and pubic hair growth and genital maturation with a standard deviation of approximately one year for the onset of each given stage.

The initial sign of sexual development in boys is the onset of testicular growth, occurring at about 11 to 11.5 years (Tanner Stage 2). The bulk of testicular volume is attributable to the sperm-producing tubules, the mass of which is considerably greater than that of the sparse androgen-producing

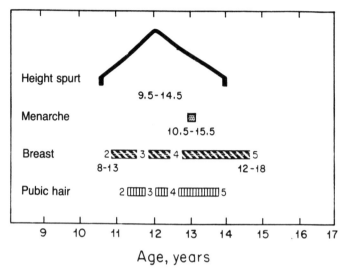

FIG. 3.3 The developmental course of four pubertal processes for girls. (From J. M. Tanner, *Growth at Adolescence*, Oxford; Blackwell Scientific, 1962, p.35. Copyright 1962 Blackwell Scientific. Reprinted with permission).

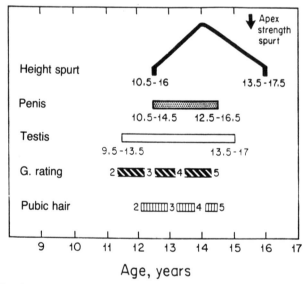

FIG. 3.4 The developmental course of four pubertal processes for boys. (From J. M. Tanner, *Growth at Adolescence*, Oxford; Blackwell Scientific, 1962, p.35. Copyright 1962 Blackwell Scientific. Reprinted with permission).

Leydig cells. Very few boys in Tanner Genital Stage 2 have acquired visible pubic hair; 41% are in Tanner Genital Stage 4 by the time pubic hair growth is first observed. Approximately three years are required for boys to pass from the first signs of genital growth to adult male genitalia, but the duration may be as long as 4.7 years and still be within normal range. The peak height velocity is achieved by a few boys by Tanner Genital Stage 3, but by 76% by Genital Stage 4. In boys, the mean age of initiation of the adolescent height spurt is approximately 11.7 years, thus beginning shortly after evidence of gonadal maturation. The age of peak height velocity is between 13 to 14 years (see Fig. 3.4). Spermarche occurs between 12 and 14 years, at a rather early stage of pubic hair growth and within an extremely wide variation of testicular volume (Laron, Arad, Gurewitz, Grunebaum, & Dickerman, 1980). Peak height velocity and maximum levels of testosterone production follow spermarche. Most boys reach spermarche by age 14.

These visible manifestations of puberty have very high social stimulus value to the young adolescent as well as to others. Meaning is attached to these changes, based on individual experiences, direct socialisation, and the cultural milieu (see Brooks-Gunn & Reiter, 1990; Brooks-Gunn, 1984; Grief & Ulman, 1982; Paige, 1983). Pubertal growth is celebrated in many cultures where it marks the acquisition of adult status (Paige, 1983). This is less true in technological than agricultural cultures, as the necessity of lengthy schooling for most adult jobs has extended the time between the completion of puberty and the taking on of adult responsibilities. Prospective research in Western countries suggests that the majority of youth report a combination of positive and negative self-feelings and very few find pubertal change extremely upsetting (Brooks-Gunn & Reiter, 1990; Brooks-Gunn & Ruble, 1982; Ruble & Brooks-Gunn, 1982).

Timing of Pubertal Changes

As is clear in Figs. 3.3 and 3.4, girls begin to develop earlier than boys. This gender difference is especially evident for the growth spurt, which begins on the average two years earlier for girls than boys (Tanner, Whitehouse, & Takaishi, 1966). Girls have acquired most of their adult height by the middle of puberty while boys often continue to grow after secondary sexual characteristic development is almost complete. The large gender difference in growth patterns and the considerable within-sex variation are hallmarks of the adolescent experience. Both the tempo of growth and the speed with which children progress through the pubertal process have been extensively documented by Tanner (1962; 1981).

The consequences of variations in physical development have also been extensively documented (Brooks-Gunn, Petersen, & Eichorn, 1985;

Brooks-Gunn, 1988). Generally, effects are seen in many domains, including peer relationships, parent–child relationships, body image, eating problems (girls only), sexual behaviour, and substance use. Of particular importance is the fact that effects are more pronounced for girls than for boys. Girls who are early maturers are more likely to exhibit eating problems, conflictual parental relationships, poor body images, and earlier onset of sexual intercourse and smoking than later maturing girls. Additionally, many of these are not direct effects, but mediated ones; for example, in a long-term follow-up of Swedish girls, early maturing girls drank and smoked earlier as well as exhibiting decrements in school and eventually work achievement. These differences were due to the friendship patterns of the early maturers, who spent more time with older, more mature peers than did the later maturers (Magnusson, Stattin, & Allen, 1985; Stattin & Magnusson, 1990).

Self-Definitional Changes Due to Pubertal Events

Adolescents construct a definition of the pubertal experience from various sources of information. For example, menarche symptom reports are correlated with girls' premenarcheal expectations, suggesting that the direct experience of menstruation is interpreted in terms of previously formed expectations (Brooks-Gunn & Ruble, 1982). In addition, individual variation in symptom reports can be predicted from the context in which self-definitions are initially formed (Ruble & Brooks-Gunn, 1982). Finally, self-definitions that are established during menarche are resistant to change, such that subsequent menstrual experiences are perceived in terms of prior definitions. Thus, perceptions of information and actual information received about menstruation during menarche and shortly thereafter may have long-lasting impact.

Pubertal events other than menarche also alter self-definitions. For example, menarche is associated with increases in social maturity, peer prestige, and self-esteem (Garwood & Allen, 1979; Grief & Ulman, 1982; Hill, 1982; Simmons, Blyth, & McKinney, 1983); at the same time, the onset of breast development is associated with better peer relationships, increases in leadership, and a more positive body image in the short-term (Brooks-Gunn, 1984; Brooks-Gunn & Warren, 1988). Reasons for these influences have not been systematically examined; however, they are probably due in part to the social stimulus value of pubertal change. Since breast growth is a normative event signalling the onset of maturity, this exhibition of "adulthood" may confer enhanced status to young adolescents. Comparisons to others, while probably covert, are common; 5th to 7th grade girls readily categorise their classmates regarding stage of pubertal development (Brooks-Gunn, Warren, Samelson, & Fox, 1986). Thus, the experience of puberty may result in a range of affective responses regarding the self, ranging from positive to negative, but essentially mild in intensity. Pubertal changes also appear to influence self-definitional processes in adolescents. It is quite likely that these responses to pubertal change will be associated with the social-cognitive abilities of the young adolescent, although few studies have explored this possibility.

Social-Cognitive Changes

Social-cognitive processes are most generally distinguished from other cognitive processes by virtue of involving reasoning with regard to the thoughts, emotions, and attributions of individuals (both others and the self) as well as with regard to the properties of social relationships (Flavell, 1977; Tagiuri, 1969). The degree to which social-cognitive processes differ substantively from other cognitive processes remains unclear (Flavell, 1977; Keating, 1990). One major distinction has to do with the level of *abstraction or inference* required in the social-cognitive domain. While many cognitive tasks in domains such as mathematics, science, or English are perceptually accessible to the individual (or could be), tasks of attributing emotions, motivations or thoughts to others (as well as tasks regarding assessment of relational properties between self and others or in larger social groupings) necessitate consideration of factors that must be inferred from the behaviour or speech of others (Damon, 1977; Flavell, 1977; Selman, 1980). In this respect, however, self-perception (a sub-topic of social cognition) may differ substantially from inferences regarding others or relationships, since individuals can be assumed to have more accurate information about their own (conscious) thoughts, feelings, and motivations than about those of others.

In addition to differences in abstraction or inference level, social cognition may differ from much of non-social cognition due to the level of affect involved (Flavell, 1977; Isen, 1985; Showers & Cantor, 1985). When tasks involve discussion or reasoning about the self, significant others, or intimate relationships, they may be expected to elicit increased levels of engagement or arousal, as well as increased involvement of emotional as well as cognitive factors in responses. Unfortunately, the majority of studies examining the role of affect in cognition have not examined this issue with regard to perceptions or expectations of known others or the self (Isen, 1985). In the majority of these studies, affect has either been induced (via promises of gifts or positive suggestion) or affect has been assumed due to particular task demands (e.g., task failure or success). Studies comparing affect or arousal levels as a function of task content are necessary to understand fully the relationship between content and arousal level. The majority of developmental investigators have attempted to avoid the influence of arousal or affective state upon child and adolescent responses by using hypothetical situations or dilemmas in their assessments. As most interpret their findings as reflective of reasoning about the individual's family or self, however, this strategy is somewhat flawed.

Within the domain of social cognition, two general types of data have been collected. In one set, investigators have focused on the *content* of social cognition, examining changes over time in what children and young adolescents say about themselves, their families, and friends (Berndt, 1986; Harter, 1983; Montemayor & Eisen, 1977; Secord & Peevers, 1974; Smetana, 1988a, b; 1989). In another set, investigators have examined the *structure* of social cognition, exploring hypotheses regarding increases in complexity, sophistication and integration in understanding the self, others, and social relationships from childhood through adolescence (Damon, 1977; Damon & Hart, 1982; Selman, 1980). We will examine both these aspects of social-cognitive processes with regard to the late childhood and young adolescent years.

Social-Cognitive Content

The Self. A number of investigators have examined the content of children and young adolescents' self-perceptions, asking participants to either list self-descriptors (Kelley, 1971; Montemayor & Eisen, 1977) or to write open ended self-descriptions (Livesley & Bromley, 1973). In both cases, investigators have reported shifts in the content of self-perceptions during middle childhood from concrete, physical descriptions to increasing use of social comparisons and psychological descriptors (Harter, 1983; Livesley & Bromley, 1973; Montemayor & Eisen, 1977) as well as increasingly complex views of the self (Ruble, Boggiano, Feldman, & Loebl, 1980). For example, Montemayor and Eisen (1977) asked 10 to 18 year olds to describe themselves using an open-ended "Who am I?" task developed by Gordon (1968). Age related increases were found in the use of descriptive categories such as self, ideology, and belief references, as well as categories related to self thoughts and feelings. Decreases were found, however, in use of categories related to the physical self and possessions.

In a separate study by Ruble, Boggiano, Feldman, and Loebl (1980) children's self-evaluations were assessed in an achievement context. In the context of a ball-throwing game, kindergarten (5 year old), second grade (7 year old) and 4th grade (9 year old) children were asked to predict later successes under conditions of task success or failure relative to other children. Only the fourth grade children were able to use this information differentially with regard to predicting future success or failure, as well as with regard to certainty of predictions. Thus, by late childhood, self-evaluation information is already becoming increasingly differentiated. In this respect, social cognition resembles other aspects of cognitive development; it proceeds from surface to depth in content (Flavell, 1977; Livesley & Bromley, 1973).

Social Relationships.   In addition to discussions of the content of self-perceptions, investigators have recently begun examining the content of perceptions regarding social relationships. In particular, friendships (Berndt, 1986; Berndt & Perry, 1990) and parent–child relationships (Smetana, 1988a, b; 1989; 1991) have been extensively studied. For our discussion, we focus on the parent–child relationship.

Smetana (1988a, b) has suggested a way that changes in the content of adolescent thinking about parent–child conflict may impact on the parent–child relationship. She proposes that parents and children view the conflict situations that arise in adolescence as falling into two different domains, conventional versus personal. The conflicts that arise in these domains are interpreted differently, thus contributing to some of the observed changes in parent–child relationships during this age period. Smetana examines how adolescents and parents interpret their social worlds, and suggests that conflict may arise because of competing goals in social situations. Adolescent perceptions of limitations in legitimate parental authority increase with age. Consequently, the adolescent increasingly interprets many situations in personal rather than conventional terms. For example, Smetana (1988a, b) found that parents were likely to argue that cleaning one's room was a legitimate matter of parental jurisdiction, and to cite social conventions in their justification of this belief. Adolescents, however, were likely to argue that cleaning one's room was a matter of personal choice, and should not be subject to parental jurisdiction. On matters within the moral domain (e.g., stealing, lying or hitting: Nucci, 1981; Smetana, 1988b; Turiel, 1983), parental authority was not disputed.

Smetana (1988a, p.81) defines social conventions as "arbitrary and agreed-upon behavioral uniformities that coordinate the interactions of individuals within social systems. Conventions . . . coordinate interactions by providing individuals with a set of expectations regarding appropriate behavior." Examples of social conventions include completing assigned chores, and keeping parents informed of one's activities. Personal issues, however, have consequences only to the individual and thus are considered beyond societal regulation; examples include sleeping late on a weekend, or talking on the phone when no one else wants to use it. In addition, Smetana examined multi-faceted items (such as dressing in punk clothes, and the room-cleaning example referred to above) to provide more ambiguous domains in which to assess parent and adolescent reasoning.

Exploring the match or mismatch between parents and adolescents in their interpretation of these situations provides a window on parent–child conflict.

Adolescents' perceptions of situations involving legitimate parental authority shifted with age from the 5th through the 7th grade (Smetana, 1989). With increasing age, children were more likely to perceive situations as involving personal choice, while parents continued to perceive situations as more appropriately regulated by social conventions regardless of adolescent age. Mismatches between parents and children increased through adolescence, with the greatest shifts occurring from 5th to 6th and from 7th to 8th grades, mirroring conflictual increases between parents and young adolescents. Although parents and children differed as to their interpretation of conflict, when they were asked to take the other's perspective in providing counter arguments, both adolescents and parents were able to do so (although specific matches and mismatches within families were not assessed). For boys, this ability increased linearly with age; for girls, however, a dip in perspective taking ability occurred at 7th and 8th grade.

In summary, Smetana's work suggests that while many adolescents understand their parents' perspective on some issues as conventional, they reject it, believing that their own personal jurisdiction is more legitimate. Parents appear to respond similarly with regard to issues where they believe social conventions should take precedence. The developmental task for young adolescents involves acceptance of higher levels of reasoning about social conventions resulting in enhanced perspective taking and understanding of the necessities and limitations of social expectations. For parents, the developmental task may involve acceptance of more personal jurisdiction by the adolescent over her or his behaviour, or the separation of their own social conventional expectations from the adolescent's more personal expectations.

Social-Cognitive Structure

The majority of investigators interested in the structure of thought during late childhood and young adolescence have adapted a neo-Piagetian framework to the study of social issues, postulating discrete stages of development in reasoning about social domains (Damon, 1977; Damon & Hart, 1982; Kohlberg, 1969; Lapsley, 1990; Selman, 1980; Youniss, 1980; Youniss & Smollar, 1985). While this research has resulted in substantial increases in our knowledge regarding the characterisation of thought processes at various ages, studies within this area have been plagued with similar problems to those adapting neo-Piagetian frameworks to non-social domains; namely, large overlapping stages that indicate non-specific developmental change, and unclear links to behaviour (Lapsley, 1990). When the structure of social cognition is considered, it is equally appropriate to consider individual variation within developmental ages or stages, as well as normative patterns of change over time; in particular, a blending of these two strategies may be necessary for a complete understanding of the structure of reasoning in social domains (Maccoby, 1984). We now briefly discuss the nature of our knowledge regarding social-cognitive structure from late childhood to young adolescence.

The Self. As mentioned earlier, studies of the structure of thinking about the self have most often involved interviews probing individuals about hypothetical situations (Selman, 1980) or more open-ended speculation about the self (Broughton, 1981). Damon and Hart (1982) provide an integration of available research on self-understanding from infancy through adolescence, suggesting that the important changes influencing the structure of young adolescent thinking about the self include: recognition of unconscious as well as conscious motivations regarding the self (Selman, 1980); recognition of the subjectivity of the self (Selman, 1980; Broughton, 1981); appreciation of the importance of individual and social characteristics in defining the self (Livesley & Bromley, 1973); views of the self as malleable, and an active processing and modifying of the self's experience (Damon & Hart, 1982). The realisation of these various factors enables the young adolescent to create new organisations of self-definitions, including dimensions such as personality, social situation, unconscious volition, relativity, and reactivity. It has been suggested that the young adolescent years may in some sense reflect an upheaval in the structure of thinking about the self, with full integration of these components being achieved during late adolescence (Broughton, 1981; Damon & Hart, 1982). Put another way, Gardner (1983) has suggested that the adolescent years are the time when intraindividual and interindividual intelligences are fused, resulting in a sense of identity (as described by Erikson, 1968).

Social Relationships. The most comprehensive treatments of the structural properties of social cognition with regard to social relationships have been provided by Selman (1980) and by Youniss (Youniss, 1980; Youniss & Smollar, 1985). From Selman's (1980) social perspective taking framework, individuals improve over the childhood and young adolescent years in their understanding of both social relatonships based on systems of mutual and reciprocal influence, as opposed to subjective, self-generated understanding of social relationships. In parent–child relationships, Selman (1980) examined dimensions of punishment and disobedience, delineating movement from unilateral dimensions of parental authority to understanding the transactional and societal functions of punishment, as well as relativity and mutuality in parent–child interactions (see also Damon, 1977; Laupa & Turiel, 1986, Tisak, 1986). Youniss (1980) also finds support for a change in children's conceptions of parent–child relationships over the ages of 9 to 14, suggesting that children increasingly recognise their own right to an active role in the parent–child relationship, in part due to changes in the structure and function of friendships during this age period. Although Youniss's (1980) research paradigm was initially based on the theories of Sullivan (1953) and Piaget (1965), he carries the argument a step further by suggesting that changes in the structure of children's social knowledge arise from interactions with significant others (see also Riegel, 1976; Vygotsky, 1978; Wertsch, 1985). Neither of these perspectives, however, has been applied directly to the study of links between structure of reasoning about the parent–child relationship and behaviour in parent–child interactions (Laursen & Collins, 1988).

Changes in Social Events

The transition to adolescence is marked by a number of changes in roles, rights, and responsibilities across societies. Although it is often asserted that the first years of adolescence are marked by a greater number and diversity of social events than the years preceding or following (Compas, 1987a; Simmons & Blyth, 1987), to our knowledge, only one study has documented such a trend. In our study of over 100 adolescent girls seen yearly, girls were asked about events that had occurred in the last six months (Baydar et al., 1991; Brooks-Gunn, Warren, & Rosso, 1991). Looking at year-by-year reports, more social events were reported in the first three years than the second three years of adolescence (see Fig. 3.5). This is the first test of the underlying premise of most of the research, namely that more social events occur in the first half of adolescence than at other ages. This finding is important because the increase in social events was highly associated with increases in negative self-feelings.

Changes in Parent–Child Relationships

Changes in parent–child relationships during the young adolescent years have received intensive study (Collins, 1990; Paikoff & Brooks-Gunn, 1991; Steinberg, 1990). While early theoretical writings on adolescence suggested that parent–child relationships experience a rupture during the child's transition to adolescence (A. Freud, 1965), researchers are now in agreement that young adolescents' relationships with their parents undergo transformations or realignments that, although likely to result in

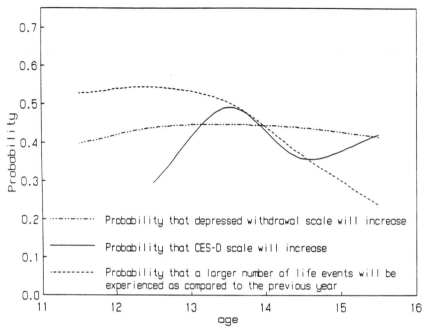

FIG. 3.5   Age dependency of changes in depressive symptoms and life event experiences.

temporary perturbations in relationships, do not damage pre-existing levels of warmth and positive feelings (Collins, 1990; Hill, 1988; Steinberg, 1988, 1990). The characterisation of parent–child relationships as conflictive has also been the focus of much research (Cooper, 1988; Hill, 1988; Montemayor, 1983, 1986; Smetana, 1988a, b, 1991). While the level of conflict betwen parents and children does appear to rise during early adolescence, stabilising during mid-adolescence and decreasing at late adolescence (Montemayor, 1983), many significant questions about parent-adolescent conflict remain. In particular, the issues of definition of conflict (Hill, 1988) and of the consequences of conflict for future adaptation (Cooper, 1988) are central for those interested in parent–child relationships at adolescence. These issues are inter-related to some degree: how conflict is defined can influence whether positive or negative adaptation is expected from conflictive parent–child relationships. In addition, consideration of the consequences of conflict for adolescent adaptation is likely to vary, dependent on whether they are assessed in the short or the long term.

Individual families vary substantially in their level of conflict (Montemayor, 1986); however, it is not clear whether these variations are linked to parent–child interactional styles. It is expected that parent–child interaction styles will be closely linked to conflict resolution strategies (Smetana, Yau, & Hanson, in press), with interactional styles that facilitate healthy adolescent separation in the context of a warm parental relationship leading to recognition and acceptance of differences in perspective (Cooper, Grotevant, & Condon, 1983; Hauser et al., 1984; Powers et al., 1983). Related research has found these interactional styles to be linked to higher levels of adolescent perspective taking and identity development (Cooper, Grotevant, & Condon, 1983; Grotevant & Cooper, 1985), ego development (Hauser et al., 1984; Leaper et al., 1989; Powers et al., 1983) and moral development (Holstein, 1972).

As indicated in our model, pubertal and social-cognitive processes may affect family relationships (see Paikoff & Brooks-Gunn, 1991), which in turn could influence self-feelings. Studies of the association between pubertal change and family relationships have consistently revealed a perturbation in parent–child relationships (via increased conflict, emotional distance, or behavioural rejection or interruption) at mid-puberty for boys and shortly after menarche for girls (Hill, 1988; Hill, Holmbeck, Marlow, Green, & Lynch, 1985a, b; Papini, Datan, & McCluskey-Fawcett, 1988; Papini & Sebby, 1985; Steinberg, 1981; Steinberg & Hill, 1978). One study found associations between level of androgens and assertive behaviour in girls but not boys (Inoff-Germain, Nottelman, Arnold, & Susman, 1989). The long-term consequences of this association, however, remain unclear, as do implications for the health of the parent–child relationship (Cooper, 1988; Hill, 1988).

Familial interactional styles and children's cognitive or social-cognitive functioning are associated (see Cooper, Grotevant, & Condon, 1983; Hauser et al., 1984; Powers et al., 1983). Few studies, however, have examined how the structure or content of thinking about the family may impact upon interactions within the family. Collins (1988; 1990; 1991) has suggested a framework for the study of interplay between social-cognitive and familial processes. He argues that experiences in school and with the peer group potentially result in changes in children's perceptions of authority and legitimacy of the parental role (see also Damon, 1977; Laupa & Turiel, 1986; Paikoff, Collins, & Laursen, 1988; Tisak, 1986), thus altering their approach to parental requests or directives. At the same time, parents may encounter difficulty in responding to the rapid, multiple changes in their offspring, persisting in previously effective interactional patterns that are now less developmentally appropriate. The meeting of these two perspectives may result in less predictable and more conflictive interactive patterns in parent–child relationships. How this might affect self-feelings is unknown.

LINKS BETWEEN SELF-FEELINGS AND CHANGES DURING THE ADOLESCENT TRANSITION

The heuristic model with which we introduced this chapter specifies pathways of influence between the four domains and self-feelings (Fig. 3.1). The research addressing these links is reviewed here.

Pubertal Growth and Self-Feelings

Hormonal changes, physical changes, and tempo variations might all influence self-feelings. The extant research focuses to a large extent on depressive symptomatology, with some studies of impulse control, aggressive symptomatology, and self-worth. Studies of tempo variations have a long history (Brooks-Gunn, Petersen, & Eichorn, 1985), and effects of secondary sexual characteristics have been examined as well (Brooks-Gunn, 1984). Work on hormonal links is much more recent, as techniques for assessing hormonal levels become more commonly used and as interdisciplinary collaborations between developmentalists and endocrinologists are forged (for recent reviews see Miller-Buchanan, Eccles, & Becker, 1992; Paikoff & Brooks-Gunn, 1990a; 1990b).

The physiological processes of puberty may contribute to self-feelings directly. For example, changes in either pubertal hormone concentration or fluctuation could render an adolescent more excitable or easily aroused, and thus more prone to sudden mood shifts or to negative mood states, or they may interact in as yet unspecified ways with the endogenous opiate or neurotransmitter systems (Paikoff, Brooks-Gunn & Warren, 1991). Physiological change may also affect self-feelings more indirectly, via the changing reactions of others to heightened self-consciousness, or self-consciousness due to physical pubertal changes that occur as a result of physiological events. It is also possible that physiological and physical changes each exert independent effects on self-feelings and/or that such effects are mediated by prior experience or self-feelings.

Direct hormonal effects on depressive and aggressive symptomatology have been reported. Changes in estradiol level seem to be implicated for girls (Brooks-Gunn & Warren, 1989; but for a contrary view see Susman et al., 1987). In boys, testosterone levels have been associated with aggressive symptomatology and behaviour (Olweus et al., 1980; Udry, 1988; Paikoff & Brooks-Gunn, 1990b). It is possible that such effects are due to the general rises in all of the gonadal and hypothalamic pituitary hormones rather than to any specific hormones (Nottelmann et al., 1987; Warren & Brooks-Gunn, 1989). Intercorrelations among the pubertal hormones are quite high, making it difficult to disentangle effects of separate hormones.

In our research, we have classified endocrine changes into four categories based on measures of estradiol levels; such measures, however, also "capture" rises in luteinising hormone (LH) and follicle stimulating hormone (FSH) levels (see Warren & Brooks-Gunn, 1989, Figure 1, p.79). Increases in depressive symptomatology were found in our study of 100 young adolescent girls across the first three estradiol categories; these effects were still seen a year later even when initial depressive symptomatology was controlled (Paikoff, Brooks-Gunn, & Warren, 1991).

Pubertal status was not associated with depressive symptomatology in our cross-sectional analysis. However, being an early maturing girl has been associated with depressive symptomatology in many other studies (Petersen, 1988; Baydar et al., 1991; Susman et al., 1987; Magnusson et al., 1985). It has also been associated with poorer self-worth (Simmons & Blyth, 1987). Tempo variation does not seem to make a difference for boys in these domains (Simmons & Blyth, 1987), but cultural differences in the effects of tempo variation on girls are seen (Stattin & Magnusson, 1990).

These findings—that maturational timing has the largest effect on self-feelings and that gender and culture mediate these results—suggest that most pubertal effects are probably mediated by girls' responses to their changing bodies as well as others' reactions. This hypothesis is further strengthened by the fact that the hormonal effects reported are quite small (1–5% of the variance), especially compared to the effects of social events upon self-feelings (20–30% of the variance in one comparative study; Brooks-Gunn & Warren, 1989).

Social Cognition and Self-Feelings

Social-cognitive processes have seldom been linked to self-feelings. However, one of the central hypotheses for explaining increases in clinical and non-clinical depressive affect during young adolescence revolves around increasing capacities for self-comparison and future-oriented thinking with regard to abstractions and possibilities (Beck, 1967; Nolen-Hoeksema, Seligman, & Girgus, 1991). The work of Nolen-Hoeksema et al. (1991) marks a significant step in making the important links necessary to test these cognitive-behavioural hypotheses. In attempting to understand why some individuals develop depressive symptomatology and why females are more prone to do so than males, Nolen-Hoeksema and her colleagues have drawn upon learned helplessness history, which characterises the ways individuals explain the good and bad events in their lives. A maladaptive explanatory style has been identified in which negative events are attributed to factors that are internal, global and stable (Abramson, Seligman, & Teasdale, 1978). Such a style is likely to result in the expectation that bad events will re-occur and that the individual is to blame for them. Research with adults suggests that such a style renders individuals at risk of depression (Peterson & Seligman, 1984). Extending this line of work, children are being followed during the transition to middle school to see if explanatory styles, over and above the number and type of negative events experienced, are predictive of depressive symptomatology. In the first two years of the study, boys were more pessimistic than girls vis-a-vis attributions for negative events while no sex differences were seen for positive events. Both groups exhibited more maladaptive explanatory styles over time, and pessimistic styles were associated with depressive symptomatology. The examination of children's attributions and self-descriptions over time promises to yield insight both into the content of such descriptions and their organisation (or structure) as a function of age, gender, and individual variation.

Social Events and Self-Feelings

The effects of multiple social events upon self-feelings have been studied using three approaches. The first considers the possible cumulative number of changes occurring during adolescence, testing the premise that self-feelings may become more negative because of the sheer number of events with which the young adolescent is faced. The second focuses upon effects of different features of life events (for example, timing, novelty, number of events, number of events relative to one's peers, and type of event). The underlying premise is that it is these features of the events experienced that contribute to changes in self-feelings, rather than their number. The third approach incorporates pubertal as well as social events, testing the proposition that both types of events influence self-feelings. Each approach will now be considered in more detail.

Cumulative Effects of Social Events

Simmons and her colleagues (1988) have conducted an elegant study using a cumulative events model to examine associations between number of life events and well-being of youth in middle school. Social events include those occurring to the individual vis-a-vis the family, the peer group, and school. Event scales have been developed focusing on adolescent experiences (Compas, 1987a). Unlike most studies, which include 20 to 30 possible events, Simmons focuses on four social events (school change in grade 7, early dating, moving to a new neighbourhood, and major family disruption since age 9) and one biological event (recent pubertal change—menarche for girls and peak height growth prior to grade 7 for boys). The number of events was associated with lower self-esteem scores, a measure of self-feeling. The associations were primarily linear and held for both boys and girls.

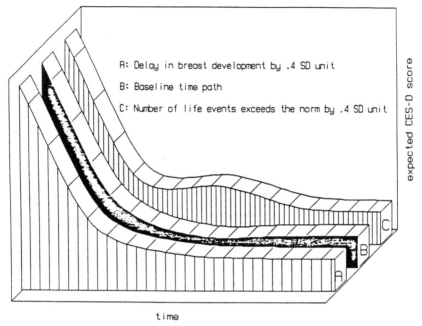

A: Delay in breast development by .4 SD unit

B: Baseline time path

C: Number of life events exceeds the norm by .4 SD unit

expected CES-D score

time

FIG. 3.6   Expected time paths of depressive symptoms based on the dynamic regression model of the CES-D scale.

The cumulative number of life events model also has been examined in our four-year longitudinal study of over 100 girls seen yearly (Baydar et al., 1991). Depressive symptoms were higher at ages 13 to 14 than earlier or later, using the Center for Epidemiological Survey Depression Scale (CES-D: Radloff, 1977; 1991). When we modelled changes in negative affect and behaviour and changes in 20 social events simultaneously using a differential linear equation regression technique, the cumulative number of events was significantly associated with depressive symptoms (Fig. 3.6; Baydar et al., 1991).

Type, Novelty, and Relativity of Social Events

Cumulative analyses of multiple life changes have been extended in several ways. Both our earlier work and that of Simmons and her colleagues demonstrated that the number of social events, particularly negative social ones, is linked to increases in negative self-feelings. We still did not know, however, what it was about these events that contributed to decrements in self-evaluations. Accordingly, we specified five hypotheses to test in our four-year longitudinal study using depressive symptomatology as our outcome measure: (a) The multitude of life experiences during a given time period will increase depressive symptoms due to their cumulative load on coping resources; our analyses confirmed this hypothesis. (b) More life events experienced relative to peers will increase negative self-feelings. Adolescents compare their pubertal and social experience to those of their peers, rendering an individual's experience relative to peers salient (Berndt, 1982; Brooks-Gunn et al., 1986; Savin-Williams & Berndt, 1990). Number of events relative to peers, not studied previously, contributed to an increase in depressive symptomatology in our study. (c) The novelty of a particular experience will increase negative self-feelings more than subsequent experiences. This premise is particularly important to test since it is believed that young adolescents experience more novel events than most other age groups (Compas, 1987a; b). However, novelty of events was not associated with an increase in negative self-feelings. (d) Occurrence of a novel experience will have more impact for younger compared with older adolescents, due to heightened emotional vulnerability prior to age 14 (Achenbach & Edelbrock, 1981; Rutter et al., 1976). This hypothesis was not substantiated in our study. (e) Some types of events will be more likely to lead to an increase in negative self-feelings than others. We believed family and peer events were the most likely candidates (Baydar et al., 1991, p.2; Compas, 1987a). Few effects of specific events were found in our analysis.

Pubertal and Social Events

A number of research groups have investigated the influence of pubertal processes and social events on the self-feelings of young adolescents. In two of these studies, puberty has been added to a series of other life changes, and the cumulative effects of these changes have been assessed (Petersen et al., 1991; Simmons, Burgeson, & Carlton-Ford, 1987). In our own work, we have examined comparatively the effects of a series of pubertal processes and social events upon the self-feelings of young adolescent girls (Baydar et al., 1991; Brooks-Gunn & Warren, 1989; Brooks-Gunn et al., 1991). Timing of maturation, but not actual pubertal status, was associated with changes in depressive symptomatology. This maturation effect was apparent after controlling for the effect of increases in number of social events. While significant, the effect was smaller than that for social events by themselves.

Another line of research has tested the hypothesis that certain social events are reacted to differently as a function of pubertal development. For example, in a study of 5th to 7th graders where depressive symptomatology was the outcome, main effects of pubertal events (such as menarche, breast growth, and timing of maturation) and negative and positive social life events (occurring in family, peer, and school contexts) were examined simultaneously. Negative social events occurring in the past six months were associated with increased negative self-feelings assessed via depressive affect, while positive events and self-feelings were not associated (as expected from the adult literature). Somewhat surprisingly, pubertal events were not associated with increases in negative self-feelings. However, analysis of the interactions between pubertal and negative social events suggested that the occurrence of negative family events during earlier stages of pubertal development was associated with depressive symptomatology (Brooks-Gunn et al., 1991). More developed adolescents are allowed (and demand) more freedom from their parents (Simmons & Blyth, 1987; Stattin & Magnusson, 1990). When family problems exist, postpubertal girls are probably more likely to be able to go to peers for comfort as they have more access to friends than their less mature counterparts.

Parent–Child Relationships and Self-Feelings

In our work, we have conducted a series of studies examining familial factors in adolescent self-feelings (Paikoff, Carlton-Ford, & Brooks-Gunn, 1991; Carlton-Ford, Paikoff, & Brooks-Gunn, 1991). In particular, we have examined mother and daughter ratings of the family environment, looking at the level of agreement, or convergence, between their ratings for family conflict and cohesion. High levels of mother-daughter disagreement on family conflict were associated with negative adolescent self-feelings. Girls who rated family conflict as higher than their mothers did, reported more feelings of ineffectiveness than girls who rated family conflict as lower than their mothers. This finding is similar to earlier work with boys on self-esteem (Offer, Ostrov, & Howard, 1981). Patterns were different for depressive symptomatology, as the absolute difference rather than the direction of the disagreement on family conflict was predictive. Girls who disagreed more with their mothers on the level of family conflict (regardless of who rated conflict as higher than whom) reported more depressive symptomatology. This finding might be due to lack of communication between mother-daughter dyads; research suggests that the degree to which families lack a subjective shared notion regarding their family seems to be associated with problems in family functioning (Carlson, Cooper, & Spradling, 1991; Moos & Moos, 1987; Olson, Russell, & Sprenkel, 1983; Youniss & Smollar, 1985). It may also be associated with alterations in what Collins (1990) has termed relational cognitions. He has suggested that divergent perceptions may be more common during transitional phases, because individual expectations do not keep up with the changes that an individual or family is experiencing.

CONCLUSION

Several of the major changes that occur during the transition towards adolescence have been reviewed in this chapter. We started with the premise, substantiated by current literature, that this life phase is characterised by increases in self-feelings. The question asked here was, what are the mechanisms underlying these increases? Given our interest in a specific life phase, our focus was on those mechanisms that are coupled with a particular transitional phase, rather than on other mechanisms that might operate across life phases. The hypothesised mechanisms are located within four domains in which changes are expected during the first half of adolescence—biology, social cognition, relationships, and social events. Changes in each are expected to account in part for the increases in self-feelings seen. Evidence supports this premise, although the empirical research is still sketchy in some areas, particularly in the social-cognitive domain. At the same time, almost no research looks at changes in the four domains simultaneously, rendering comparisons among the strength of effects difficult. The exception is the literature on biological change and social events.

We propose three different models that would be useful in future research aimed at explicating the links between changes in self-feelings and changes in biology, social cognition, relationships, and social events. These are termed direction of influence, mediational, and transactional models.

Direction of Influence Models. Research on adolescent development is now ready to follow the trends evident in research on infancy and early development regarding bi-directionality of influence between social agents, as well as between individual and contextual variables. Such research could involve sequential analyses of behavioural interactions (Patterson, 1982; Vuchinich, Emery, & Cassidy, 1988) or analysis of questionnaire data as dyadic or systemic units rather than as individual units (Carlton-Ford et al., 1991). Implications of dyadic or systemic variables for the well-being of all members of the social interaction also could be considered.

Mediational Models. Mediational models that are theoretically derived are beginning to be tested. For example, attachment theories of early development suggest that relationships with parents are carried into other social situations (Sroufe, Egeland, & Kreutzer, 1990). Extrapolation of these ideas to the study of social relationships in adolescence might lead to hypotheses regarding translation of family interactions to school or peer group interactions via individual variables (such as individual's social-cognitive level in thinking about relationships). Another illustration is the work of Stattin and Magnusson (1990) discussed earlier.

Transactional Models.   In development studies, we are often interested in predicting change from change. It is only quite recently, however, that statistical techniques are being used to test such questions directly (Brooks-Gunn, Phelps, & Elder, 1991). Testing of such models will be possible only with longitudinal data, and should address many of the central questions of influence over developmental change both during the transition towards adolescence and in other life phases.

REFERENCES

Abramson, L. Y., Seligman, M. E. P., & Teasdale, J. (1978). Learned helplessness in humans: Critique and reformulation. *Journal of Abnormal Psychology, 87,* 49–74.

Achenbach, T. M., & Edelbrock, C. (1981). Behavioral problems and competencies reported by the parents of normal and disturbed children aged 4 through 16. *Monographs of the Society for Research in Child Development, 46* (1. Serial No. 188).

Baydar, N., Brooks-Gunn, J., & Warren, M. P. (submitted 1991). *Determinants of depressive symptoms in adolescent girls: A four year longitudinal study.* Manuscript submitted for publication.

Beck, A. (1967). *Depression: Causes and treatment.* Philadelphia: University of Philadelphia Press.

Berndt, T. J. (1982). The features and effects of friendship in early adolescence. *Child Development, 53,* 1447–1460.

Berndt, T. J. (1986). Children's comments about their friendships. In M. Perlmutter (Ed.), *Cognitive perspectives on children's social and behavioral development: The Minnesota Symposia on Child Psychology* (Vol. 18, pp. 189–212). Hillsdale, N.J.: Lawrence Erlbaum Associates Inc.

Berndt, T. J., & Perry, T. B. (1990). Distinctive features and effects of early adolescent friendships. In R. Montemayor, G. R. Adams, & T. P. Gullotta (Eds.), *From childhood to adolescence: A transitional period?* (pp. 269–287). Newbury Park, Cal.: Sage Publications.

Brooks-Gunn, J. (1984). The psychological significance of different pubertal events to young girls. *Journal of Youth and Adolescence, 13* (3), 181–196.

Brooks-Gunn, J. (1986). The relationship of maternal beliefs about sex-typing to maternal and young children's behaviour. *Sex Roles, 14* (12), 21–35.

Brooks-Gunn, J. (1988). Transition to early adolescence. In M. Gunnar, & W. A. Collins (Eds.), *Development during transition to adolescence: Minnesota symposia on child psychology,* (Vol. 21, pp. 189–208). Hillsdale, N.J.: Lawrence Erlbaum Associates Inc.

Brooks-Gunn, J., & Paikoff, R. L. (1992). "Sex is a gamble, kissing is a game": Adolescent sexuality, contraception, and pregnancy. In S. P. Millstein, A. C. Petersen, & E. Nightingale (Eds.), *Promotion of Health Behavior in Adolescence.* New York: Carnegie Corporation.

Brooks-Gunn, J., & Petersen, A. C. (1983). *Girls at puberty: Biological and psychosocial perspectives.* New York: Plenum Press.

Brooks-Gunn, J., & Petersen, A. C. (Eds.) (1991). The emergence of depression and depressive symptoms during adolescence. *Journal of Youth and Adolescence, 20* (2–3).

Brooks-Gunn, J., Petersen, A. C., & Eichorn, D. (Eds.) (1985). Time of maturation and psychosocial functioning in adolescence. *Journal of Youth and Adolescence, 14* (3–4).

Brooks-Gunn, J., Phelps, E., & Elder, G. H. (1991). Studying lives through time: Secondary data analyses in developmental psychology. *Developmental Psychology, 27,* 899–910.

Brooks-Gunn, J., & Reiter, E. O. (1990). The role of pubertal processes in the early adolescent transition. In S. Feldman, & G. Elliot (Eds.), *At the threshold: The developing adolescent* (pp. 16–53). Cambridge, Mass.: Harvard University Press.

Brooks-Gunn, J., Rock, D., & Warren, M. P. (1989). Comparability of constructs across the adolescent years. *Developmental Psychology, 25* (1), 51–60.

Brooks-Gunn, J., & Ruble, D. N. (1982). The development of menstrual-related beliefs and behaviours during early adolescence. *Child Development, 53*, 1567–1577.

Brooks-Gunn, J., & Warren, M. P. (1988). The psychological significance of secondary sexual characteristics in 9- to 11-year-old girls. *Child Development, 59*, 161–169.

Brooks-Gunn, J., & Warren, M. P. (1989). Biological contributions to affective expression in young adolescent girls. *Child Development, 60*, 372–385.

Brooks-Gunn, J., Warren, M. P., & Rosso, J. T. (submitted 1991). *The impact of pubertal and social events upon girls' problem behavior.* Manuscript submitted for publication.

Brooks-Gunn, J., Warren, M. P., Samelson, M., & Fox, R. (1986). Physical similarity of and disclosure of menarcheal status to friends: Effects of age and pubertal status. *Journal of Early Adolescence, 6* (1), 3–14.

Broughton, J. M. (1981). The divided self in adolescence. *Human Development, 24*, 13–32.

Cantwell, D. P., & Baker, L. (1991). Manifestations of depressive affect in adolescence. *Journal of Youth and Adolescence, 20*, 121–133.

Carlson, C. I., Cooper, C. R., & Spradling, V. Y. (1991). Developmental implications of shared versus distinct perceptions of the family in early adolescence. *New Directions for Child Development, 51.*

Carlton-Ford, S., Paikoff, R. L., & Brooks-Gunn, J. (1991). Methodological issues in the study of divergent views of the family. In R. L. Paikoff (Ed.), *Shared views in the family during adolescence: New directions for child development* (Vol. 51, pp. 87–102). San Francisco: Jossey-Bass.

Collins, W. A. (1988). Developmental theories in research on the transition to adolescence. In M. R. Gunnar, & W. A. Collins (Eds.), *Minnesota symposia on child psychologoy* (Vol. 21, pp. 1–15). Hillsdale, N.J.: Lawrence Erlbaum Associates Inc.

Collins, W. A. (1990). Parent–child relationships in the transition to adolescence: Continuity and change in interaction, affect, and cognition. In R. Montemayor, G. Adams, & T. Gullotta (Eds.), *Advances in adolescent development: Vol. 2. The transition from childhood to adolescence* (pp. 85–106). Beverly Hills, Cal.: Sage.

Collins, W. A. (1991). Shared views and parent–adolescent relationships. In R. L. Paikoff (Ed.), *Shared views in the family during adolescence: New directions for child development* (Vol. 51, pp. 103–110). San Francisco: Jossey-Bass.

Compas, B. E. (1987a). Coping with stress during childhood and adolescence. *Psychological Bulletin, 101* (3), 1–11.

Compas, B. E. (1987b). Stress and life events during childhood and adolescence. *Clinical Psychology Review, 7*, 272–302.

Cooper, C. R. (1988). Commentary: The role of conflict in adolescent–parent relationships. In M. R. Gunnar, & W. A. Collins (Eds.), *Development during the transition to adolescence, Minnesota Symposia on Child Psychology* (Vol. 21). Hillsdale, N.J.: Lawrence Erlbaum Associates Inc.

Cooper, C., Grotevant, H., & Condon, S. (1983). Individuality and connectedness in the family as a context for adolescent identity formation and role-taking skill. In H. Grotevant, & C. Cooper (Eds.), *Adolescent development in the family: New directions for child development* (pp. 43–59). San Francisco: Jossey-Bass.

Csikzentmihalyi, M., & Larson, R. (1984). *Being adolescent: Conflict and growth in the teenage years.* New York: Basic Books.

Damon, W. (1977). *The social world of the child.* San Francisco: Jossey-Bass.

Damon, W., & Hart, D. (1982). The development of self-understanding from infancy through adolescence. *Child Development, 53*, 841–864.

Entwisle, D. R. (1990). Schools and adolescence. In S. Feldman, & G. Elliott (Eds.), *At the threshold: The developing adolescent* (pp. 197–224). Cambridge, Mass.: Harvard University Press.

Erikson, E. (1968). *Identity: Youth and crisis.* New York: W. W. Norton & Co.

Feldman, S. S., & Elliott, G. R. (1990). *At the threshold: The Developing adolescent.* Cambridge, Mass.: Harvard University Press.

Flavell, J. H. (1977). *Cognitive development: Second edition.* Englewood Cliffs, N.J.: Prentice-Hall.

Freud, A. (1965). *Normality and pathology in childhood.* New York: International Universities Press.

Gardner, H. (1983). *Frames of mind: The theory of multiple intelligence.* New York: Basic Books.

Garwood, S. G., & Allen, L. (1979). Self-concept and identified problem differences between pre- and postmenarcheal adolescents. *Journal of Clinical Psychology, 35* (3), 528–537.

Gordon, C. (1968). Self-conceptions: Configurations of content. In C. Gordon, & K. J. Gergen (Eds.), *The self in social interaction.* New York: Wiley.

Grief, E. B. & Ulman, K. J. (1982). The psychological impact of menarche on early adolescent females: A review of the literature. *Child Development, 53,* 1413–1430.

Grotevant, H. D., & Cooper, C. R. (1985). Patterns of interaction in family relationships and the development of identity exploration in adolescence. *Child Development, 56* (2), 405–428.

Gunnar, M. R., & Collins, W. A. (Eds.) (1988). *Transitions in adolescence: Minnesota symposia on child psychology* (Vol. 21). Hillsdale, N.J.: Lawrence Erlbaum Associates Inc.

Harter, S. (1983). Developmental perspectives on the self-system. In E. M. Hetherington (Vol. Ed.), *Socialization, personality, and social development.* New York: Wiley.

Harter, S. (1990). Adolescent self and identity development. In S. Feldman, & G. Elliott (Eds.), *At the threshold: The developing adolescent* (pp. 352–387). Cambridge, Mass.: Harvard University Press.

Hauser, S. T., & Bowlds, M. K. (1990). Stress, coping, and adaptation within adolescence: Divesity and resilience. In S. S. Feldman, & G. R. Elliott (Eds.), *At the threshold: The developing adolescent* (pp. 388–413). Cambridge, Mass.: Harvard University Press.

Hauser, S. T., Powers, S. I., Noam, G., Jacobson, A. M., Weiss, B., & Follansbee, D. J. (1984). Familial contexts of adolescent ego development. *Child Development, 55,* 195–213.

Hill, J. P. (1981). Secondary schools, socialization and social development during adolescence. In F. M. Newman, & C. E. Sleeter (Eds.), *Adolescent development and secondary schooling* (pp. 163–200). Madison, Wis.: Wisconsin Centre for Education Research.

Hill, J. P. (1982). Early adolescence. (Special issue). *Child Development, 53* (6), 1409–1412.

Hill, J. P. (1983). Early adolescence: A research agenda. *Journal of Early Adolescence, 3* (1–2), 1–21.

Hill, J. P. (1988). Adapting to menarche: Familial Control and Conflict. In M. R. Gunnar, & W. A. Collins (Eds.), *Development during the transition to adolescence* (Vol. 21, pp. 43–77). Hillsdale, N.J.: Lawrence Erlbaum Associates Inc.

Hill, J. P., Holmbeck, G. N., Marlow, L., Green, T. M., & Lynch, M. E. (1985a). Menarcheal status and parent–child relations in families of seventh-grade girls. *Journal of Youth and Adolescence, 14,* 301–316.

Hill, J. P., Holmbeck, G. N., Marlow, L., Green, T. M., & Lynch, M. E. (1985b). Pubertal status and parent–child relations in families of seventh-grade boys. *Journal of Early Adolescence, 5,* 31–44.

Holstein, C. (1972). The relation of children's moral judgment level to that of their parents and to communication patterns in the family. In R. Smart, & M. Smart (Eds.), *Readings in child development* (pp. 484–494). New York: Macmillan.

Inoff-Germain, G., Nottelman, E. D., Arnold, G. S., & Susman, E. J. (1988). Adolescent aggression and parent–adolescent conflict: Relations between observed family interactions and measures of the adolescents' general functioning. *Journal of Early Adolescence, 8* (1), 17–36.

Isen, A. M. (1985). Toward understanding the role of affect in cognition. In R. S. Wyer & T. K. Srull (Eds.), *Handbook of social cognition* (Vol. III, pp. 179–227). Hillsdale, N.J.: Lawrence Erlbaum Associates Inc.

Kandel, D. B., & Davies, M. (1982). Epidemiology of depressive mood in adolescents. *Archives of General Psychiatry, 39,* 1205–1212.

Kandel, D. B., & Davies, M. (1986). Adult sequelae of adolescent depressive symptoms. *Archives of General Psychiatry, 43,* 225–262.

Katchadourian, H. (1990). Sexuality. In S. S. Feldman, & G. R. Elliott (Eds.), *At the Threshold: The developing adolescent* (pp. 330–351). Cambridge, Mass.: Harvard University Press.

Keating, D. P. (1990). Adolescent thinking. In S. Feldman, & G. Elliott (Eds.), *At the threshold: The developing adolescent* (pp. 54–89). Cambridge, Mass.: Harvard University Press.

Kelley, H. H. (1971). *Casual schemata and the attribution process.* Moristown, N.J.: Ceneral Learning Press.

Kohlberg, L. (1969). Stage and sequence: The cognitive-developmental approach to socialization. In D. A. Goslin (Ed.), *Handbook of socialization theory and research* (pp. 82–172). Chicago: Rand McNally.

Lapsley, D. K. (1990). Continuity and discontinuity in adolescent social cognitive development. In R. Montemayor, G. R. Adams, & T. P. Gullotta (Eds.), *Advances in adolescent development: Vol. 2: From childhood to adolescence: A transitional period?* (pp. 183–204). Newbury Park: Sage.

Laron, Z., Arad, J., Gurewitz, R., Grunebaum, M., & Dickerman, Z. (1980). Age at first conscious ejaculation: A milestone in male puberty. *Helvetica Paediatrica Acta, 5,* 13–20.

Larson, R., Csikszentmihalhyi, M., & Graef, R. (1980). Mood variability and the psychosocial adjustment of adolescents. *Journal of Youth and Adolescence, 9,* 469–490.

Larson, R., & Lampman-Petraitis, C. (1989). Daily emotional states as reported by children and adolescents. *Child Development, 60* (5), 1250–1260.

Laupa, M. & Turiel, E. (1986). Children's conceptions of adult and peer authority. *Child Development, 57,* 405–412.

Laursen, B., & Collins, W. A. (1988). Conceptual changes during adolescence and effects upon parent–child relationships. *Journal of Adolescent Research, 3,* 119–140.

Leaper, C., Hauser, S. T., Kremen, A., Powers, S. I., Jacobson, A. M., Noam, G. G., Weiss-Perry, B., & Follansbee, D. (1989). Adolescent–parent interactions in relation to adolescents' gender and ego development pathway: A longitudinal study. *Journal of Early Adolescence, 9* (3), 335–361.

Lerner, R. M., Petersen, A. C., & Brooks-Gunn, J. (Eds.) (1991). *Encyclopedia of adolescence.* New York: Garland Publishing, Inc.

Levine, M., & McAnarney, E. R. (Eds.) (1988). *Early adolescent transitions.* Lexington, Mass.: D.C. Health Publications.

Lipsitz, J. (1977). *Growing up forgotten: A review of research and programs concerning young adolescents.* Lexington, Mass.: Heath.

Livesley, W. J., & Bromley, B. D. (1973). *Person perception in childhood and adolescence.* London: Wiley & Sons.

Maccoby, E. E. (1984). Socialization and developmental change. *Child Development, 55* (2), 317–328.

Magnusson, D., Stattin, H., & Allen, V. L. (1985). Biological maturation and social development: A longitudinal study of some adjustment processes from mid-adolescence to adulthood. *Journal of Youth and Adolescence, 14* (4), 267–283.

Marshall, W. A., & Tanner, J. M. (1969). Variations in the pattern of pubertal changes in girls. *Archives of Diseases and Childhood, 44*, 291–303.

Marshall, W. A., & Tanner, J. M. (1970). Variations in the pattern of pubertal changes in boys. *Archives of the Diseases of Childhood, 45*, 13–23.

Miller-Buchanan, C., Eccles, J. S., & Becker, J. B. (1992). Are adolescents the victims of raging hormones?: Evidence for activational effects of hormones on moods and behaviour at adolescence. *Psychological Bulletin, 111*, 62–107.

Montemayor, R. (1983). Parents and adolescents in conflict. All families some of the time and some familes most of the time. *Journal of Early Adolescence, 3*, 83–103.

Montemayor, R. (1986). Family variation in parent–adolescent storm and stress. *Journal of Adolescent Research, 1* (1), 15–31.

Montemayor, R., Adams, G. R., & Gullotta, T. P. (Eds.) (1990). *From childhood to adolescence: A transitional period?* Newbury Park: Sage Publications.

Montemayor R., & Eisen, M. (1977). The development of self-conceptions from childhood to adolescence. *Developmental Psychology, 13* (4), 314–319.

Moos, R. H., & Moos, R. B. (1987). *The Family Environment Scale manual.* Palo Alto, Cal.: Consulting Psychologists Press.

Nolen-Hoeksema, S., (1987). Sex differences in unipolar depression: Evidence and theory. *Psychological Bulletin, 101*, 259–282.

Nolen-Hoeksema, S. Seligman, M. E. P., & Girgus, J. S. (1991). Sex differences in depression and explanatory style in children. *Journal of Youth and Adolescence, 20* (2/3).

Nottelmann, E. D., Susman, E. J., Blue, J. H., Inoff-Germain, G., Dorn, L. D., Loriaux, D. L., Cutler, G. B., Jr., & Chrousos, G. P. (1987). Gonadal and adrenal hormone correlates of adjustment in early adolescence. In R. M. Lerner, & T. T. Foch (Eds.), *Biological-psychosocial interactions in early adolescence* (pp. 303–324). Hillsdale, N.J.: Lawrence Erlbaum Associates Inc.

Nucci, L. (1981). Conceptions of personal issues: A domain distinct from moral or societal concepts. *Child Development, 52*, 114–121.

Offer, D. (1987). In defense of adolescents. *Journal of the American Medical Association, 257*, (24), 3407–3408.

Offer, D., Ostrov, E., & Howard, K. I. (1981). *The adolescent: A psychological self-portrait.* New York: Basic Books.

Olson, D. H., Russell, C. R., & Sprenkel, D. H. (1983). Circumplex model of marital and family systems IV: Theoretical update. *Family Process, 23*, 69–83.

Olweus, D., Mattsson, A., Schalling, D., & Low, H. (1980). Testosterone, aggression, physical, and personality dimensions in normal adolescent males. *Psychosomatic Medicine, 42* (2), 253–269.

Olweus, D., Mattsson, A., Schalling, D., & Low, H. (1988). Circulating testosterone levels and aggression in adolescent males: A causal analysis. *Psychosomatic Medicine, 50*, 261–272.

Paige, K. E. (1983). A bargaining theory of mencheal responses in preindustrial cultures. In J. Brooks-Gunn, & A. C. Petersen (Eds.), *Girls at puberty: Biological and psychosocial perspectives* (pp. 301–322). New York: Plenum Press.

Paikoff, R., & Brooks-Gunn, J. (1990a). Associations between pubertal hormones and behavioural and affective expression. In C. S. Holmes (Ed.), *Psychoneuroendocrinology: Brain, behavior, and hormonal interactions* (pp. 205–226). New York: Springer-Verlag.

Paikoff, R. L., & Brooks-Gunn, J. (1990b). Physiological processes: What role do they play during the transition to adolescence? In R. Montemayor, G. Adams, & T. Gullotta (Eds.), *Advances in adolescent development: Vol. 2, The transition from childhood to adolescence* (pp. 63–81). Newbury Park, Cal.: Sage.

Paikoff, R. L., & Brooks-Gunn, J. (1991). Do parent–child relationships change during puberty? *Psychological Bulletin, 110*, 47–66.

Paikoff, R. L., Brooks-Gunn, J., & Carlton-Ford, S. (1991). Effect of reproductive status changes upon family functioning and well-being of mothers and daughters. *Journal of Early Adolescence, 11*, 201–220.

Paikoff, R. L., Brooks-Gunn, J., & Warren, M. P. (1991). Effects of girls' hormonal status on depressive and aggressive symptoms over the course of one year. *Journal of Youth and Adolescence, 20*, 191–215.

Paikoff, R. L., Carlton-Ford, S., & Brooks-Gunn, J. (submitted 1991). *Mother–daughter dyads view the family: Associations between divergent perceptions and daughter well-being.* Manuscript submitted for publication.

Paikoff, R. L., Collins, W. A., & Laursen, B. (1988). Perceptions of efficacy and legitimacy of parental influence techniques by children and early adolescents. *Journal of Early Adolescence, 8* (1), 37–52.

Papini, D. R., Datan, N., & McCluskey-Fawcett, K. A. (1988). An observational study of effective and assertive family interactions during adolescence. *Journal of Youth and Adolescence, 17* (6), 477–492.

Papini, D. R., & Sebby, R. A. (1985, April). *Mutivariate assessment of adolescent physical maturation as a source of family conflict.* Paper presented at the Changing Family Conference XIV: Adolescents and Families. University of Iowa, Iowa City, Iowa.

Patterson, G. R. (1982). *Coercive family process.* Eugene, Ore.: Castalia.

Petersen, A. C. (1988). Adolescent development. *Annual Review of Psychology, 39*, 583–607.

Petersen, A. C., Sarigiani, P. A., & Kennedy, R. E. (1991). Adolescent depression: Why more girls? *Journal of Youth and Adolescence, 20*, 247–271.

Peterson, C., & Seligman, M. E. P. (1984). Causal explanations as a risk factor for depression: Theory and evidence. *Psychological Review, 91*, 347–374.

Piaget, J. (1965). *The moral judgement of the child.* New York: Free Press.

Powers, S. I., Hauser, S. T., Schwartz, J. M., Noam, G. G., & Jacobson, A. M. (1983). Adolescent ego development & family interaction: A structural-developmental perspective. In H. D. Grotevant, & C. R. Cooper (Eds.), *Adolescent development in the family. New directions for child development* (pp. 5–25). San Francisco: Jossey-Bass.

Puig-Antich, J., & Gittelman, R. (1982). Depression in childhood and adolescence. In E. S. Piazket (Ed.), *Handbook of affective disorders* (pp. 379–392). New York: Guilford Press.

Radloff, L. S. (1977). The CES-D Scale: A self-report depression scale for research in the general population. *Applied Psychological Measurement, 1* (3), 385–401.

Radloff, L. S. (1991). The use of the center for epidemiologic studies depression (CES-D) scale in adolescents and young adults. *Journal of Youth and Adolescence, 20*, 149–166.

Reiter, E. O. (1987). Neuroendocrine control processes. *Journal of Adolescent Health Care, 8* (6), 479–491.

Reiter, E. O., & Grumbach, M. M. (1982) Neuroendocrine control mechanisms and the onset of puberty. *Annual Review of Physiology, 44*, 595–613.

Riegel, K. F. (1976). The dialectics of human development. *American Psychologist, 31*, 689–700.

Ruble, D. N., & Brooks-Gunn, J. (1982). The experience of menarche. *Child Development, 53*, 1557–1566.

Ruble, D. N., Boggiano, A. K., Feldman, N. S., & Loebl, J. H. (1980). Developmental analysis of the role of social comparison in self-evaluation. *Developmental Psychology, 16*, 105–115.

Rutter, M., Graham, P., Chadwick, O. F., & Yule, W. (1976). Adolescent turmoil: Fact or fiction. *Journal of Child Psychology and Psychiatry, 17*, 35–56.

Rutter, M., Izard, C. E., & Read, P. B. (1986). *Depression in young people: Developmental and clinical perspectives.* New York: The Guilford Press.

Savin-Williams, R. C., & Berndt, T. J. (1990). Friendships and peer relations. In S. Feldman, & G. Elliott (Eds.), *At the threshold: The developing adolescent* (pp. 277–307). Cambridge, Mass.: Harvard University Press.

Savin-Williams, R. C., & Demo, D. H. (1984). Developmental change and stability in adolescent self-concept. *Developmental Psychology, 20,* 1100–1110.

Secord, P., & Peevers, B. H. (1974). The development of person concepts. In T. Mischel (Ed.), *Understanding other persons.* Oxford: Blackwell.

Selman, R. L. (1980). *The growth of interpersonal understanding: Developmental and clinical analyses.* New York: Academic Press.

Showers, C., & Cantor, N. (1985). Social cognition: A look at motivated strategies. *Annual Review of Psychology, 36,* 275–305.

Simmons, R. G., & Blyth, D. A. (1987). *Moving into adolescence: The impact of pubertal change and school context.* New York: Adline De Gruyter.

Simmons, R. G., Blyth, D. A., & McKinney, K. L. (1983). The social and psychological effects of puberty on white females. In J. Brooks-Gunn, & A. C. Petersen (Eds.), *Girls at puberty: Biological and psychosocial perspectives* (pp. 229–272). New York: Plenum Press.

Simmons, R. G., Burgeson, R., Carlton-Ford, S., & Blyth, D. A. (1987). The impact of cumulative change in early adolescence. *Child Development, 58* (5), 1220–1234.

Simmons, R. G., Burgeson, R., & Reef, M. J. (1988). Cumulative change at entry to adolescence. In M. Gunnar, & W. A. Collins (Eds.), *Development during transition to adolescence: Minnesota symposia on child psychology, Vol. 21* (pp. 123–150). Hillsdale, N.J.: Lawrence Erlbaum Associates, Inc.

Smetana, J. G. (1988a). Concepts of self and social convention: Adolescents' and parents' reasoning about hypothetical and actual family conflicts. In M. Gunnar, & W. A. Collins (Eds.), *Development during transition to adolescence: Minnesota Symposia on Child Psychology, Vol. 21.* Hillsdale, N.J.: Lawrence Erlbaum Associates Inc.

Smetana, J. G. (1988b). Adolescents' and parents' conceptions of parental authority. *Child Development, 59* (2), 321–335.

Smetana, J. G. (1989). Adolescents' and parents' reasoning about actual family conflict. *Child Development, 60,* 1052–1067.

Smetana, J. G. (1991). Adolescents' and mothers' evaluations of justifications for conflicts. In R. L. Paikoff (Ed.), *Shared views in the family during adolescence: New Directions for Child Development* (Vol. 5, pp. 71–86). San Francisco: Jossey-Bass.

Smetana, J. G., Yau, J., & Hanson, S. (in press). Conflict resolution in families with adolescents. *Child Development.*

Spencer, M. B., & Dornbusch, S. M. (1990). Challenges in studying minority youth. In S. S. Feldman, & G. R. Elliott (Eds.), *At the threshold: The developing adolescent* (pp. 123–146). Cambridge, Mass.: Harvard University Press.

Sroufe, L. A., Egeland, B., & Kreutzer, T. (1990). The fate of early experience following developmental change: longitudinal approaches to individual adaptation in childhood. *Child Development, 61* (5), 1363–1372.

Stattin, H., & Magnusson, D. (1990). *Pubertal maturation in female development.* Hillsdale, N.J.: Lawrence Erlbaum Associates Inc.

Steinberg, L. D. (1981). Transformation in family relations at puberty. *Developmental Psychology, 17,* 833–840.

Steinberg, L. D. (1988). Reciprocal relations between parent–child distance and pubertal maturation. *Child Development, 24,* 451–460.

Steinberg, L. D. (1990). Autonomy, conflict, and harmony in the family relationship. In S. S. Feldman, & G. R. Elliott (Eds.), *At the threshold: The developing adolescent* (pp. 255–276). Cambridge, Mass.: Harvard University Press.

Steinberg, L. D., & Hill, J. P. (1978). Patterns of family interaction as a function of age, the onset of puberty, and formal thinking. *Developmental Psychology, 14*, 683–684.

Sullivan, H. S. (1953). *The interpersonal theory of psychiatry.* New York: Norton.

Susman, E. J., Inoff-Germain, G., Nottelmann, E. D., Loriaux, D. L., Cutler, G. B., & Chrousos, G. P. (1987). Hormones, emotional dispositions, and aggressive atributes in young adolescents. *Child Development, 58*, 1114–1134.

Tagiuri, R. (1969). Person perception. In G. Linddzey, & E. Aronson (Eds.), *The handbook of social psychology* (Vol. 3). Reading, Mass.: Addison-Wesley.

Tanner, J. M. (1962). *Growth at Adolescence.* Oxford: Blackwell Scientific Publications.

Tanner, J. M. (1981). *A history of the study of human growth.* Cambridge: Cambridge University Press.

Tanner, J. M., Whitehouse, R. H., & Takaishi, M. (1966). Standards from birth to maturity for height, weight, height velocity and weight velocity: British children, 1965. *Archives of Disease in Childhood, 41*, 454–471; 613–635.

Tisak, M. S. (1986). Children's conception of parental authority. *Child Development, 57*, 166–176.

Turiel, E. (1983). Interaction and development in social cognition. In E. T. Higgins, D. N. Ruble, & W. W. Hartup (Eds.), *Social cognition and social development: A sociocultural perspective* (pp. 333–355). New York: Cambridge University Press.

Udry, J. R. (1988). Biological predispositions and social control in adolescent sexual behaviour. *American Sociological Review, 53*, 709–722.

Vuchinich, S., Emery, R. E., & Cassidy, J. (1988). Family members as third parties in dyadic family conflict: Strategies, alliances, and outcomes. *Child Development, 59*, 1293–1302.

Vygotsky, L. S. (1978). *Mind in society: The development of higher psychological processes.* Cambridge: Harvard University Press.

Warren, M. P., & Brooks-Gunn, J. (1989). Mood and behaviour at adolescence: Evidence for hormonal factors. *Journal of Clinical Endocrinology and Metabolism, 69* (1), 77–83.

Wertsch, J. V. (1985). *Vygotsky and the social formation of mind.* Cambridge, Mass.: Harvard University Press.

Wylie, R. E. (1979). *The self-concept, Vol. 2: Theory and research on selected topics.* Lincoln, Nebr.: University of Nebraska Press.

Youniss, J. (1980). *Parents and peers in social development: A Sullivan-Piaget perspective.* Chicago: University of Chicago Press.

Youniss, J., & Smollar, J. (1985). *Adolescent relations with mothers, fathers and friends.* Chicago: The University of Chicago Press.

4 Joint Involvement Episodes as Context for Development

H. Rudolph Schaffer
University of Strathclyde, Glasgow, U.K.

INTRODUCTION

These days it seems eminently sensible to most psychologists to view the development of cognition as taking place within a social context. The distinction between cognitive and socio-emotional aspects is becoming increasingly blurred; Vygotsky's rapid overtaking of Piaget in the citation stakes is just one indication of this trend.

Formerly, accounts of psychological development were almost entirely of an intra-individual nature. The issues they addressed concerned such matters as the age at which particular functions first emerge, the course they subsequently take, their amount or intensity or range at particular ages, their manifestation in different groups, and so forth. Questions about processes were also dealt with at an intra-individual level, i.e. in terms of beneath-the-skin events of either a psychological or a physiological nature. Little note was taken of the social context in which the child functioned and the possible role which that context might play in development; even social behaviour was treated entirely as though it were the property of individuals, while the idea that cognitive functions might be shaped by the child's interpersonal experiences was given little credence.

An individual-centred approach is, of course, justified for certain kinds of questions, in particular those concerning the way in which a particular function manifests itself. However, as soon as one's enquiry widens to encompass questions relating to the origins of that function, as well as to the factors responsible for individual differences in its manifestation, the role of the context in which its development occurs needs to be examined. Extreme maturationist accounts are clearly invalid for most aspects of human behaviour; the assumption that psychological development can be fully understood within the boundaries of the individual organism cannot be sustained. It is thus necessary to provide some sort of conceptualisation of the psychological environment and the part it plays at different stages of development. In Piagetian theory this issue is faced squarely and constitutes the centrepiece of the account of development given therein. Piaget fully recognised that development does not occur in a vacuum but that knowledge is constructed as a result of the child's active engagement of the environment. However, the nature of that environment in his account is conceived very largely in asocial terms: during the sensori-motor period in particular the infant's life appears to be devoid of other people and transactions with things occur entirely on the child's initiative. Thus this account is also very much individual-based; the notion that development is a joint endeavour involving both the child and its caretakers in a finely orchestrated enterprise fails to gain recognition

Under the current Zeitgeist such asocial treatment is no longer acceptable. Other people are not just mere objects, to be perceived and progressively assimilated by the infant; they play a vital role in supporting, structuring and extending the child's efforts to make sense of the world and thus act as partners with the child in shaping the course of development. That much is now widely recognised (as shown, for instance, in the recent surge of interest in Vygotsky's work); the details of the social influence process, however, require further study.

In this chapter we shall concentrate on certain kinds of social interactions that appear to play a particularly important role in influencing development, referring to them as Joint Involvement Episodes (JIEs). We shall examine these by asking a series of questions, namely:

1. What characterises such episodes?
2. What evidence is there that they exert an influence on cognitive development?
3. What are the interactive events occurring in JIEs that have a bearing on their outcome?
4. What are the mechanisms whereby such events produce an effect on the course of cognitive development?

THE NATURE OF JOINT INVOLVEMENT EPISODES

Much of the earlier work on social influence processes was of a highly indirect nature. Measures were taken from parents; other measures, conceptually related to the former, were obtained from their children, and the resulting correlations were then regarded as an indication of the extent to which parental socialising shaped children's developmental progress. As is now generally appreciated, such an approach has its limitations. For one thing, correlations provide no information about the cause-and-effect sequence; the possibility of child effects on parental practices has been demonstrated forcefully and repeatedly ever since Bell (1968) first drew attention to it; a far more complex system of reciprocal influences is clearly indicated than the previous unilateral model would suggest. And for another thing, the correlation approach tells one little about what is actually going on between parent and child: it treats each of the partners involved in isolation and cannot therefore make statements about how the influence process works.

In more recent years a different approach has accordingly been taken, i.e. one that concentrates on the analysis of social interaction situations and that aims to examine in precise detail how parent and child interweave their respective contributions and how children's behaviour is changed thereby. Parent–child interaction serves, of course, many different functions, among which affectional exchange and caretaking are prominent. However, our present concern is with those that are of a primarily formative nature, i.e. those in which the adult is actively involved in extending the child's behavioural repertoire by helping it to master some new problem and thus progress to a higher level of competence in coping with environmental demands. It is these that we shall refer to as Joint Involvement Episodes, meaning any encounter between two individuals in which the participants pay joint attention to, and jointly act upon, some external topic. In so far as we shall be concentrating primarily on early development, the child's partner in JIEs is most likely to be an adult, though the influence of other children as partners has also received attention and is an aspect to which we shall return later. For that matter JIEs may involve more than two individuals, but in view of the reduced potential of polyadic situations for interactive responsiveness (Schaffer & Liddell, 1984) we shall focus on dyadic exchanges here. The topic of the exchange is some specified object, event or other environmental feature that is incorporated in the social interaction and thus becomes a focus for the partners' joint involvement (although as children get older topics are increasingly likely to assume a verbal form, the JIE thus becoming a conversation not necessarily supported by physically present referents).

For a meaningful encounter to occur the participants must in the first place agree on a topic which they will jointly address. How this initial step takes place in interactions involving a young child and an adult has been investigated by a number of studies (summarised by Schaffer, 1984), which have shown that in the early years the establishment of joint attention is very much an asymmetrical process, in which the child leads and the adult follows. Initially, that is, children appear to lack the ability to home in on another person's focus of attention, and even when this ability does emerge it is often not exercised. For a large part of early childhood it is therefore left to the adult to follow the child's interests and so ensure that a dyadic interaction becomes established. A number of attentional devices—gazing, pointing, manipulation and referential speech in particular—are available whereby one partner can indicate to the other (purposely or not) what the topic of exchange can be; however, it is only gradually in the course of development that topic sharing becomes symmetrical and the initiative is no longer left entirely to the adult.

Establishing a common attentional focus is an essential first step in setting up JIEs, for it is only in the context of the child's own interests that the adult can then introduce additional material: a verbal label for the object that the child is looking at, a demonstration of the various properties of the toy the child has just picked up or an extension of the verbalisation the child has just uttered. Once set up, such episodes may provide opportunity for all sorts of enriching exchanges, and much of what we shall discuss below will examine the evidence relevant to this proposition and consider its developmental implications. However, as much of that evidence comes from interaction situations specifically set up for that purpose under laboratory conditions let us first note what observational studies have found about their occurrence in the child's natural environment. The study by White and his colleagues (1977; 1979), conducted in preschool children's homes, is particularly informative in this respect, for they noted not only the form and content of such interactions but also their relationship to the children's development of competence. As the observations show, more often than not the episodes were initiated by the children rather than by the mother: they would turn to her when encountering some interesting or difficult situation; she would usually respond quickly, pause only to identify the topic of the child's interests and then provide whatever was needed, including support, information or some extended idea as well as shared enthusiasm, whereupon she would let the child return to private exploration and herself would resume whatever activity she had been engaged in. The whole episode might last no more than 20 to 40 seconds, but these occurred dozens of times each day and appeared to be the core teaching situations involved in promoting development. Mothers, that is, got an enormous amount of teaching in "on the sly", and the more children experienced such episodes the more likely they were to develop intellectual and motivational competence in the preschool years.

Whether or not the mother's teaching was responsible for the development of competence cannot, of course, be substantiated with such observational data. Nevertheless, the question of the role that JIEs play in children's development is raised thereby, and may best be considered on the basis of the following two propositions (derived largely from Vygotsky, 1962, 1978):

1. During JIEs children's behaviour is richer and more complex than at other times. JIEs, that is, can elicit a child's optimal and developmentally most advanced performance.

2. The long-term development of psychological functions is crucially dependent on involvement in JIEs, and the more the child experiences such encounters the more its developmental progress will be furthered.

We shall examine some of the data bearing on these propositions; in more general terms, however, the area is important because it leads on to the issue that is at the core of the debate about socialisation mechanisms: the way in which the child comes to internalise social influence.

ASPECTS OF COGNITIVE SOCIALISATION

The notion that *social* skills require an interpersonal context for their acquisition and development can readily be accepted, for the ability to deal successfully with other individuals can only emerge during social interaction and is bound to depend to a considerable extent on the co-operation and support of the child's partners. The proposal that the development of *cognitive* abilities is similarly tied to a social context has met with more scepticism; it does not have the same intuitive appeal and in the past has been rejected in favour of searches for intra-personal processes that might explain the course of development. Convincing evidence is therefore needed that adult interaction has effects on children's subsequent independent performance.

A number of methodological requirements must be met if the evidence is indeed to be convincing. Thus, if one is to show that adult–child interaction is a necessary precursor to cognitive competence, a comparison condition of children working on their own needs to be included. A variant of this might be the child working with a peer, in order to check on the degree of competence required from the partner to elicit raised performance. In any case, baseline measures need to be obtained from children in order to assess pre- to post-task progress in independent functioning. And, ideally, the post-task measures should not be confined to the end of the observational session but be extended over a follow-up period, so that one can check on the extent to which achievement has indeed become a lasting feature of the child's behaviour.

There are unfortunately few studies that satisfy such methodological requirements, and as we shall see unequivocal conclusions about the two aforementioned propositions are accordingly difficult to reach. The research that has been reported has concerned itself with the development of a variety of cognitive functions; here we shall examine three of these:

problem-solving, play and attention. The role of JIEs in language development has been discussed elsewhere (Schaffer, 1989).

Problem Solving

Overtly didactic interactions with adults, where the interaction revolves
around a set task with a precisely defined goal, have been the most
common situations investigated. Yet depressingly few enable one to
establish whether the role played by the adult does exert an essential
influence on subsequent performance by the child.

To some extent this is because many of the studies have been concerned
with different issues, in particular with the kind of interactive processes to
be found within the encounter. This is, of course, a perfectly legitimate
enquiry and one to which we shall turn later; it does, however, leave open
the basic question whether the interaction "works". At best one obtains
somewhat indirect evidence, as seen in Wood's (1980) study of mothers
teaching their 4-year old children an assembly task. When scoring the
extent to which mothers contingently adjusted their level of control to the
child's successes or failures a range of variabilty among the mothers
emerged in this respect; these scores turned out to be highly correlated
with the child's performance when working alone. A measure of maternal
effectiveness in teaching, that is, appeared to be associated with child
effectiveness in learning; the reason for the association, however, cannot
be stated with certainty.

A study by Freund (1990) provides firmer evidence. Three- and five-
year old children worked with their mothers on a sorting task; measures of
performance ability on the same task but working independently were
obtained from the children both before and immediately after the interactive session. When compared with a group of children who did not
experience interaction (though they were given feedback on completion as
to the errors they had made), it was found that mother-interaction children
made significantly greater gains than the control group children. Thus the
joint involvement with the adult appeared to be directly responsible for a
rise in performance level. What is more, those mothers who provided more
verbalisations concerned with goal direction, monitoring, strategy and
planning in the course of the joint session with the child had children
making the greatest improvement in independent problem solving. Thus
the more the adult exposed the child to processes necessary for successful
problem solving the greater were the chances that the child would be able
in due course to cope with the task alone—an individual difference analysis
that bears out the comparison of the experimental groups in pinpointing
the mothers' active involvement with their children's task-related attempts
as the crucial factor.

Freund's study is an exceptionally neat demonstration that JIEs are effective. Various other investigations also provide supportive evidence (e.g. Heber, 1981; Henderson, 1984a,b; Rogoff, Ellis & Gardner, 1984). However, the support is by no means unanimous, the fly in the ointment being a series of studies by Kontos (Kontos, 1983; Kontos & Nicholas, 1986), which also incorporated control conditions of children working independently throughout and the administration of both pre- and post-tests. The children ranged in age from 3 to 8 years; their adult partners included mothers, fathers and experimenters; and the task in each case involved a set of form-board puzzles. At all ages both the social interaction groups and the control groups improved from pre-test to post-test, the rate of improvement being comparable. Self-directed problem-solving was as effective as adult guidance; there was no reason to conclude from these results that interaction with an adult partner is a necessary precursor to the development of this particular problem-solving skill.

There are so many differences between studies in subjects, tasks, conditions and measures that it is virtually impossible to know what can account for any divergence of results. On the whole there is rather more evidence to suggest that joint problem solving does lead to improved independent problem-solving—in the short-term at any rate, for we have no data bearing on the longer-term implications.

Play

Play is a less structured, more open-ended type of activity than problem-solving, with less precisely specified goals. Here too, however, developmental changes occur in the nature of play activities, which have until quite recently been studies entirely in individual terms and have customarily been ascribed to the periodic emergence of new cognitive competencies within the child (Fein & Apfel, 1979;, Rubin, Fein, & Vandenberg, 1983). A number of scales have accordingly been developed to chart children's progression in play maturity, beginning with the sensori-motor patterns that are typically found in infancy and extending to sophisticated symbolic and representational actions appearing in later years (Belsky & Most, 1981; Nicolich, 1977). The level reached by any given child is then regarded as reflecting the stage that child has reached in its cognitive growth, the development proceeding according to the same rules that govern cognitive development generally.

However, this approach presents only a partial view. Children's play frequently occurs in social interaction contexts and there are indications that a partner, under certain conditions at least, can elicit higher maturity levels in play in the context of JIEs than when the child is alone, with the further possible implication that developmental progress is fostered by the opportunity to engage in interactions of this type.

Let us look at some representative studies. In a longitudinal investigation of maternal involvement in children's play, Slade (1987) observed toddlers between the ages of 20 and 28 months at home, and classified occurrences of symbolic play according to the mother's availability at the time. Both the level of play (using Nicolich's 1977, five-step category system for increasingly complex acts) and the length of play episodes increased when the mother participated in the child's activities in contrast to periods when children were on their own. The effect varied, however, according to the nature of maternal involvement, being greatest when mothers actively entered into the child's activities or encouraged them via explicit suggestions. Merely providing a verbal commentary, though also capable of raising the maturity level, was not effective to the same degree. Similarly Zukow (1986), in observations of children at the one-word stage, categorised play sequences as interactive or non-interactive (the latter including instances of the caregiver being near and talking but not actually joining in with the child). She too found that play performance was significantly more advanced during interactive than during non-interactive periods. And likewise DeLoache and Plaetzer (1985), in a comparison of two separate sessions, found children aged 15 to 30 months reaching higher levels of sophistication when playing jointly with the mother than during a solitary session—partly, the authors believe, because the mothers provided the necessary motivation simply by making play more fun!

These findings all come from studies in which an adult and a child were observed in entirely unrestricted situations, with no control being imposed as to the amount or nature of the adult's contribution. Belsky and his colleagues have taken this a step further by imposing such controls, i.e. by asking what happens to a child's play maturity when adult interventions assume a particular, specified form. Thus Belsky, Goode, and Most (1980), having first noted that one-year-old infants with the greatest competence in exploratory play tended to have mothers who frequently focus the child's attention on objects and events in the environment. This association between attention-focusing strategies and competence at play was put to experimental test in order to check on the aetiological relationship involved. Infants were assigned either to a treatment or to a control condition. The former group was observed at play on three successive occasions, during which the mothers were actively encouraged to provide attention-focusing strategies (pointing, demonstrating, naming, highlighting, etc.); the latter group was also observed but with no such treatment being provided. In subsequent assessments it was found that infants in the experimental group significantly exceeded their control counterparts in the level of competence that they showed in play—a clear indication that adult stimulation did indeed have an enhancing effect on infant functioning. A similar conclusion comes from a study by Vondra and Belsky (1989), again involving one-year-old infants whose play behaviour was assessed on a 14-level developmental scale. Through verbal suggestions and demonstrations, all pitched at the level immediately above the child's highest spontaneous achievement, an experimenter actively attempted to elicit cognitively more sophisticated play from the child, continuing until ceiling level had clearly been reached. There was no doubt about the success of this strategy: children were found to perform on average two steps above the level characterising their spontaneous behaviour, indicating a clear gap between competence and performance.

Yet another demonstration, that children's performance level when interacting with an involved adult can be raised over and above the level attained in solitary situations, comes from a study by O'Connell and Bretherton (1984). Children at two ages, 20 and 28 months, were seen in an independent play session and in a joint session with the mother. When their play activities were categorised into four groupings (exploratory combinatorial, symbolic and ambiguous) and compared for the two conditions, it was found that the diversity of activities within each group increased significantly when the mother joined in. The maternal effect differed, however, according to the children's age: at 20 months exploration and combination were affected by the mother's presence; at 28 months only symbolic play showed an increase. As the mothers provided guidance to an equal extent in all four categories the children appeared to act selectively in their use of the mother according to age—an important conclusion to which we shall return.

Attention

It has been known for a long time that the ability to attend increases with age (Gutteridge, 1935). More recently it has also been proposed that there are individual differences in attentional capacity that are already evident in infancy and have predictive significance for later cognitive ability (Bornstein & Sigman, 1986). Both age differences and individual differences have been ascribed to intra-personal influences such as maturation and temperament; the notion that this is a psychological function that can be shaped by inter-personal experience has only lately been given credence.

Yet there are hints to this effect from studies concerned with the consequences for attentional deployment of being reared under certain atypical family conditions. Thus children brought up without families and experiencing only institutional care during the early years have been described as restless and lacking in concentration, especially in school settings; what is more, while adverse effects on other functions such as attachment formation and intelligence appear to be reversible, attentional pathology tends to persist (Tizard, 1977). In addition, children with mothers suffering from certain kinds of psychopathology, in particular depression, have repeatedly been found to display poor attentional skills (e.g. Weissman et al., 1984). This relationship could be genetic in origin but it has also been interpreted by some authors as due to the mothers' lack of psychological availability to their children (Longfellow, Zelkowitz, & Saunders, 1982) and by others, such as Breznitz and Friedman (1988), as stemming from the less than optimal concentration strategies that such mothers teach their children. The latter authors backed up their claim by examining mother–child dyads in a play session and finding that depressed mothers initiated and terminated attentional bouts to objects significantly more often than well mothers. This relatively more controlling behaviour was seen as inducing similar attentional strategies in the children, who also engaged with more objects for shorter durations than did children of non-depressed mothers. In view of the close correlations between maternal behaviour and children's attention it is at least plausible that the latter were inculcated by the former.

There are, of course, alternative explanations. A common genetic basis is one; a tendency on the part of the mothers to be sensitive to the characteristics of their children and to react accordingly is another. Teasing apart cause-and-effect chains is a problem common to virtually all aspects of socialisation research (Schaffer, 1986). As we shall see, observational studies of dyads in JIEs at least enable the contributions of the two partners to be examined in sequence and so help understand the influence process more clearly than by merely correlating summed adult and summed child scores.

Unfortunately much of the observational research on mutual attention regulation is of such a correlational nature and therefore leaves open the question of who influences whom and how. What it does do is to place the study of attentional development squarely in the realm of social interaction and so at least enables us to consider how effects might be brought about. Thus Dunn and Wooding (1977), observing two-year-old children at home, found length of attention bouts to be significantly greater when both mother and child were paying joint attention to the focus of the child's play than when mother did not join in. This applied to each child in the sample and could be demonstrated for various categories of activity such as pretend play, household activity, etc. Joint involvement was thus the forum in which the child's attention span was particularly long, but while the authors were able to rule out the possibility that mothers were paying selective attention to those activities that are likely to go on longer anyway, they were not able to explain how the effect was actually brought about.

A similar effect in the context of daycare has been reported by Hutt, Tyler, Hutt, and Christopherson (1989). Children were observed with nursery staff in various types of preschool provision during free play and measures of concentration (referred to as activity spans) were obtained from the length of time children continuously engaged in any particular kind of activity. In all types of preschool provision the spans were significantly increased when an adult was present; the effect was greatest, however, in day nurseries (generally attended by children from less privileged family backgrounds): there the concentration span increased by 113.5% when the child was with an adult compared with periods without an adult. In nursery schools, on the other hand, the increase was 49.5%, the difference between the two figures being accounted for largely by the much lower attentional level from which the day nursery children started when playing on their own.

The latter finding illustrates an important point to which we shall return in greater detail later, namely that the effectiveness of the adult varies according to child characteristics. This is also emphasised in a study by Parrinello and Ruff (1988), in which the amount of adults' intervention during 10-month-old infants' play with objects was controlled by systematically varying the manner and frequency with which the objects were presented, the extent to which the adult talked to the infant, and her physical proximity. Each infant was assigned to one of four conditions; high, medium, low or no intervention. Overall attention was found to be greatest in the medium group; however, this occurred primarily in infants who had previously been classified as low spontaneous attenders when on their own. For these infants higher levels of intervention were of greater help in extending attention span than were low levels; with infants who were spontaneous high attenders, on the other hand, the adult's actions were ineffective at all levels in modifying their attentional behaviour.

It appears that already from a very early age onwards, adults can (under certain circumstances at least) extend children's concentration. For instance, Lockman and McHale (1989), in a preliminary report, found infants as young as 6 months to show more focused and prolonged visual exploration of objects while playing with their mothers than while playing alone. Slightly older infants, aged 8 and 10 months, additionally fingered the objects more in the dyadic than in the solitary situation, and at all ages infants tended to handle the objects more *without* looking at them when on their own. There was, however, no indication that the benefits of the JIE carried forward to a subsequent solitary session: the effectiveness of the social context in this study was confined to the social context itself.

Duration of attention is not the only feature that appears to be affected by adult involvement; other aspects such as flexibility in attentional deployment can also be influenced. This was shown by Bakeman and

Adamson (1984) in a longitudinal study of infants between 6 and 18 months, concerned with the ability to coordinate attention to objects and persons. This ability increased over age; however, it was more likely to occur when the child was playing with the mother rather than a peer. The mother, that is, was a considerably more efficient partner in helping the infants' early attempts to embed objects in social interaction; yet with peers, too, developmental trends were apparent, which suggested that as attentional skills develop even a quite unskilled partner may help to elicit the necessary skills.

Comments on Evidence

We can conclude from these studies that enough evidence is available to suggest that cognitive processes are indeed open to socialisation influences and that JIEs do provide an effective context for their extension. Whether the social support is *necessary* for all developing functions we do not know; even Vygotsky confined his "inter-mental to intra-mental" progression to higher cognitive functions only (though whether attention is to be regarded as "high" might be debatable). The findings by Kontos (Kontos, 1983; Kontos & Nicholas, 1986) are a warning not to make sweeping generalisations and disregard the possibility that children, acting independently on the physical environment, may work out solutions and achieve adaptations without a social partner.

Nevertheless, what we might refer to as the JIE effect does seem real: children's performance is raised when interacting with a supportive adult. This has also been shown for functions other than those mentioned above. Take the emergence of numeracy: for the most part this development has been considered from an intra-individual point of view (Gelman & Gallistel, 1978; Hughes, 1986). However, while such work has thrown valuable light on the way in which children construe the world in quantitative terms and on the principles underlying their concepts at different ages, it neglects the fact that from the beginning children are exposed to adults who spontaneously incorporate number concepts in all their interactions (Durkin et al., 1986). Work by Saxe, Guberman, & Gearhart (1987) in particular has illustrated how numerical skills emerge in and are transformed by interactions with the mother who creates contexts in which children can achieve higher levels than when alone—the JIE effect!

This bears on the first of our propositions—the notion that children's behaviour is more advanced and more complex during JIEs. The second proposition, that long-term development is dependent on the extent of involvement in JIEs, has received scant attention from research. Such ignorance derives largely from the lack of longitudinal studies; work cited earlier is exclusively of a cross-sectional nature, which cannot tell us anything about long-term implications. The JIE effect refers to performance rather than to development. Thus post-tests of the child's ability to work independently have usually been conducted immediately after the joint session with the adult; whether the child has indeed internalised the help and guidance offered, and progressed from other-regulation to self-regulation, cannot be established from such short term studies. Follow-up of children with varying amounts of JIE experience is a more complex undertaking, but necessary if the role of social experience in children's cognitive development is to be taken seriously (though Tamis-LeMonda & Bornstein, 1989, have provided one provocative attempt to spell out the details of this relationship). For that matter the lack of longitudinal work also accounts for our inability to examine Vygotsky's proposal that skills invariably make their initial appearance in social contexts rather than during solitary activity. Once again the need to trace the course of a particular psychological function over time rather than merely contrast performance in different settings at one particular point is highlighted.

COOPERATIVE EFFORTS OF ADULTS AND CHILDREN

Comparing JIEs in which a child is performing with or without an adult may be sufficient to answer questions about the effects of adult presence; it is not sufficient to understand how such effects are brought about. For that purpose one must examine what is happening inside the episode, i.e. describe and analyse the nature of adults' input and compare the effectiveness of different kinds of adult contributions. Research designs need to move away from the "child-alone versus child-with-adult" type and concentrate instead on the different strategies adopted by adults and the way in which these are manifested in the interaction with the child.

There are now a number of reports available in which detailed descriptions appear of mothers' behaviour in JIEs. These draw attention to such specific response patterns as prompting, suggesting, demonstrating, correcting, elaborating and facilitating (DeLoache & Plaetzer, 1985) or to more general strategies such as providing bridges between familiar and new skills, arranging and structuring problem-solving situations and gradually transferring responsibility from adult to child (Rogoff, 1989). Such descriptions are, of course, useful; indeed essential. What becomes very apparent, however, is that to concentrate on the contribution of one partner without taking into account that of the other is a fruitless enterprise. The adult does not impinge upon and shape an inert child but instead must act within the context of the child's characteristics and ongoing activity. Whatever effects are produced emerge from a joint enterprise to which the child as well as the adult contributes.

The Child's Contribution

Children bring certain organismic characteristics to a situation, which will determine adults' behaviour towards them. Of these the most obvious is age: as studies including age comparisons have shown (e.g. DeLoache & DeMendoza, 1987), mothers appear to calibrate their input according to the child's age by means such as providing more complex types of information, increasing their demands and handing over a greater share of the responsibility as children get older. In fact it is not chronological age as such that is responsible for such variation; rather it is the child's developmental status as reflected by the child's ongoing behaviour in the interactive situation to which adults respond. This is clearly shown by Heckhausen (1987a), who observed a group of infants on five occasions between the ages of 14 and 22 months attempting two tasks (tower building and form sorting) jointly with their mothers. Changes took place during this period in the mothers' supportive behaviour, but these depended more on the children's perceived performance than on their chronological age. Using log-linear modelling, information about infants' age was compared with information about the infants' performance (as reflected by their attempts at the tasks). In so far as the results show the performance-based model to be decidedly superior to the age-based model, one can conclude that mothers adapt their behaviour not so much to an abstract notion such as age, but rather to the child's competence as perceived in the here-and-now situation.

The influence of child characteristics on adults' attempts to help and support becomes particularly evident in cases of pathology. In the case of attention-directing strategies, the attempts of mothers to focus their children's attention on relevant objects are highly distinctive with pre-term infants or children with Down's Syndrome, reflecting the difficulties such children have in spontaneously employing or maintaining attention (Landry & Chapieski, 1989; Landry, Chapieski, & Schmidt, 1986). However, in non-pathological samples too it has been demonstrated that individual differences in children's attentional characteristics influence the nature and effectiveness of adults' interventions. In a controlled study of the level of intervention, Parinello and Ruff (1988) found effectiveness to depend on the spontaneous attentional behaviour of 10-month-old infants. For those who were naturally attentive on their own the amount of adult intervention was of little account, in contrast to infants who attended relatively little to objects on their own and who therefore required considerable effort on the part of the adult. Similarly with individual differences in the exploratory level of 3- to 6-year olds, as Henderson (1984a) has shown, the extent of children's exploration in a joint mother-child play session depended both on the mother's efforts and on the child's spontaneous exploratory behaviour. Low-exploratory children required considerable input from the mother, whereas high-explorers actually showed reduced levels of exploration in joint play as compared to solitary play. The social context, it appears, has different meanings for different children according to the predispositions they bring to that context; for some children the adult's presence may in fact have a suppressant rather than a facilitative effect.

No doubt there are many other organismic factors that influence adults' interactions with children in playful and in problem-solving encounters. For that matter, there are temporary interests and goals that children pursue during the interaction which adults must take into account in pursuing their own goals. That children are active participants in their own socialisation is widely accepted now; however, moving beyond the general principle to spelling out how this is accomplished in given contexts remains to a large extent a task for the future. As far as JIEs are concerned, descriptive data from various studies illustrate how active children tend to be in structuring the interaction and selecting from what the adult offers according to their own interests and skills. This point is particularly well made by O'Connell and Bretherton's (1984) observations of mother-child joint play sessions held when the children were 20 months and again when they were 28 months old. During play the mothers provided the children with a constant flow of suggestions; the children, however, appeared quite systematically to select from these only the ones that fitted in with their own capabilities. Thus at 20 months old they used their mothers' assistance for exploratory and combinatorial play activities, which predominated at that age, whereas at 28 months they took advantage of those suggestions that fitted in with the rather more advanced symbolic type of play of which they were then capable. It is thus the *child* who appears to be determining the effectiveness of the mother's instructions, many of which may not be particularly suitable at that developmental stage but which the child simply ignores. In that sense the child is the member of the dyad who shapes the course of the interaction rather than the mother.

The Adult's Contribution

What the adult does has to slot in with the child's contribution. But while there are quite a number of descriptions available of typical adult behaviour in JIEs, one cannot tell from such data alone what ingredients are necessary to advance child performance. For that purpose a more analytic approach is needed, and so far only a limited number of efforts have been made experimentally to tease apart the different components of adult input.

One component concerns the mere presence of the adult. To perform satisfactorily, children need security; during the early years the mother's physical availability is usually required for that. There is evidence, however, that on its own this component is insufficient to account for the JIE effect. It comes from various studies (e.g. Dunn & Wooding, 1977; O'Connell & Bretherton, 1984; Slade, 1987) in which comparisons were made between the child's performance while the mother was present but not interacting and performance during bouts of active participation on the part of the mother. In each case the latter was superior, suggesting that the effect was brought about not so much by maternal presence alone as by more direct aspects of the mother's involvement in the child's activity.

One constituent of that involvement relates to the motivation that an adult can provide. Simply in joining their children at play, mothers can make the experience more fun: they can convey an interest and excitement that will keep the child glued to the activity at the time and more likely to return to it subsequently, even when alone. That attention span is prolonged in this way seems plausible. More problematic is the effect on the complexity and developmental sophistication of the child's actions; here rather more specific techniques are likely to be required.

One such concerns the adult's attention focusing efforts. In so far as joint involvement requires both partners to be oriented to the same topic, ways of sharing that topic must be found by means such as pointing, gaze direction and verbal reference. Thus during control-compliance sequences mothers tend to work within the framework of the child's attention (Schaffer & Crook, 1979; 1980). Requests and suggestions are made with respect to objects to which the child is already attending or, alternatively, an attention directing device (tapping, holding up, pointing, etc.) is employed to get the child appropriately oriented before some action on that object is demanded. Bringing about topic sharing is, of course, an essential first step before adult and child can jointly carry out activities; a shared frame of reference is needed before the adult can introduce new material. Subsequently, however, the adult must also continuously monitor the child's attentional behaviour in order to ensure, first, that the child remains on task and second that the relevant features of that task are picked out in the right order and at the right time. Thus the ability to organise children's attention would appear to be one essential component of adult's behaviour in JIEs, and there are indications that individual differences in this ability are related to various child outcome measures (Belsky et al., 1980). In so far as the onus for topic sharing during the early years is very much on the child's partner, it seems probable that one reason for the ineffectiveness of peers as partners in JIEs lies in the difficulty that young children have in fitting their own interests into the framework of another individual. Adults, on the other hand, are more prepared to start where the child already is and lead on from there. Within the shared frame of reference, adult activities mostly take one of two forms: supportive or challenging. The former serves to maintain the child's current behaviour and to facilitate it. Under this heading one may include techniques such as holding objects steady, arranging material for easier access, giving praise and verbally labelling events and actions. But other adult interventions take a more proactive form, and especially so in problem-solving situations where the child has to be helped to reach a definite goal. It is here that challenging becomes essential: the adult must sensitively gear any demands to the child's particular abilities and achievements in order to carry the child forward in a series of carefully graduated steps at a pace appropriate to that individual. As Wood and Middleton (1975) showed, mothers attempting to teach their children a construction task are continually adjusting the level of their instruction: on the one hand withdrawing assistance whenever the child had succeeded at a particular step, and on the other hand increasing the level of help in response to failure. According to Heckhausen (1987b), the optimal strategy to adopt in such a situation is based on the principle of "one step ahead"—the adult focuses on those aspects of the task that lie just beyond the level that the child has currently attained. There are many indications (see Schaffer, 1979) that adults quite spontaneously adopt such a strategy in interacting with young children; as we shall see later, it may well be that the essence of this strategy lies in the conflict generated thereby between the child's and the adult's perspective of the task. Cognitive socialisation can thus be regarded as very much dependent on the ability of adults to generate graded conflict in the context of joint task involvement with the child.

All this demands considerable sensitivity on the part of the adult to the characteristics and achievements of the child. Performance has to be monitored on a moment-to-moment basis. Decisions have to be made as to the optimal degree of challenge required at each stage, and for this purpose the adult needs to be closely tuned in to the relevant signals the child is providing with respect to task performance. Adult sensitivity is a general characteristic that has been associated with child progress in various developmental spheres (Schaffer & Collis, 1986), and it certainly seems plausible that individual differences in this respect among parents may have wide-ranging implications not just for socio-emotional but also for cognitive aspects of their children's development.

However, there are a number of reservations. For one thing, an association between parental sensitivity and child progress does not tell one anything about how the effect is brought about. Sensitivity is perhaps a general prerequisite, but it has no direct causal influence on children's growing competence. As Bornstein and Tamis-LeMonda (1989) have suggested for the closely linked concept of parental responsiveness, such a characteristic is embedded in other caretaking activities which in themselves foster growth. Any aetiological link therefore still needs to be spelled out. Then again, the extent to which there is parental sensitivity can easily be exaggerated: O'Connell and Bretherton (1984) have provided a useful warning signal in this respect with their observation that much of maternal input tends to be inappropriate to the level of the child's competence and that it is left to the child to pick out what is relevant and helpful. And finally there is also a case for the argument that a certain degree of insensitivity may be beneficial (Schaffer & Collis, 1986): one can maintain, for instance, that the experience of having overtures for attention ignored or refused by the adult throws the child back on its own resources and thus encourages self-reliance. There is clearly a point beyond which such treatment will be unhelpful; nevertheless, the assumption "the more the better" as generally applied to sensitivity is not necessarily a valid one.

An adult interactive style characterised by directiveness is sometimes discussed as representing the opposite of sensitivity, it is widely regarded as an undesirable type of treatment. There certainly seems to be some evidence to suggest that children's developmental achievements are not facilitated by adult behaviour in which commands, controls and directions predominate (cf. Nelson, 1973; McDonald & Pien, 1982, with respect to language development; Rubenstein & Howes, 1979, regarding play level; White & Watts, 1973, concerning developmental competence generally). But just as the lauding of sensitivity can so easily be overdone, so it may be that the condemnation of directiveness could be too hasty. Under some circumstances such a style may well be appropriate, and in particular with children characterised by certain kinds of special needs such as mental handicap, deafness and language delay (Cunningham, Reuler, Blackwell, & Deck, 1981; Marfo, 1990; Siegel & Cunningham, 1984). Where it is necessary to convey guidance to a child in a form that is simple and straightforward and will not overload capacity for information processing, commands have the advantage that they are brief, to the point and syntactically less complex than more indirect forms of conveying instruction. Under such circumstances the communication process is not necessarily of an inferior quality; rather it takes a different form in which the mother adjusts to the child's particular characteristics by suitably modifying the nature of her contribution to the child-parent system (Schaffer, 1990).

What is more, with children generally, directives do not necessarily indicate a pattern of increased dominance on the part of the adult, where the latter intrusively imposes certain aims on the child irrespective of the child's own intentions. As shown in studies of control techniques (Schaffer & Crook, 1979; 1980), mothers tend to take considerable care in checking children's orientational focus before asking for some action to be carried out on a particular object—either by timing their request to coincide with the child's spontaneous attention or by preceding the action control with an attention control. The action control may well take the form of a direct command; it is nevertheless far from intrusive, in that the mother first ensures that she is working within the child's own orientation framework. There is therefore no justification for regarding directives *per se* as denoting lack of sensitivity; there is also no reason to think that they are necessarily any less successful in achieving desired results (Marfo, 1990; Schaffer & Crook, 1980).

So far only a few studies are available in which different kinds of parental input to JIEs have been compared for their effectiveness. The focus in these is accordingly on individual differences in adult behaviour rather than on a comparision of child-alone and child-with-adult conditions. The individual differences may reflect the parents' natural inclinations or result from experimental manipulation. An example of the former is a study by Pratt, Kerig, Cowan, and Cowan (1988), in which parents were compared according to a typology of parenting style derived from Baumrind's (1967) classification. Both mothers and fathers were observed interacting with their children in three tasks (matrix classification, block-model copying and retelling a story). Parents classified as authoritative were found to be generally more sensitive in their tutoring of children and more effective in bringing about success in task performance than other types of parents.

While such a comparison is useful, it is still based on characteristics too global to show precisely what the essential components are. Experimentally manipulating parental behaviour by instructing adults to behave in contrasting ways is likely to provide more precise information in this respect. We see this in a study by Slade (1987), in which three conditions were set up: mothers actively interacting with their children and encouraging them with explicit suggestions; mothers providing only verbal commentary, e.g. affirmation or elaboration; and mothers present but taking no part in the child's activity. Results indicate that both the duration and the complexity of pretend play were raised by the first two conditions relative to the third, with the most active involvement producing the most marked results. Any sign of interest on the part of the adult thus appears to be effective, but adopting the role of play partner is more effective than providing passive commentary alone. Observations by Freund (1990) indicate similar conclusions: in one condition mothers actively helped their children in any way they chose to learn a sorting task, in another the children worked independently but were then provided with corrective feedback regarding the mistakes they had made. Subsequent performance by the children while working on their own on the task was superior for those from the first condition, suggesting that it was not just the learning of correct solutions but rather the process of adult-child interaction itself that accounted for the children's improved performance.

Such analyses still leave many questions unanswered as to the precise components of social interaction that bring about particular effects, and considerable more work needs to be done in analysing adult input before these components can be identified. What is clear is that the adult's contribution cannot be examined in isolation; it must be seen in relation to the child's contribution, with reference to such characteristics as age and ability, and also with respect to the nature of the child's ongoing behaviour, which demands moment-to-moment decisions on the part of the adult as to the optimal kind of input to be provided at any particular point.

CONFLICT IN THE CONTEXT OF COOPERATION

How adults and children behave in the context of JIEs needs to be established, so that we understand the kinds of interactions that appear to give rise to cognitive achievements. That alone, however, is not sufficient to help explain why cognitive development is furthered by social encounters; for that we must consider the mechanisms whereby the adult's efforts produce mental reorganisation in the child. This lies, of course, at the very heart of the socialisation problem, and though the absence of a satisfactory all-embracing answer remains a major obstacle to our understanding of the nature of child development (Schaffer, 1986), a number of explanations have been advanced to account for the types of effects we have considered here.

Scaffolding

To do justice to the many supportive efforts made by mothers in JIEs, the concept of scaffolding has been advanced by Bruner and by Wood (e.g. Wood, Bruner & Ross, 1976). As Bruner (1975) put it, mothers often help "the child in achieving an intended outcome, entering only to assist or reciprocate or 'scaffold' the action". Thus the term designates all those strategies that an adult uses in order to help children's learning efforts through supportive interventions, the form of which may vary but which are all aimed at ensuring that children achieve goals that would be beyond them without such support.

Scaffolding is a useful umbrella term to describe a wide range of adult actions. As Rogoff (1989) points out, the term scaffold may seem to imply a rigid structure or one that does not involve the child; however, Wood and

Bruner use it flexibly to denote continuous revision of action in response to the child's ongoing activity. The major limitation of the term, however, is that it is no more than a metaphor—a vivid one, but one that does not explain the problem of internalisation, i.e. how a child becomes self-regulated after a period of other-regulation. This is the basic issue that needs to be addressed. While it is clear that sensitive adults at first provide support in JIEs and then gradually withdraw it as the child becomes progressively independent, accounts of scaffolding do not in themselves help one to understand the processes responsible for the mental reorganisation which underlies that independence.

Vygotsky and the Zone of Proximal Development

The rekindling of interest in Vygotsky's writings (1962; 1978) indicates well the widespread appreciation that cognitive development needs to be seen as closely tied to its social context. Vygotsky's statement (1978, p. 57) was a strong one: "All the higher functions originate as actual relationships between human individuals". If one were to look for concrete evidence it would be difficult to bear this out in a literal sense; it remains a declaration of faith rather than a substantiated conclusion. As such, however, it asserts Vygotsky's belief that the processes which the child needs to cope with the environment and solve problems independently originate in processes found initially in the course of interacting with adults—a progression, that is, from the *intermental* to the *intramental* level. Thus all skills and knowledge are said to be first encountered in the course of social interaction and then to become internalised and decontextualised as a result of the child gradually taking over responsibility from the adult.

The child must, however, have achieved some specified level of competence before it can benefit from interacting with adults in problem solving situations, and Vygotsky proposed the *zone of proximal development* (ZPD) to define the range within which the instructions of adults are likely to be most effective. The boundaries of the ZPD are defined by the level of the child's independent functioning on the one hand and its functioning as the junior partner in an instructional social interaction on the other. The ability of adults to pitch their tutorial efforts within this zone is thus a crucial factor in helping the child to progress to independence; what is more, variations in the type of social experience provided will form part of what the child internalises and what will later affect variations in individual performance.

Vygotsky's view is frequently contrasted with that of Piaget, in that the latter paid little attention to social contexts and saw the child's developmental progress primarily mediated by interaction with the physical world. Vygotsky redresses the balance, though his *sine qua non* view of the adult's part in children's acquisition of competence may well be too extreme a statement. More to the point, however, the question is left open as to the mechanisms whereby the child comes to internalise adult instruction. Thus Vygotsky talks vaguely of such instruction "awakening and rousing to life those functions which are in a state of maturing" (Rogoff & Wertsch, 1984). In general, however, he tends to draw a highly didactic picture of the adult's role: the very fact that he talks of *instruction* and *tuition* suggests a teaching-learning process in which the child is a relatively passive recipient of adult action, and his emphasis on *limitation* under the guidance of adults (Vygotsky, 1978, p. 87–88) reinforces this one-sided picture. As we have seen, however, the child's contribution to the interaction is a very much more active one and by no means confined to imitation; for that matter the adult does more than merely provide tuition through modelling. Vygotsky did consider the role of private speech as a link between inter- and intra-mental functioning, proposing that adults' verbal regulations became internalised as verbal self-regulation. There is, however, little convincing evidence for this proposition, and the question of internalisation and the manner whereby the child's mental approach to problems is reorganised thus receive no satisfactory answer by Vygotskian theory.

Socio-Cognitive Conflict

Studies using the scaffolding metaphor and those derived from Vygotsky's conceptions of cognitive development have placed major emphasis on the *supportive* and *cooperative* role of the child's partner. There is, however, another body of literature, originally based on Piagetian theory but extended to include social interactive phenomena, which sees *conflict* as the essential ingredient of any joint involvement intended to bring about cognitive change in the child. The relevant studies are mostly based on somewhat older children—of mid- rather than pre-school age—and initially at least were confined to orthodox Piagetian tasks such as conservation; they were also primarily concerned with peer interaction rather than that between child and adult. Nevertheless, they are highly pertinent here because in them the problem of internalisation has been squarely faced and explicit consideration given to the mechanisms whereby change is brought about in the child through social interaction.

Working in Geneva, Doise and his colleagues (e.g. Doise & Mackie, 1981; Doise & Mugny, 1984; Mugny, DePaolis & Carngati, 1984; Perret-Clermont, 1980) have demonstrated in an extensive programme of research that children working in pairs solve problems at a more advanced level than children working on their own. The research design in these studies generally involved a pre-test in which the child's basal level was established, followed by random assignment to dyadic or individual problem-solving conditions and, subsequently, by a post-test when the child's performance on that problem (or sometimes also other related problems) was again assessed in an individual session. The superior performance of children assigned to the dyadic condition was found not to depend on being paired with a more knowledgeable partner; children made progress as a result of working with another child at the same initial level or even at a less advanced level. Such progress could therefore not be due to imitation; moreover, as individual children observing an interacting dyad showed no cognitive gains it appears that the giving of task-relevant information is also not the crucial factor.

Instead, the mechanism responsible for change is to be found in "the conflict of centrations which the subject experiences during the interaction" (Perret-Clermont, 1981, p. 184). Coming up against an alternative (though not necessarily correct) viewpoint in the course of joint problem-solving the child is forced to coordinate his or her own viewpoint with that of the partner. The conflict can only be resolved if cognitive restructuring takes place—on the lines, that is, of Piagetian equilibration, except that the mental change occurs as a result of *social* interaction. Thus social interaction stimulates cognitive development by permitting dyadic coordinations to facilitate inner coordinations. However, this cannot happen merely through the passive presentation of alternative viewpoints; children must be actively engaged in opposing their particular opinion and reasoning with those of other individuals, thereby experiencing a confrontational socio-cognitive conflict. The mental restructuring that follows in turn allows each partner to adopt an approach to this class of problems that is more advanced than that adopted previously when working as an individual.

That peer interaction (at least among children of primary school age or over) can promote cognitive change has now been demonstrated by a considerable number of writers, including those from outside the Geneva tradition (e.g. Ames & Murray, 1982; Damon & Killin, 1982) and with tasks other than Piagetian ones. The superiority of social interaction to individual performance has not been found in every study (Bearison, Magzamon, & Filarde, 1986; Roy & Howe, 1990). Clearly there is still work to be done to investigate the conditions under which one kind of condition produces better results than the other, and clearly caution is meanwhile necessary in making generalisations about the effectiveness of social interaction in this kind of setting. What does matter about this line of investigation is that it is closely tied to a theory about cognitive advancement that addresses itself directly to the issue of internalisation and change. Following the Piagetian tradition the child is seen as actively participating in its own development through attempting to resolve conflict. The disequilibrium that occurs when differences between two perspectives become apparent forces the child to restructure its representations and alter its strategy. This reflects the fact that mental reorganisation has taken place and that the child has thus internalised the lessons learned from the social encounter. It follows that only those social interactions that contain an element of conflict will be effective—a point not brought out by studies stressing the supportive ("scaffolding") role of the child's partner. Accordingly, either mechanisms of learning and imitation are proposed to account for change (unsuccessfully so, in view of the evidence on giving task information and on modelling) or alternatively leave the question of internalisation simply unanswered. The necessity of a conflict element also explains why peer interaction is initially ineffective. A juxtaposition of different points of view, as found in early peer interaction, does not on its own force a child to alter its perspective; this can only occur when the child is drawn into active task participation, and for this purpose an adult is required when dealing with younger children.

Although Vygotsky did not explicitly discuss the role of conflict in adult-child interaction, it can be said to be implicit in his statement that instruction can only bring about change when it proceeds ahead of the child's development. As Wertsch (1984) has put it, adult and child provide different situational definitions; the adult, possessing a more encompassing view of the task, can challenge the child by means of a "one-step-ahead" strategy (Heckhausen, 1987b), and it is through such challenge that conflict can be brought about. That the child requires support is not disputed, nor that the adult must be capable of sensitivity to produce the right degree of challenge. The key to change, however, lies in the conflict generated by the challenge, in that it stimulates the child actively to resolve the perceived discrepancy and thus to attain a new, more advanced functional level.

CONCLUSIONS

There is little doubt that cognitive processes can be affected by the social interactions in which they are embedded and that joint involvement episodes do provide an effective context for their growth. Yet before we are swept away by any wave of enthusiasm for explaining all cognitive development in social interactional terms let us summarise the various reservations and gaps in our knowledge that caution against sweeping generalisations. These apply to the following aspects:

Immediate versus Long-Term Effects

We have found plenty of evidence that, under certain circumstances at least, a child performs at a higher level in interaction with a social partner than under solitary conditions (the JIE effect, as we referred to it). The other proposition, however, that such interactions do not merely raise the immediate performance level but also have long-term implications for development, has not as yet been substantiated. This is largely due do the absence of longitudinal studies; most investigators have confined themselves to post-tests that immediately follow the interaction session and cannot therefore comment on the issue of internalisation. The transfer from other-regulation to self-regulation thus remains an interesting idea looking for supportive evidence.

Range of Psychological Functions Affected

Even if we confine ourselves to immediate effects there is still uncertainty as to the range of functions whose development is crucially dependent on their social context. Problem-solving, play and attention were reviewed in this chapter and language development elsewhere (Schaffer, 1989), and in each case there is at least some evidence for the link with social context variables. Yet even Vygotsky's otherwise quite extreme assertions regarding such a link are restricted to "higher" psychological functions and make no claim that all behaviour patterns originate to the same extent in interactions with other people. Whether there are indeed differences between psychological functions in their susceptibility to social influence remains to be established.

Age Effects

Most research workers have concerned themselves with only one age group, and we do not know therefore whether social interactions play the same facilitating role at all ages. Intuitively it seems plausible that this role is most prominent in the earlier years and it is thus no coincidence that the majority of studies have concentrated on the preschool period. Yet Vygotsky placed no age restrictions on his "intermental to intramental" progression, and the work by Doise and his colleagues suggests that in older children, too, cognitive attainments are brought about by means of social experiences. Whether the mechanisms underlying cognitive socialisation change as children become older and more capable is an open question.

Adult versus Peer

The nature of the child's partner required to bring about change is one respect in which there may be age differences. There are indications that at younger ages children require a person of greater competence than themselves, while later on a partner of equal or even lesser capability will suffice. However, the two sets of studies dealing with younger and older children respectively are not directly comparable in such matters as tasks, conditions and research design, and no conclusions are therefore possible. Uncertainty remains in particular with regard to the role of peer interaction in the preschool period.

Nature of Interactive Processes

What transpires within JIEs that brings about cognitive change? We now have a substantial number of descriptive accounts of behaviour in such settings, and as a result it is generally appreciated that justice must be done to the interactive nature of what goes on between adult and child. Thus accounts concentrating only on adult instruction are too one-sided and didactic. Even the youngest and most naive child does not start from zero but always provides some perspective, however primitive, that must form the starting point for any effort to lead the child further. The interweaving of adult and child contributions clearly provides the key to developmental change; however, precisely what aspects of this multi-faceted exchange form the crucial components responsible for change remain obscure. Thus it seems highly likely that attentional manipulation is one of the more important contributions of adults, though it has also become apparent that what the adult does in this respect must be based on awareness of the child's own spontaneous behavioural tendencies. Similarly, directive strategies may not deserve the condemnation they have received so far but may be effective under certain circumstances and with certain kinds of children. As yet, however, few attempts have been made to tease out which of the many adult strategies observed represent the necessary ingredients of bringing about cognitive change. For that purpose it is essential to go beyond descriptive accounts and make use of experimental analysis.

The Question of Mechanisms

This leads us to the basic problem of how social interactions can affect children's cognition in such a way that joint solutions become the child's own internalised solutions, to be applied independently on all future occasions. Socio-cognitive conflict theory has probably gone furthest in providing provocative ideas for considering this issue, in that it has directly addressed the question of mental restructuring, which mediates between social interaction and independent functioning. In so doing it has drawn attention away from support and cooperation to conflict and confrontation. However, these two kinds of rational qualities are not really as antithetical as may appear at first sight, for conflict cannot be useful unless the participants have a common aim on which they have first agreed, just as challenge cannot be effective without the adult sensitively grading the discrepancy presented to the child. The ideas of socio-cognitive conflict theory have been derived from studies with older children participating in peer interaction; whether they are equally applicable to children in the early years interacting with an adult needs to be established. It seems unlikely that completely different mechanisms are operative at different age periods, and it may well be that the "one-step-ahead" strategy described for younger children is based on the same processes as socio-cognitive conflict in the case of older children.

Socially Mediated versus Independent Problem Solving

Uncertainty remains as to the extent to which cognitive functions are initially dependent on social interactions. The evidence obtained so far is contradictory: while the majority of studies have found superior performance in interaction settings compared with control conditions of children working independently, a few have failed to find such a difference. In view of the many variables involved (age, type and difficulty of task, nature and timing of measures, and so forth) it is impossible to explain this divergence. In general terms, doing things with a partner has many advantages ("two heads are better than one"): quite apart from the variety of perspectives introduced thereby, it is often more fun and thus raises the level of motivation and persistence; it may introduce a competitive element and it may have various practical advantages such as making easier the physical manipulation of task materials. Yet any global statement, to the effect that the social setting is essential for cognitive advancement, is surely unjustified. There are circumstances where self-directed activity, even in young children and even at the very early stages of acquiring task competence, enhances problem solving; for that matter there are circumstances where adults hinder rather than help. Thus it is not a matter of Piaget versus Vygotsky but rather a matter of defining the conditions under which independent or joint functioning is the most effective way of promoting cognition.

   In short, there are considerable dangers in making too strong claims for the part played by the social context: interacting with others can facilitate cognitive development under many circumstances and under some circumstances may in fact be essential. It is unlikely, however, that all skills acquired at all stages of development originate in social interactions. There is still a need therefore to establish what kinds of social interactions promote what kinds of cognitive achievements at what ages and in what manner.

REFERENCES

Ames, G., & Murray, F. (1982). When two wrongs make a right: Promoting cognitive change by social conflict. *Developmental Psychology*, *18*, 894–897.

Bakeman, R., & Adamson, L. B. (1984). Coordinating attention to people and objects in mother-infant and peer-infant interaction. *Child Development*, *55*, 1278–1289.

Baumrind, D. (1967). Child care practices anteceding three patterns of pre-school behavior. *Genetic Psychology Monographs*, *75*, 43–88.

Bearison, D. J., Magzamen, S., & Filarde, E. K. (1986). Socio-cognitive conflict and cognitive growth in young children. *Merrill-Palmer Quarterly*, *32*, 51–72.

Bell, R. Q. (1968). A reinterpretation of the direction of effects in studies of socialisation. *Psychological Review*, *75*, 81–95.

Belsky, J., Goode, M. K., & Most, R. K. (1980). Maternal stimulation and infant exploratory competence: Cross-sectional correlational and experimental analysis. *Child Development*, *51*, 1168–1178.

Belsky, J., & Most, R. K. (1981). From exploration to play: A cross-sectional study of infant free play behavior. *Developmental Psychology*, *17*, 630–639.

Bornstein, M. H., & Sigman, M. D. (1986). Continuity in mental development from infancy. *Child Development*, *57*, 251–274.

Bornstein, M. H., & Tamis-LeMonda, C. S. (1989). In M. H. Bornstein (Ed.), Maternal responsiveness: Characteristics and consequences. *New Directions for Child Development No. 43*. San Francisco: Jossey-Bass.

Breznitz, Z., & Friedman, S. L. (1988). Toddlers' concentration: Does maternal depression make a difference? *Journal of Child Psychology and Psychiatry*, *29*, 267–280.

Bruner, J. S. (1975). The ontogenesis of speech acts. *Journal of Child Language*, *2*, 1–19.

Cunningham, C. E., Reuler, E., Blackwell, J., & Deck, J. (1981). Behavioural and linguistic developments in the interactions of normal and retarded children with their mothers. *Child Development*, *52*, 62–70.

Damon, W., & Killin, M. (1982). Peer interaction and the process of change in children's moral reasoning. *Merrill-Palmer Quarterly*, *28*, 347–367.

DeLoache, J. S., & DeMendoza, O. A. P. (1987). Joint picturebook interactions of mothers and 1-year-old children. *British Journal of Developmental Psychology*, *5*, 111–124.

DeLoache, J. S., & Plaetzer, B. (1985). *Tea for two: Joint mother–child symbolic play*. Unpublished paper, Society for Research in Child Development, Toronto.

Doise, W., & Mackie, D. (1981). On the social nature of cognition. In J. P. Forgas (Ed.), *Social Cognition: Perspectives on Everyday Understanding*. London: Academic Press.

Doise, W., & Mugny, G. (1984). *The social development of the intellect*. Oxford: Pergamon Press.

Dunn, J., & Wooding, C. (1977). Play in the home and its implications for learning. In B. Tizard, & D. Harvey (Eds.), *Biology of Play*. London: Heinemann.

Durkin, K., Shire, B., Riem, R., Crowther, R. D., & Rutter, D. (1986). The social and linguistic context of early number word use. *British Journal of Developmental Psychology*, *4*, 269–288.

Fein, G. G., & Apfel, N. (1979). The development of play: Style, structure and situations. *Genetic Psychology Monographs*, *99*, 231–250.

Freund, L. (1990). Maternal regulation of children's problem-solving behaviour and its impact on children's performance. *Child Development*, *61*, 113–126.

Gelman, R., & Gallistel, C. R. (1978). *The child's understanding of number*. Cambridge, Mass.: Harvard University Press.

Gutteridge, M. V. (1935). *The duration of attention in young children*. Melbourne: Melbourne University Press.

Heber, M. (1981). Instruction versus conversation as opportunities for learning. In W. P. Robinson (Ed.), *Communication in development*. London: Academic Press.

Heckhausen, J. (1987a). How do mothers know? Infants' chronological age or infants' performance as determinants of adaptation in maternal instruction? *Journal of Experimental Child Psychology, 43*, 212–226.

Heckhausen, J. (1987b). Balancing for weaknesses and challenging developmental potential: A longitudinal study of mother–infant dyads in apprenticeship interactions. *Developmental Psychology, 23*, 762–770.

Henderson, B. B. (1984a). Parents and exploration: The effect of context on individual differences in exploratory behavior. *Child Development, 55*, 1237–1245.

Henderson, B. B. (1984b). Social support and exploration. *Child Development, 55*, 1246–1251.

Hughes, M. (1986). *Children and number*. Oxford: Blackwell.

Hutt, S. J., Tyler, S., Hutt, C., & Christopherson, H. (1989). *Play, exploration and learning*. London: Routledge.

Kontos, S. (1983). Adult-child interaction and the origins of metacognition. *Journal of Educational Research, 77*, 43–54.

Kontos, S., & Nicholas, J. G. (1986). Independent problem solving in the development of metacognition. *Journal of Genetic Psychology, 147*, 481–495.

Landry, S. H., & Chapieski, M. L. (1989). Joint attention and infant toy exploration: Effects of Down Syndrome and prematurity. *Child Development, 60*, 103–118.

Landry, S. H., Chapieski, M. L., & Schmidt, M. (1986). Effects of maternal attention-directing strategies on preterms' response to toys. *Infant Behavior and Development, 9*, 257–269.

Lockman, J. L., & McHale, J. P. (1989). Object manipulation in infancy: Developmental and contextual determinants. In J. L. Lockman, & N. L. Hazen (Eds.), *Action and Social Context*. New York: Plenum.

Longfellow, C., Zelkowitz, P., & Saunders, E. (1982). The quality of mother-child relationships. In D. Bell (Ed.), *Lives in stress. Women and depression*. Beverly Hills: Sage Publications.

McDonald, L., & Pien, D. (1982). Mother conversational behaviour as a function of interactional intent. *Journal of Child Language, 9*, 337–358.

Marfo, K. (1990). Maternal directiveness in interactions with mentally handicapped children: An analytic commentary. *Journal of Child Psychology and Psychiatry, 31*, 531–550.

Mugny, G., DePaolis, P., & Carngati, F. (1984). Social regulations in cognitive development. In W. Doise, & A. Palmonari (Eds.), *Interaction in individual development*. Cambridge: Cambridge University Press.

Nelson, K. (1973). Structure and strategy in learning to talk. *Monographs of the Society for Research in Child Development, 38*, (nos. 1–2, Serial no. 149).

Nicholich, L. M. (1977). Beyond sensori-motor intelligence: Assessment of symbolic maturity through analysis of pretend play. *Merrill-Palmer Quarterly, 23*, 89–99.

O'Connell, B., & Bretherton, I. (1984). Toddlers' play alone and with mother: The role of maternal guidance. In I. Bretherton (Ed.), *Symbolic play: The development of social understanding*. London: Academic Press.

Parrinello, R. M., & Ruff, H. A. (1988). The influence of adult intervention on infants' level of attention. *Child Development, 59*, 1125–1135.

Perret-Clermont, A. N. (1980). *Social interaction and cognitive development in children*. London: Academic Press.

Pratt, M. W., Kerig, P., Cowan, P. A., & Cowan, C. P. (1988). Mothers and fathers teaching 3-year-olds: Authoritative parenting and adult scaffolding of young children's learning. *Developmental Psychology, 24*, 832–839.

Rogoff, B. (1989). The joint socialisation of development by young children and adults. In A. Gellatly, D. Rogers, & J. A. Sloboda (Eds.), *Cognitive and social worlds*. Oxford: Clarendon Press.

Rogoff, B., Ellis, S., & Gardner, W. (1984). Adjustment of adult-child instructions according to child's age and task. *Developmental Psychology, 20*, 193–199.

Rogoff, B., & Wertsch, J. V. (Eds.) (1984). *Children's learning in the "zone of proximal development"*. New Directions in Child Development no. 23. San Francisco: Jossey-Bass.

Roy, A. W. N., & Howe, C. J. (1990). Effects of cognitive conflict, socio-cognitive conflict and imitation on children's socio-legal thinking. *European Journal of Social Psychology, 20*, 241–252.

Rubenstein, J. L., & Howes, C. (1979). Caregiving and infant behavior in day care and in homes. *Developmental Psychology, 15*, 1–24.

Rubin, K. H., Fein, G. G., & Vandenberg, B. (1983). Play. In E. M. Hetherington (Ed.), *Handbook of child psychology, vol. 4, Social development*. New York: Wiley.

Saxe, G. B., Guberman, S. R., & Gearhart, M. (1987). Social processes in early number development. *Monographs of the Society for Research in Child Development, 52* (no. 2, Serial no. 216).

Schaffer, H. R. (1979). Acquiring the concept of the dialogue. In M. Bornstein, and W. Kessen (Eds.), *Psychological development from infancy: Image and intention*. Hillsdale, N.J.: Lawrence Erlbaum Associates Inc.

Schaffer, H. R. (1984). *The child's entry into a social world*. London: Academic Press.

Schaffer, H. R. (1986). Child psychology: The future. *Journal of Child Psychology and Psychiatry, 27*, 761–780.

Schaffer, H. R. (1989). Language development in context. In S. von Tetzchner, L. S. Siegel, & L. Smith (Eds.), *The social and cognitive aspects of normal and atypical language development*. New York: Springer-Verlag.

Schaffer, H. R. (1990). The mutuality of parental control in early childhood. In M. Lewis, & S. Feinman (Eds.), *Social influences and socialization in infancy*. New York: Plenum Press.

Schaffer, H. R., & Collis, G. M. (1986). Parental responsiveness and child behaviour. In W. Sluckin, & M. Herbert (Eds.), *Parental behaviour in animals and humans*. Oxford: Blackwell.

Schaffer, H. R., & Crook, C. K. (1979). Maternal control techniques in a directed play situation. *Child Development, 50*, 989–998.

Schaffer, H. R., & Crook, C. K. (1980). Child compliance and maternal control techniques. *Developmental Psychology, 16*, 54–61.

Schaffer, H. R., & Liddell, C. (1984). Adult-child interaction under dyadic and polyadic conditions. *British Journal of Developmental Psychology, 2*, 33–42.

Siegel, L. S., & Cunningham, C. E. (1984). Social interactions: A transactional approach with illustrations from children with developmental problems. In A. Doyle, D. Gold, & D. S. Moskowitz (Eds.), *Children in families under stress. New Directions for child development no. 24*. San Francisco: Jossey-Bass.

Slade, A. (1987). A longitudinal study of maternal involvement and symbolic play during the toddler period. *Child Development, 58*, 367–375.

Tamis-LeMonda, C. S., & Bornstein, M. H. (1989). Habituation and maternal encouragement of attention in infancy as predictors of toddler language, play, and representational competence. *Child Development, 60*, 738–751.

Tizard, B. (1977). *Adoption: A second chance*. London: Open Books.

Vondra, J., & Belsky, J. (1989). Infant play at one year: Characteristics and early antecedents. In J. J. Lockman, & N. L. Hazen (Eds.), *Action and social context*, New York: Plenum

Vygotsky, L. S. (1962). *Thought and language*. Cambridge, Mass.: M.I.T. Press.

Vygotsky, L. S. (1978). *Mind in society*. Cambridge, Mass.: M.I.T. Press.

Weissman, M. M., Leckman, J. F., Merikangas, K. R., Gammon, G. D., & Prusoff, B. A. (1984). Depression and anxiety disorders in parents and children. *Archives of General Psychiatry, 41*, 845–852.

Wertsch, J. V. (1984). The zone of proximal development: Some conceptual issues. In B. Rogoff, & J. V. Wertsch (Eds.), *Children's learning in the "zone of proximal development"*. San Francisco: Jossey-Bass.

White, B. L., Kaban, B. T., & Attanucci, J. S. (1979). *The origins of human competence*. Lexington, Mass.: D. C. Heath.

White, B. L., Kaban, B., Shapiro, B., & Attanucci, J. (1977). Competence and experience. In I. C. Uzgiris, & F. Weizmann (Eds.), *The structuring of experience*. New York: Plenum.

White, B. L., & Watts, J. C. (1973). *Experience and environment: Major influences on the development of the young child*. Englewood Cliffs, N.J.: Prentice-Hall.

Wood, D. (1980). Teaching the young child: Some relationships between social interaction, language and thought. In D. Olson (Ed.), *The social foundations of language and thought*. New York: Norton.

Wood, D., Bruner, J. S., & Ross, G. (1976). The role of tutoring in problem-solving. *Journal of Child Psychology and Psychiatry, 17*, 89–100.

Wood, D., & Middleton, D. (1975). A study of assisted problem solving, *British Journal of Psychology, 66*, 181–191.

Zukow, P. G. (1986). The relationship between interaction with the caregiver and the emergence of play activities during the one-word period. *British Journal of Developmental Psychology, 4*, 223–235.

5 Parent and Peer Relations in the Emergence of Cultural Competence

James Youniss
The Catholic University of America, Washington D.C., U.S.A.

INTRODUCTION

In the second half of the nineteenth century, social reformers in the United States viewed children as the hope for the nation's future. Founded on Christian and liberal tenets, the 100-year-old nation faced the challenge of assimilating the immigrant masses that had come in a continuous stream after the Civil War. The immigrants who populated the urban centres, were a visible sign of diversity that posed a threat to a traditional way of life. In response, a reform effort to transform the immigrants into Protestant-Americans was mounted, but after experiencing only minor successes, reformers redirected their focus to children who were more pliable and open to socialisation. Focusing on families, schools, and the work place, reformers hoped to eliminate poverty, stop delinquency, and enculturate the immigrants. This effort had some success and appeared sufficiently promising that, as the century ended, children were characterised as the next generation of voters who would carry on the traditions that sustained American society.

G. Stanley Hall, the acknowledged "father of developmental psychology", entered the field of child study in the midst of this reform movement and seems to have shared its central focus. He was personally steeped in the American ethos, tracing his ancestry to the Mayflower settlers (Hall, 1923). Hall graduated from Williams College and took his PhD at Harvard University. Hall's first European trip was encouraged by Henry Ward Beecher of New York's Union Theological Seminary. In his writings, Hall forthrightly expressed his belief in the central role of

131

Christianity in psychology as well as in the nation's identity. He voiced concern about preserving the nation in light of the immigrant "masses", which he saw in need of cultural education in the broad sense. Hall believed tradition could be sustained by promoting those institutions that were part of the core value system—the National Education Association, the Boy Scouts, the Young Men's, and Women's, Christian Association, the Sunday School movement, and, of course, those colleges to which the education of the nation's elite was entrusted.

Hall died in 1924 and with his death, American developmental psychology seems to have severed its intellectual and ideological ties with the nineteenth century. No sharper contrast than John B. Watson need be cited to illustrate the chasm between the nineteenth century ethos of reform and the twentieth century's approach to children through scientific psychology. Whereas Hall and his intellectual kin sought to remake immigrant children into Christian Americans, Watson wanted to create healthy human beings able "to cope with the world in which they must later live" (Watson, 1928, p. 44). Whereas Hall recognised the cultures from which the immigrant children had come as sources of racial types, Watson believed that culture-free individuals, regardless of parental background, could be created with proper psychological techniques. Hall's aim was to preserve the Christian American ideal. Watson, in contrast, hoped to teach parents how to produce new kinds of citizens who would not duplicate their parents' cultures but form the base for a new and better society: "Will not these children, . . ., with their better ways of living and thinking, replace us as a society and, in turn, bring up their children in a still more scientific way, until the world finally becomes a place fit for human habitation?" (Watson, 1925, p. 248).

Ever since Watson, the study of child rearing and development has been focused on a culture-free individual who can operate adaptively in all social situations. The culture in which the parents are steeped is considered largely irrelevant to the practices they might be taught to adopt. If parents were aware of proper rearing techniques, they could produce competent individuals who would be adapted to society, even if it were only distantly related to the cultural values of their parents. Watson was confident that parents would adopt proper techniques and that results would free the individal from the impediment of family background. He boasted: "I would feel perfectly confident in the ultimately favourable outcome of careful upbringing of a *healthy well-formed baby*, born of a long line of crooks, murderers and thieves, and prostitutes (Watson, 1925, p. 82).

The form of thinking expressed by Watson, became etched in our discipline and characterised the central stance towards child rearing for several decades thereafter. Researchers designed studies to discover rearing techniques that were most conducive to desired psychological outcomes. Analysis of techniques was shaped mainly by considerations of basic processes of acquisition, which for Watson were "conditioning and unconditioning". Outcomes were designated in general terms as behaviours that would be adaptive for whichever situations might arise. Through several generations of research, parents, the techniques they used, and the outcomes that followed, became increasingly abstracted from cultural considerations. Aggression or altruism, for instance, became topics on their own and were studied without regard for their situational relevance or their cultural meaning.

In recent years, a general critique has evolved within the field to counteract this drift away from culture. It is known through several guises, one of the clearest being contextual analysis. Its chief tenet is that children should be understood as products of the social circumstances in which they develop. Child rearing is an obvious point of focus because it is the immediate means of contact between children and society, and because it may be, itself, shaped by society. The major aim of the present chapter is to review work done during the past decade that illustrates the importance of this perspective, in particular, for the study of parents' socialisation of children. The chapter has two major parts. In the first, two areas of research that illustrate this emerging viewpoint will be briefly reviewed. One includes studies of language socialisation insofar as this work demonstrates the role of social structure in shaping parents' everyday practices with children. The other includes studies of parents' beliefs about children's development. These studies show the value of viewing parents' rearing practices as tactics that are devised to help children become adaptive members of particular societies. Both types of data illustrate the gains that come from locating parents in a cultural system. One sees that parents' habitual ways of interacting with, and beliefs about, children are grounded in a culture. Further, one recognises that parents' actions and understanding of their actions are directed to helping their offspring become members of a culture.

Part two of this chapter considers the kind of theory the field would need to deal with culture and psychological development. Beginning with George Herbert Mead (Davidson & Youniss, 1991), one sees that contextual theories tend to have a cost, in that they simplify development by construing acquisition as internalisation. The premise has been that children acquire that which first exists in culture and is transmitted inward through the parents' agency. Today, this model is not adequate to explain the constructive side of development, which researchers have uncovered through 30 years of empirical research (Corsaro & Eder, 1990). The challenge is to integrate an adequate theory of social constitution with proper attention to what we know of children's own constructions. A model that potenially meets these needs is sketched by combining elements from Piaget's epistemology with insights from research on children's interactive and discourse skills through relations with peers (Corsaro, 1985) and parents (Miller & Sperry, 1987).

LANGUAGE SOCIALISATION

Recent studies of the manner in which parents communicate with their children have been framed as much from an anthropological as a psychological position. Until recently, psychologists' interests were focused on which of parents' speech patterns promoted the acquisition of "mature" grammar. One finding was that parents' simplification of speech was an effective form of communication, and another was that parents' expansion of children's utterances effectively helped children move towards more adult-like productions. Simplification and expansion played a role similar to that of well-known rearing techniques such as "love withdrawal" or "induction" in the area of personality development, in that they were effective procedures for promoting optimal development (Maccoby & Martin, 1983).

During the past decade, researchers have taken a different approach to the study of language socialisation. They have looked at caretaker-child verbal exchanges as constituent acts, which promote socialisation and make discourse patterns part of children's cultural identity. Further, they have viewed the parents' part in this process as being based in the culture and not just coming from their individual minds. It follows that participation in language routines embeds children in a culture and provides means for participating further in that culture with other persons. A small sample of findings that illustrate these points will now be presented.

Ochs (1984) reports observations on caretaker-child interactions in rural Western Samoan society, which she compares with findings from white middle class (WMC) families in the United States. One of her central observations is focused on ways Samoan mothers clarify ambiguous or incomplete utterances of their children. Findings from WMC families, in which mothers typically clarify children's speech with strategies of expansion or simplification, are the comparative referent. Mothers in the Samoan sample do not typically expand or simplify but either do not react, say "I don't understand", or offer a puzzled look indicating incomprehension. From a WMC perspective, these mothers appear as cold, unsympathetic teachers, but in the context of their culture, one sees their behaviour differently.

Mothers in WMC families are usually adept at imputing viewpoints to children and making clarifications from children's supposed viewpoints. Their tactics include prods, guesses, simplifications, and expansions. In contrast, the Samoan mothers place the burden of clarification on children, forcing them to figure out what adults want and expect. Ochs attempts to understand this posture by considering the place of perspective taking in the culture. She refers to the importance of social stratification in relation to Samoan culture's dominant theory of knowledge and learning; to wit, a person of higher rank is not expected to take the perspective of a person of lower rank but a person of lower rank is to take the perspective of someone higher in rank. Among other things, rank applies to age; hence, parents rank higher than children who "are expected to notice and anticipate the wishes" of parents, more than vice versa (Ochs, 1984, p. 333).

This expectation is conveyed to children through several means, including putting the burden on children to discover parents' perspectives. By not providing cues and forcing children to clarify for others, caretakers are teaching children to participate in a recurrent cultural routine. Apparently this teaching begins at an early age as, for instance, children are often held so that they face outward towards other persons rather than facing inwards towards the caretaker. This spatial orientation presumably encourages children to be sensitive to cues given by the audience: "Sib and parental caregivers work hard to get children, even before the age of two years, to take the perspective of others. This demeanour is a fundamental component of showing respect, a most necessary competence in Samoan daily life" (Ochs, 1984, p. 333). Hence, the acquisition of discourse routines allow children to conduct everyday communication as it is conducted in this particular culture. In interacting with mothers, children partake of general structures, such as stratification, that are shared by adult members of the culture. Parents' ways of interacting with children are based in these structures and help children become members of the culture.

A complementary set of studies is reported by Heath (1983), Stack (1974), and Ward (1971), who offer observations of linguistic interactions between black children and adult caretakers. Ward studied a sample of seven families in rural Louisiana, in the 1960s; Heath observed black families in rural North Carolina and, for comparison, studied white families in a small town in North Carolina, during the 1970s; Stack studied black families in an urban setting, in the 1960s. Each reported typical caretaker-child discourse along with descriptions of living conditions and broader cultural patterns.

A few of the more interesting observations illustrate the general point of this section. Heath found that adults rarely repeated or elaborated on young children's words, while Ward also found that adults did not pay close attention to young children's utterances. Heath reported that adults conversed infrequently with children. Ward also reported that mothers rarely conversed with children; in fact, they said that children's talking was "bad" and that children made them "nervous". Heath noted that children were parties to ongoing adult-adult interactions without being shielded from adult topics and Ward observed that adults took pleasure in children's participation in their activities; for example, children were encouraged to gossip, such as telling who was sleeping with whom. Heath found that mothers used expansion when children's utterances were unclear, but Ward reported that adults tended to expand their own, rather than children's speech. Heath found that parents told children fanciful stories that were laced with exaggeration and that mothers infrequently accommodated speech "downward" for children; Ward reported that mothers used a kind of child-directed speech, but said it was general and lacked adjustment to individual children. Heath and Ward both observed that adults seemed unconcerned when children used incorrect grammar; grammatical errors were unattended and rarely corrected. Ward noted that mothers did not view themselves as "language instructors". Heath and Ward reported that adults enjoyed verbal play with children—Heath observed a kind of public teasing in which adult male passers-by provoked children with negative name-calling in a challenging manner; Ward observed children's participation in gossip episodes, as was noted earlier.

Heath, Ward, and Stack have interpreted these examples as reflecting the cultures in which they occurred. For present purposes, culture refers to a shared system of relationships among persons from which they assign meaning to their actions. Even general properties provide insight into the practices that have just been described. First, in these settings, children "belong to" the community and are not viewed as offspring of particular parents (Heath, 1983; Stack, 1974). Any adult, especially a relative, can care for an infant (Ward, 1971). Child care is the obligation of adults who compromise a "durable network of kin and non-kin, who interact daily, providing domestic needs of children and assuring their survival" (Stack, 1974, p. 31). The terms "mama" or "parent" may vary over time and apply to whichever adults take the role at a given time.

Second, adults seem to lose interest in children at just about the time they begin the language acquisition process (Ward, 1971). After age 2 or 3, children are often cared for by siblings or mixed-aged peer groups (Heath, 1983; Stack, 1974; Ward, 1971). Belonging to communities and not exclusively to biological parents, children experience life in common, in contrast to the segregated privacy of nuclear families. In this context, it is not surprising to find the kind of teasing relationship of adult men to little boys whereby the men seek to "toughen them up" so that the boys can better deal with harsh social reality (Heath, 1983, p. 79; cf, Miller & Sperry, 1987).

Third, caretakers do not adopt the role of "teacher" but believe that children should learn on their own. In Stack's sample, parenthood was "elastic", the "parent" being the caretaker currently in charge. According to Ward, children by age 3 are no longer considered in need of close monitoring and are left to interact within the defined community. In Heath's sample, children were valued in themselves and not as offspring of a particular parent. The role of teacher is not attached to the child's mother as it is in typical WMC families. Language instruction is not unique in this regard but is only one domain in which children are left to learn from their own experience.

Fourth; Heath, Ward, and Stack concur that children spend much time in crowded spaces witnessing ongoing life. Children are parties to, although not major agents in, discourse. In Ward's view, this impedes children from learning how to control situations verbally (Ward, 1971, p. 88). Adults talk more *to* than *with* children, so that children lack experience in conversational give-and-take. Children are not construed as needing attention or as being in the process of developing. They are assigned the status of "children" at a young age and are expected to behave in accordance with the community's norms for child behaviour.

PARENT BELIEFS

The functionalist sociological tradition assumes that parents' rearing practices are grounded in their station in society and that rearing practices are designed to help offspring adapt to society and get an edge over others. Riesman's (1950) classic work, *The lonely crowd*, provides an articulate statement on behalf of this position. Riesman offers a historical analysis of three types of rearing patterns, which he calls *traditional, inner directed*, and *other directed*. Each type is a joint product of society's structure and parents' desire for offspring who are successful in society, as parents know it.

Riesman proposes that during the traditional era, which ended roughly with industrialisation in the second half of the eighteenth century, adults experienced a relatively stable and repetitive social structure. Economics were grounded in tried agricultural practices and everyday life was guided by norms that were unchanging. Population remained stable due to a match between a high rate of death and a replacement birth rate. Individuals identified with their families and deferred to norms that served the community's interest. It follows that rearing was oriented towards obedience and conformity because individuality was not prized so much as the willingness to support norms that allowed the community to function smoothly.

In contrast, Riesman described the contemporary era as marked by rapid changes in the economic order, tolerance of pluralistic views, and rewards for persons who can make quick reconnaissance of fluctuating situations. Demographically, the population is again relatively stable, but now because both death and birth rates have been reduced. In this context, adaptive rearing has switched from an emphasis on obedience and compliance to stressing the ability to assess social cues that signal other people's thoughts and desires. It follows that *other directed* rearing consists in skills of appraising other people and taking the role of others (Gadlin & Rubin, 1977: Youniss, 1983). This is because social skills, which allow rapid adaptation to changing contexts, have advantages over sheer obedience to standards, since standards are open to change.

Riesman's analysis offers a speculative framework for viewing major shifts in rearing patterns in relation to social structural change in Western society over the past 300 or so years (see Gadlin, 1978, for a complementary review of the history of childrearing techniques). Research stemming from this thesis illustrates a relationship between parents' strategies of rearing and parents' understanding of society. Miller and Swanson (1958), and Kohn (1969), for instance, hypothesised that fathers' social status, defined through type of work and socio-economic status (SES), determined the dominant goals in their rearing of sons. Miller and Swanson differentiated "entrepreneurial" fathers, who worked with their minds and were expected to encourage sons to think creatively, from "bureaucratic" fathers, whose work entailed following set rules and who were expected to encourage compliance in their sons.

Kohn (1969) pursued the same general relationship through a comparative analysis of fathers who either managed other people or worked with inanimate objects, and who either made managerial decisions or mainly filled prescribed roles. Kohn observed that managerial fathers, also relatively high in SES, wanted sons to think for themselves in a logical, self-directed manner. Lower SES fathers, who filled more functionary roles, wanted their sons to be conforming, obedient, and orderly.

Psychologists, with some exceptions (Bjornsson, Edelstein, & Kreppner, 1977) were slow to pursue this approach. As Maccoby and Martin (1983) noted, psychologists' main quest has been to find the most effective rearing procedures for producing the healthiest personality. They might have added: "... with no regard for the cultural or social conditions in which the parents live or for which the practices might be adaptive". While some researchers have specified parent SES, geographic location, or educational level, these factors were not treated as constitutive forces that inhere in culture and create individuals accordingly. The literature on parent training verifies this point, its central premise being that any parent can be taught to use rearing tactics that benefit children. Such a view ignores the possibility that parents operate from a culturally constructed set of premises about what society is, what its norms are, and how children ought to fit into society. If rearing practices are constituted in parents' understandings of society, they are part of the taken-for-granted cognition by which parents operate and cannot be simply imported from without or made to change with verbal instruction.

Bronfenbrenner's (1958) assessment of historical changes in child rearing patterns was another exception. He suggested that working- and middle-class parents in the United States had reversed child rearing practices between 1930 and 1950. Surveys in the 1930s showed middle-class parents to be demanding and strict, relative to working-class parents who were permissive and lenient. After the Second World War, the classes switched orientations, although both became more flexible. Bronfenbrenner attributed this switch to a mix of "cultural background, urban vs. rural upbringing, and exposure to particular ideologies of child rearing" (p. 424).

About a decade ago, a new outlook was adopted as researchers once again began to study what parents thought about childrearing rather than simply measuring parenting behaviours. Parents were recognised as being steeped in ideology and holding beliefs about the ways children develop. They did not merely react to situations as they came up, but designed actions to fit the roles they saw for their children, on the one hand, and the roles they saw for themselves in their children's development, on the other hand. This shift in perspective allowed researchers to study how experiences in parenting affected subsequent rearing and how approaches to rearing were grounded in culture, which recursively operated on parents' cognition

McGillicuddy-De Lisi (1982), and McGillicuddy-De Lisi and Sigel (1982), published early work that addressed parents' beliefs about development. They documented types of theories parents held and demonstrated that parents' theories were correlated with children's behaviour. This work granted cognition to parents, who had previously been construed as acting without thinking; parents were now allowed to use thinking for constructing rearing strategies, which they framed for social purpose.

Grusec and Kuczynski (1980) added to this work by classifying parental actions into types. Some parental actions were said to be directed towards handling immediate problems that required direct intervention and control. When a child faced impending danger, procuring safety seemed more critical than delivering action in a warm manner, for example. Other actions, however, were seen as pertaining to long-term aims that were served in various ways. If parents want children to think for themselves, as fathers in Kohn's studies wanted, then they can use whichever situations arise to encourage children to take the initiative.

Other researchers (Goodnow, 1988; Goodnow, Cashmore, Cotton, & Knight, 1984; Goodnow, Knight, & Cashmore, 1985) have taken the further step of connecting beliefs to their cultural roots. They have compared parents from different cultural backgrounds to assess their respective beliefs about children's development. Parents from diverse backgrounds had varied expectations about "schedules" or ages at which children ought to manifest developmental achievements, for instance, coping with peer conflict or being verbally assertive. Parents vary regarding expectations about developmental stages as well as ways in which children make developmental progress (see Goodnow, 1985, for a review).

Thus, it can be seen that psychologists are currently evolving an outlook on child rearing that grounds parents' behaviour and beliefs in culture. When parents are considered in cultural context, and given normal cognitive status, they are allowed to have beliefs, long-range goals, and the capacity to plan actions. This viewpoint gives new meaning to parents' behaviour, which can be seen in terms of their views of children and of society. Although these studies are preliminary, they are prerequisite for reconnecting parents with their cultural constitution and with conviction for action, which is founded in ideologies that direct rearing practices.

A CULTURALLY SENSITIVE DEVELOPMENTAL PROCESS

The remainder of this chapter describes elements required of a developmental theory that can adequately integrate a cultural viewpoint of parents and child rearing. The outline for such a theory is taken from Piaget's epistemology, specifically his early writings, which have recently attracted renewed interest (Bearison, 1989; Chapman, 1986; Damon, 1978; Davidson & Youniss, 1991; Furth, 1980; Youniss, 1980; Youniss & Damon, in press). A summary viewpoint will be described and then supplemented by work from two contemporary investigators, Corsaro and his colleagues, who have studied children's peer relations; and Miller and her colleagues, who have studied discourse in mother-daughter relations. The former work conceptualises peer relations in cultural terms and specifies a different kind of conjuction with adult relations than did Piaget, who sharply contrasted the two. Miller, et al.'s work, on the other hand, demonstrates ways in which children and parents collaborate in constructing knowledge and achieving shared understanding. This amends Piaget's narrow construal of adult relations as leading to "egocentric" (Piaget, 1932a, p. 36), or "sociocentric" thinking (Piaget, 1970, p. 723). It further shows how forms of discourse clarify Piaget's concept of procedures and serves children's acquisition of culture.

Piaget's Contribution

Piaget (1932a; 1932b) studied children's social life at two levels; interactive procedures and interpersonal relationships. They comprise the basis of his position and provide the connection to his general epistemology. Piaget argued that knowledge begins in action, which, in the social domain, entails interpersonal interaction. This is because children's initiatives elicit other persons' actions, which produce contingent effects. The equivalent in scientific knowledge is interaction between the child and physical objects. In that domain, objects offer resistance, which force children to reflect in an accomodative fashion. In the social area, the actions of others not only offer resistance, but "differences", which can be discussed by the respective persons. These discussions constitute reflective mental activity, which is public, not private, and collaborative, not individualistic.

Collaborative reflection produces, as in reflective abstractions in the scientific sphere, invariant properties of interactions (Davidson & Youniss, 1991). Piaget (1932a) called them procedures, which include *discussion, debate, compromise, negotiation*, and the like. Guided by rules, children can generate new interactions in cooperation with other people.

Piaget proposed that procedures are organised in terms of relationships, which he depicted with two ideal types. Relationships with adults are marked by unilateral authority or constraint, which is founded on asymmetry, or complementariness. Relationships with peers are founded on reciprocity and lead to procedures that are cooperative in nature. The former relationships are inadequate for cooperation because authority figures are unable to negotiate fully with children to explicate meaning. In addition, although children realise that adults have views different from their own, they are unable to achieve mutual understanding with adults because of procedural impediments. Procedures based on reciprocity, however, are conducive to the achievement of mutuality because each person's expression of an idea engenders a reciprocal expression, so that the two literally co-construct new ideas from their respective starting points.

Relationships persist through time. The rules and understandings that people co-construct provide them with a continuing context in which they interact in a generative manner. Sustaining relationships, with the understandings they have engendered, becomes a goal in itself. That is why persons subjugate individual interests to norms of reciprocity and discussion, which are needed to assure them of being understood by others and of understanding others. (Piaget, 1932a, p. 95).

In his classic study of moral judgment, Piaget (1932a) considered two alternatives as sources of morality. In one, attributed to Kant, moral principles are derived from private logical reflection. When pressed to justify a principle, an individual would recount its logical derivation. Piaget rejected this view as too individualistic for the reality of socal life, which surrounds children from birth. The second option, attributed to Durkheim, based morality in authority and tradition. Children would gain moral knowledge through direct transmission from adults, and beliefs would be justified by referring back to authority. Piaget rejected this view because knowledge that is not constructed through children's own actions is necessarily mystified. Therefore, Piaget chose a third route by basing morality on mutual respect, which developed as people voluntarily co-operated in the co-construction of rules they practised to sustain relationships. This is why Piaget's individual feels solidarity with others, senses an obligation to adhere to procedures, and feels *alienation* or *anomie* when norms of reciprocity and discussion are violated.

This position has several strengths. It offers a coherent account of the *social* construction of knowledge and the individual. It builds from the unit of interaction to interpersonal relationship, which stand relative to one another as procedures to the organisation of procedures. Society proceeds outward from relations and the individual derives similarly from relations. Children do not see themselves as isolated individuals but think of themselves as members of society (see also Furth & Kane, Chapter 6 in this volume). Lastly, it accounts for solidarity and mutual respect, which are central to morality.

The position's weaknesses are equally evident. It idealises peer relations in contrast to adult relations, and it does not recognise that procedures as well as relationships may be rooted in culture, even though they are co-constructed by persons. These weaknesses are not essential in the basic epistemology, however, and they can be remedied by empirical evidence as we shall now see.

Corsaro's Work

Corsaro and his colleagues have described children's peer relations and shown their relevance to social development; their work will now be described insofar as it clarifies this position. Corsaro and his colleagues acknowledge the value of basing knowledge on interactions rather than attributing it to internalisation of forms extant in society (Corsaro & Eder, 1990; Corsaro & Rizzo, 1988). From the perspective of children, culture consists in habitual interactional routines and shared understandings, which permit the individuals to participate further in social activity. This view is amenable to a developmental analysis because it does not start with an external definition of culture, but deals with the child's means for acting in a cultural manner.

In common with Piaget, Corsaro considers peer relations to be positive forces in children's social development (Corsaro, 1985). At the same time, Corsaro believes that the Piagetian view is too focused on the individualistic outcomes of social construction and insufficiently concerned with "how interpersonal relations reflect cultural systems, become part of and in turn, collectively reproduce these cultural patterns . . ." (Corsaro & Eder, 1990, p. 199). In this view, procedures used in peer relations embed ·

children in peer culture and provide them with skills and knowledge that facilitate their participation in adult culture as well. Peer relations constitute a culture for the following reasons. They offer a context in which a collective process for the socialisation of knowledge is operative. Children enter this cultural system by partaking of interactive routines through which they conduct everyday play and other social discourse. They fight, share, play games, and concoct pretend dramas. Using shared routines, like Piaget's procedures, peers negotiate meaning so that they naturally achieve understandings of reality. With these routines and knowledge in hand, peers can "produce and reproduce" their shared cultural system in a generative manner. "By interacting and negotiating with others [children] establish understandings that become fundamental social knowledge on which they continually build" (Corsaro & Eder, 1990, p. 200).

Corsaro and his colleagues recognise differences between peer and adult cultures, but, unlike Piaget, do not draw a sharp boundary between them or argue that the disparity is "resolved" by transforming adult relations into reciprocal relationships later in development. First, Corsaro et al. propose that there is not one, but a series of peer cultures, which children reconstruct as they develop from the preschool through the adolescent years. Second, habitual routines that apply to peer relations overlap with routines that apply in adult relations. Third, as children function with peers, they appropriate features from adult culture into the peer domain, and probably vice versa. For example, children import age ranking from the adult world into their relations with peers and begin to negotiate around it (Corsaro, 1985). And fourth, the routines and knowledge that peers engender are so fundamental to cultural membership that they implicitly facilitate participation in adult culture: "The habitual, taken-for-granted character of routines provides actors with the security and shared understanding of belonging to a cultural group" (Corsaro & Rizzo, 1988, p. 880).

Corsaro's (1985; 1990), observations of children's pretend play are noteworthy. While Piaget (1932a) also studied play, he focused on games with definite rules, rather than pretend play in which children cooperate in producing stories, continually checking that they share understanding as they serially take turns (see also, Cook-Gumperz & Corsaro, 1977). Pretend play, thus, provides insight into a major cultural characteristic of using agreed procedures for establishing and maintaining mutual understanding.

Miller's Work

Miller and her colleagues have studied mother-daughter relations and conceived of their findings much as Corsaro, et al., have for peer relations. They have focused on discourse patterns in which mothers and pre-school age daughters negotiate meaning. They report several types of routines through which children become embedded in culture. As in the studies with peers, the routines are recurrent and habitual, and become the means for acting productively in new situations, as they are to agreed patterns "on which the children can continually build" (Corsaro & Rizzo, 1988, p. 880).

Three aspects of this work bear on and clarify the Piagetian position. First, the work shows that children's relations with adults entail more than unilateral authority. Although, it may be the dominant role, mother-daughter interactions can function in symmetrical and cooperative modes as well. Haight and Miller (1991) have reported episodes of mother-daughter pretend play that exemplify the point clearly. They noted that mothers were partners in pretend play to children of 12 months and continued in this role with children of 48 months of age. Mothers typically initiated play with very young children, but older children also initiated play with mothers. For example, a 36-month-old said, "I drive car", adding the appropriate gesture of steering. The mother supported this initiative by asking, "Oh, where are you going?" Importantly, it was found that mothers' parts in pretend episodes were contingent on and fluent with children's initiatives. It is noted finally that mother-daughter pretend play begins at an early age and continues through the pre-school years, thus affording numerous opportunities for interplay between adult and peer cultures (Corsaro, 1985).

Miller and Sperry (1987) offer a second example of mother-daughter interaction that pertains to the establishment of rule-like routines. They report episodes dealing with the expression of anger and aggression involving either the immediate expression of emotion between the parties or reframing of emotion-provoking events in past experience. In an instance of the former, a mother initiated "playful fistfights" with her daughter, justifying this as preparation for real-life events in the daughter's future (Miller & Sperry, 1987, p. 17):

Now she likes to wrestle with me. I'll take her upstairs and we go on the bed and start wrestling. And I'll say, "Take your fist and hit me." 'Cause I try to teach in case somebody else is doin' it. 'Cause some kids do take their fist and hit you hard. (*laughs*) I let her punch me. Sometimes she sneaks a good one in on me.

Abstracting from their observations, Miller and Sperry (1987) proposed a set of organising rules regarding mother-daughter interactions. They were: (1) When another child hurts you, defend yourself. (2) Don't respond aggressively without cause. (3) When your mother acts like a bullying child and teases you, defend yourself. (4) Don't aggress or act with anger to adults without cause. These rules provide evidence for the kind of invariant procedures Piaget believed would bring order to interactions. However, in contrast to Piaget, these data illustrate the permeable boundary between adult and peer worlds, the rules for adults being compatible with the rules for peers. As with Corsaro, et al., rules applicable in one culture are useful for participation in the other culture.

The third set of data consists of stories that adults tell about everyday experiences of the adult, the child, and other persons (Miller & Sperry, 1988). These narratives recount past events, present them in an evaluative manner, and mark their cultural significance. They not only portray "personal experience [in] dramatic form" (p. 311) but also give social meaning to everyday events by making the personal public and making the child's private experience available for shared consideration. The use of narratives in the child rearing process seems an especially apt illustration of how children's experience is organised in cultural form. Parents select episodes from the flow of experience and endow them with importance by recounting selective features and offering an evaluative, dramatic reading.

CONCLUSION

In the 1920s, Watson expressed a forward-looking view of parenting and child rearing with the hope that a break from "ignorance" and folk tradition would allow production of a new kind of individual who was formed through application of scientific principles to function in the modern world. For several decades thereafter, researchers sought to discover the best rearing techniques for producing healthy personalities. Parents' cultural background, ideologies, or status in society were consciously ignored and soon became irrelevant to theory. During the past decade, critics have come to doubt generality in the sense Watson envisioned, and have come to see the techniques uncovered through research as little more than culture-specific practices. In a positive vein, new research has been designed to identify the cultural basis of practices and beliefs and to show their relation to the child's cultural formation.

This research raises new challenges for theories of development. If a simple model of children's internalisation of existing cultural forms is unacceptable—and there are good grounds for rejecting it—then theories must take account of children's abilities to construct knowledge through interactions with parents. The question is how these constructions are cultural rather than simply individual. A potential solution is provided by Piaget's epistemology supplemented by Corsaro's work with peers and Miller's work with parent-child relations.

This sketch approaches interpersonal interactions and relationships from the perspective of children's development and avoids the problematic approach that equates socialisation with internalisation. The key elements are recurrent interactive routines that are known as rules, relations that organise rules, and negotiation of understandings, or shared meaning, which is an essential characteristic of culture that differentiates members of a culture from non-members. In this sketch, children gain cultural identification by participating in rule-governed procedures, when those same procedures are the means for generating shared understandings.

REFERENCES

Bearison, D. J. (1989). Interactional contexts of cognitive development: Piagetian approaches to sociogenesis. In L. Tolchinsky (Ed.) *Culture, cognition, and schooling* (pp. 56–70). Norwood, N.J.: Ablex.

Bjornsson S., Edelstein, W., & Kreppner, K. (1977). *Explorations in social inequality: Stratification dynamics in social and individual development in Iceland.* Berlin: Max Planck Institute for Development, No. 38.

Bronfenbrenner, U. (1958). Socialization and social class through time and space. In E. E. Maccoby, T. M. Newcomb, & E. L. Hartley (Eds.) *Readings in social psychology* (pp. 400–425). New York: Holt, Rinehart, & Winston.

Chapman, M. (1986). The structure of social exchange: Piaget's sociological theory. *Human Development, 29*, 181–194.

Cook-Gumperz, J., & Corsaro, W. A. (1977). Social ecological constraints on children's communicative strategies. *Sociology, 11*, 411–434.

Corsaro, W. A. (1985). *Friendship and peer culture in the early years.* Norwood, N.J.: Ablex.

Corsaro, W. A. (1990). The underlife of the nursery school: Young children's social representations of adult rules. In B. Lloyd, & G. Duveen (Eds.) *Social representations and the development of knowledge*, (pp. 11–26). Cambridge: Cambridge University Press.

Corsaro, W. A., & Eder, D. (1990). Children's peer cultures. *Annual Review of Sociology, 16*, 197–220.

Corsaro, W. A., & Rizzo, T. A. (1988). *Discussione* and friendship: Socialization processes in the peer culture of an Italian nursery school. *American Sociological Review, 53*, 879–894.

Damon, W. (1978). *The social world of the child.* San Francisco: Jossey-Bass.

Davidson, P., & Youniss, J. (1991). Which one comes first, morality or identity? In W. M. Kurtines, & J. L. Gewirtz (Eds.), *Handbook of moral behaviour and development, Vol. 1: Theory* (pp. 105–121). Hillsdale, NJ: Lawrence Erlbaum Associates Inc.

Furth, H. G. (1980). *The world of grown-ups: Children's conceptions of society.* New York: Elsevier.

Furth, H. G., & Kane, S. R. (this volume). Children constructing society: A new perspective on children at play. In H. McGurk (Ed.) *Childhood social development: Contemporary perspectives.* Hove, U.K. Lawrence Erlbaum Associates Ltd.

Gadlin, H. (1978). Child discipline and the pursuit of self. In H. W. Reese, & L. Lippsitt (Eds.) *Advances in child development and behavior. Vol. 13*, New York: Academic Press.

Gadlin, H., & Rubin, S. H. (1979). Interactionism: A non-resolution of the person-situation controversy. In A. Buss (Ed.) *Psychology in social context.* New York: Irvington.

Goodnow, J. J. (1985). Change and variations in parents' ideas about childhood and parenting. In I. E. Sigel (Ed.) *Parental belief systems* (pp. 235–264). Hillsdale, N.J.: Lawrence Erlbaum Associates Inc.

Goodnow, J. J. (1988). Parents' ideas, actions, and feelings: Models and methods from developmental and social psychology. *Child Development, 59*, 286–320.

Goodnow, J. J., Cashmore, J., Cotton, S., & Knight, R. (1984). Mothers' developmental timetables in two cultural groups. *International Journal of Psychology, 19*, 193–205.

Goodnow, J. J., Knight, R., & Cashmore, J. (1985). Adult social cognition: Implications of parents' ideas for approaches to development. In M. Perlmutter (Ed.) *Social cognition: Minnesota symposia on child development. Vol. 18* (pp. 287–324). Hillsdale, N.J.: Lawrence Erlbaum Associates Inc.

Grusec, J. E., & Kuczynski, L. (1980). Direction of effects in socialization: A comparison of the parent's vs. the child's behavior as determinants of disciplinary techniques. *Developmental Psychology, 16*, 1–9.

Haight, W. L., & Miller, P. J. (1991). *The social nature of early pretend play: Mothers' participation in everyday pretending.* Unpublished manuscript.

Hall, G. S. (1923). *Life and confessions of a psychologist.* New York: D. Appleton.

Heath, S. B. (1983). *Ways with words: Language, life, and work in communities and classrooms.* Cambridge: Cambridge University Press.

Kohn, M. L. (1969). *Class and conformity.* Homewood, Ill: Dorsey.

Maccoby, E. E., & Martin, J. A. (1983). Socialization in the context of the family: Parent-child interaction. In P. H. Mussen (Ed.) *Carmichael's manual of child psychology* (pp. 1–101). New York: Wiley.

McGillicuddy-De Lisi, A. V. (1982). Parental beliefs about developmental processes. *Human Development, 25*, 192–200.

McGillicuddy-De Lisi, A. V., & Sigel, I. E. (1982). Family constellations and parental beliefs. In G. L. Fox (Ed.) *The childbearing decision: Fertility attitudes and behavior* (pp. 161–177). Beverly Hills, Cal.: Sage.

Miller, P. J., & Sperry, L. L. (1987). The socialization of anger and aggression. *Merrill-Palmer Quarterly, 33*, 1–31.

Miller, P. J., & Sperry, L. L. (1988). Early talk about the past: The origins of conversational stories of personal experience. *Journal of Child Language, 15*, 293–315.

Miller, D. R., & Swanson, G. E. (1958). *The changing American parent: A study in the Detroit area.* New York: Wiley.

Ochs, E. (1984). Clarification and culture. In D. Shiffrin (Ed.) *Georgetown University roundtable on language and linguistics* (pp. 325–341). Washington, D.C.: Georgetown University Press.

Piaget, J. (1932a). *The moral judgment of the child.* London: Routledge & Kegan Paul.

Piaget, J. (1932b). *Social evolution and the new education.* London: New Education Fellowship.

Piaget, J. (1970). Piaget's theory. In P. H. Mussen (Ed.) *Carmichael's manual of child psychology* (pp. 703–732). New York: Wiley.

Riesman, D. (1950). *The lonely crowd: A study of changing American character.* Garden City, N.Y.: Doubleday.

Stack, C. B. (1974). *All our kin: Strategies for survival in a black community.* New York: Harper and Row.

Ward, M. C. (1971). *Them children: A study in language learning.* New York: Holt, Rinehart, & Winston.

Watson, J. B. (1925). *Behaviorism.* New York: Norton.

Watson, J. B. (1928). *Psychological care of infant and child.* New York: Norton.

Youniss, J. (1980). *Parents and peers in social development.* Chicago: University of Chicago Press.

Youniss, J. (1983). Beyond ideology to the universals of development. In D. Kuhn, & J. A. Meacham (Eds.) *On the development of developmental psychology* (pp. 31–52). Basel: Karger.

Youniss, J., & Damon, W. (in press). Social construction in Piaget's theory. In H. Beilin, & P. Pufall (Eds.) *Piaget's theory, its past and its future.* Hillsdale, N.J.: Lawrence Erlbaum Associates Inc.

6 Children Constructing Society: A New Perspective on Children at Play

H. G. Furth and S. R. Kane
The Catholic University of America, Washington D.C., U.S.A.

During the first stage [till 2–3 years] it can be said that the real is purely and simply what is desired. The "pleasure principle" of which Freud speaks deforms and fashions the world accordingly. The second stage [from 2–3 years up to 7–8 years] ushers in two heterogeneous and equally real realities: the world of play and the world of observation. . . . For us play is based on fiction. For children it is much more. . . . In fact, play is not opposed to reality for in both cases belief is arbitrary or rather lacking in logical reasons. Play is a reality in which children tend to believe when by themselves, exactly as the real is a play which children tend to play with adults and all those who believe likewise. In both cases belief . . . requires no intrinsic justification. One must therefore say that the play of children constitutes an autonomous reality, understanding that the "true" reality to which it is opposed is much less "true" for children than it is for us.

—Piaget, 1924, pp. 91–93.

INTRODUCTION

In previously published explorations of young children's images and conceptions of society (Furth, Baur, & Smith, 1976; Furth 1978a;b; 1980) school children, ages 5 to 11, were encouraged to talk freely about the town they lived in, what things they thought important for its routine functioning. We expected that some coherent conceptualisation regarding social institutions and customs would emerge, somewhat along the lines of

149

what Piaget had described as typical for that age in terms of the beginning of concrete operations. We were not prepared to find major logical inconsistencies, gaps and personalistic preconceptions in the societal thinking of the vast majority of the 195 children interviewed. Immature features were generally characteristic of the Stage One societal thinking of nearly all 5- and 6-year old children, but were still present, albeit to a lesser extent, in later stages.

Two transitional stages were identified. A Stage Two understanding of observable transactions in personally experienced societal events was typical of 7- and 8-year old children, but unobservable transactions were interpreted in playful and person-centred images. Stage Three showed part-systems through which the children interpreted societal transactions beyond those observed in personal experience. These systems were incomplete and thereby led to logical conflicts and inconsistencies. Such conflictual thinking was characteristic of nearly all the older children, ages 9 to 11. Only eleven of the 91 older children worked out a sufficiently adequate interpretative framework so as to eliminate serious logical inconsistencies. These children were considered to have reached Stage Four, a first logical plateau in societal thinking. It seemed reasonable to suggest that as the children became aware of the logical gaps and inconsistencies they felt motivated to improve their societal comprehension, hence the transition to the final stage.

Overall the progession from Stages One to Four illustrated well Piaget's (1985) equilibration model of knowledge development as driven from within the child's own actions on social objects. At the same time these findings highlighted a remarkable discrepancy in the individual's logical development. These were school children, none of whom had serious scholastic difficulties. So it can reasonably be assumed that the vast majority had acquired the early forms of understanding logical implications (Piaget's concrete operations) and used them in their everyday activities. It is clear therefore that in young children mental actions on physical objects acquire a logically consistent quality at a much earlier age than actions on societal objects.

The findings themselves are hardly controversial; they have been replicated in a number of more recent studies (Berti & Bombi, 1988; Jahoda, 1984). However, the reasons for the apparent logical immaturity are less obvious. It should be noted that Stage Four societal thinking, mentioned earlier, is by no means an adequate adult comprehension of societal institutions, nor is logical immaturity in societal comprehension limited to younger children. A few studies (Furth & McConville, 1981; Rosenberg, 1988) have attempted to measure adolescent and adult societal comprehension. They do not paint a flattering picture of mature understanding. Journalistic and other anecdotal evidence points in the same direction—namely, that society is not an object of lucid logical consistency. The logical discrepancy found in young children merely mirrors a state of affairs that persists through adulthood.

Such results suggest that verbal interviews or questionnaires may not be appropriate methods for investigating societal thinking. After all, children belong to a particular culture or society from birth, and more or less successfully play the roles appropriate to their age and gender. Their success does not require the consciously articulate verbalisation that interviews and questionnaires demand. Just as all children at first, and probably most adults throughout their lives, speak and comprehend language without being able to articulate even the most basic phonetic and grammatical rules they are using, so there is a difference between knowing the society's rules and playing by them.

Apart from this methodological objection it is possible that a more substantive issue looms behind children's immature societal conceptions. When we ask children about linguistic rules, at least we are referring to actions that they constantly do, namely, speaking. But when we ask children about social institutions, these are action-removed objects that confront them from outside. The very questions reinforce the picture of a societal object as being outside the child's own person.

Without going into philosophical discussion here about the society-person relation, it is clear that young children are an integral part of society, certainly by the time they have acquired language. Rather than asking them what some of the institutions that they meet in their surroundings are, would it be not be nice if we could ask them to respond to the question: Tell me in what way you are part of society? Of course this is impossible to do with children—or adults. However, we can observe the spontaneous activities of the children and relate them to societal factors. It would seem that a privileged instance of such activity is children's social pretend play.

CHILDREN'S PRETEND PLAY

Pretend play has its precursors in infant-parent interaction, which sometimes—at least from the adult's viewpoint—involves make-believe. Adults are the child's primary playmates during the first two years; they take the lead in initiating and elaborating on playful episodes (Haight & Miller, 1991; Miller & Garvey, 1984). By the end of the second year, however, children can be observed performing brief, unconnected symbolic actions when playing alone (Piaget, 1962) or with peers (Howes, Unger & Seidner, 1989). Play in infant-parent interaction has a distinct quality of teasing that is frequently marked by joyful laughter, whereas solitary pretend play and social pretend play with peers are related more to the

serious business of comprehending reality, such as is evident in sensorimotor mastering of physical situations. When a 2- to 3-year old boy plays
aircraft with a wooden stick, he is seriously intent on what he is doing. He
may be imitating some event that excited him, but he is at the same time
spontaneously creating his own imaginary reality. Who is to say that this
reality is not more "real" to the boy than the adult reality? After all, it is of
his own making and corresponds effortlessly to his personal affect and
desire.

As children develop, their pretend play becomes more and more
sophisticated. Symbolic actions are gradually dissociated from their
own bodily actions, freed from environmental cues and integrated into
multiple-action sequences (Fenson & Ramsay, 1980; Nicholich, 1977). At
the same time, their play with peers becomes more sociable. The pre-
dominant activity among peers of 1½ to 3 years of age shifts, first, from
parallel action to simple turn-taking with identical roles and then to
reciprocal interaction with complementary roles (Mueller & Lucas, 1975).
At the peak of these developments, roughly between 3 and 6 years of age,
children can co-construct with peers elaborate fictitious events involving
transformed props, sustained imaginary characters, and continuous play
themes.

A variety of models has been proposed in terms of which children's play
is interpreted. Some authors view play in relation to cognitive development, such as Vygotsky (1976), Bruner (1972), Sylva (1977), and Sutton-
Smith (1979) who stress the benefits of playing with meaning and consider
play in relation to creativity and problem-solving skills. For Piaget (1924;
1962) play indicates the development of symbol-formation, which is
contrasted with serious observation-based learning. Other authors focus on
play's contribution to social development. Along this line Rubin (1980)
points to social skill learning, Garvey (1977; Garvey & Kramer, 1989) to
the learning of linguistic strategies, and Corsaro (1985; Corsaro & Eder,
1990) to participation in the peer culture. A third group of authors
emphasise psychodynamic considerations. Following Freud (1959) and
psychoanalytically-oriented child therapists some researchers such as Fein
(1989) see play as a largely beneficial compromise formation for dealing
with the unconscious past and present anxiety. Still others argue that play
should be treated as an end in itself and an expression of wishes and
hopes (Vandenberg, 1983; 1986), as an opportunity to expand biological
and cultural creativity (Cobb, 1977), or to create imaginary situations
(Franklin, 1983).

Our aim is to add an integrating perspective to these various approaches.
We suggest that beyond the many different functions pretend play may
serve in each particular case, it has a general concrete content. This
content is society. In other words, whatever else they may play at, children

pretending always "play society". In social pretend play episodes, we propose, children co-construct a societal framework. From this perspective we can expect to find some answers to the research question posed earlier regarding the societal thinking of young children.

Specifically, we analyse the pretend play episode of three children, highlighting features of their play that indicate spontaneous societal understanding. Following Goffman's (1974) approach to the coordination of meaning in face-to-face interactions, we expect the discourse during the play period to be framed by the shared intent to produce a meaningful sequence of pretend scenes. Two interrelated categories of societal know-how should be observable: First, in directing and performing their play, the children should implicitly build a societal framework of shared presuppositions, values, traditions, customs, norms and other specifically societal factors. Second, when competing for possessions or status, the children should strategically use the pretend societal framework to their personal advantage.

In the next section we present a brief outline of the play observed. This is followed by a detailed description and excerpts from the play text that illustrate the children's societal thinking. In a subsequent discussion we elaborate on the claim that children's pretend play is in fact the instituting of a societal framework and, moreover,that from a developmental and evolutionary standpoint this is a fairly adequate explanation of social play in general.

THE PLAY: GETTING READY FOR THE ROYAL BALL

The text of the pretend play episode described here was taken from one of several videotaped play sessions arranged in an afterschool daycare classroom for children between $4\frac{1}{2}$ and 6 years of age. Two of the students for whom parents' consent was obtained, Annie, (age 5 years 11 months) and Beth (5 years 2 months), volunteered to stay inside and play while the rest of the class was outside on the playground. This atypical arrangement alongside the presence of the observer and videocamera seemed to inspire an unusually animated play, but the staging and enactment of this play were spontaneous. Beyond the request that play begin in the dramatic play corner of the classroom, no further explicit constraints were imposed on the activity. The children were free to devise a theme, plan a course of action, adopt roles, and define props.

The play began with Annie's proposal to "get things ready for tomorrow night's ball". After 19 minutes into the play—choosing clothes, laying them out, making plans and preparing for bed—Annie and Beth were joined by Celia (age 4 years 9 months) who had come in early from the

TABLE 6.1
The Royal Ball Play: Discourse Units, Coded In Four Senses

Act	Scene	Duration	Title	Acting	Framing	Arguing	Not-Play
I		19:32	A Distant Ball for Annie & Beth				
	1	3:36	Dresses, money & make-up	21	11	5	3
	2	4:13	Looking ahead to a distant Ball	13	–	20	1
	3	3:03	Telephone & table	12	–	19	–
	4	3:37	Settling down for the evening	10	–	7	–
	5	3:54	Telephone conversation	21	3	10	–
	6	1:09	Who sleeps where	11	1	3	–
II		13:44	Enter Celia: The Night Before				
	7	2:47	Money and tea for Celia	16	3	18	–
	8	2:34	Wardrobes & telephone	29	–	27	–
	9	2:40	Party things for Celia	22	2	27	–
	10	2:18	Clean up before bed	17	7	3	–
	11	3:25	"Good-night Glorias"	34	14	11	–
III		15:16	The Next Morning				
	12	6:00	Getting ready & assigning ages	30	9	26	7
	13	3:04	Dressing	6	–	26	1
	14	6:12	Choosing Royal titles	6	46	23	–
IV		8:28	"Let's Off to the Royal Ball"				
	15	3:05	Donning the Queen's coat	29	2	16	3
	16	2:08	Who will marry the Prince?	1	4	17	14
	17	1:36	The procession	7	3	18	–
	18	1:39	The Royal Ball	12	5	5	1

playground. During the next 30 minutes, further preparations were made, "good night" wishes exchanged and costumes put on for the Royal Ball. Finally, in the last 8 minutes, aware that other students were returning, the three girls hastened the concluding events of proceeding to the ball, meeting the prince and becoming queens, towards which the entire play was a preamble.

Treating the play as a dramatic whole, we divided the entire discourse sequence into four acts and 18 scenes. These acts and scenes with appropriate titles and durations in minutes and seconds are shown in Table 6.1. In addition, we coded the children's discourse in terms of its *sense* in relation to the play frame. Different modes of discourse represented distinct senses of reality, corresponding to what Goffman (1974) called varying degrees of engrossment in the in-frame activity. Enactment of the play theme was considered the most in-frame sense and, in the direction of increasing distance from full engrossment, three other senses were identified: framing (metacommunication), partly out-of-frame (argumentative) discourse, and out-of-frame (not-play) discourse. Discourse units were delimited by speakers' turns and by changes in the sense or reference of speech. Table 6.1 summarises the number of discourse units in each of the four senses for all the scenes. This provides a picture of how, throughout the play, the girls moved between levels of reality and, even after arguing or stepping out of the play, managed (largely due to Annie's skill) to sustain the in-frame continuity.

In connection with the play sequence briefly summarised here—a fuller description and coding criteria can be found in Kane and Furth (in press)— we highlight, in the following five sections, features of the play that give it a societal character. These features include shared presuppositions and values, traditions, customs and history, rules, consensus and respect, and the interactional use of pretence.

SHARED PRESUPPOSITIONS AND VALUES

"Let's pretend that we had a ball tomorrow night and we had to get our stuff ready," proposed Annie (scene 1: turn 1). She seemed to take for granted that co-producing a pretend play was a valuable project for two little girls and that preparing to attend an elegant party was an appropriate pastime for two pretend women. Beth apparently agreed. "This was my dress," she replied (1:2). "Yeah and I had this dress," said Annie (1:3), "Let's pretend we set everything up on a chair" (1:4).

These first few utterances introduced the primary point of contention in the first act and a recurrent topic of discussion throughout the play; the possession of props. Beth held her dress up to admire it. "I had a real long dress," she said (1:5). "I had a long dress too," Annie answered (1:6). Annie and Beth placed a premium value on private property. From the moment they claimed their dresses, they competed for material gain. In Scene 1, they proudly displayed their costumes on chairs, laying them out for the next morning. "The ball isn't tonight," Annie explained. "Let's pretend we just was trying it on for tomorrow night and you were gonna wear that. There." (1:11,12). During the next two scenes, they haggled over "fancy clothes", a telephone, a table and a pair of binoculars. By Scene 4, successful trades were made and compromises reached so that the issue of possessions was fairly well settled. However, in Act II when Celia joined the play, this issue was raised anew. Annie and Beth reasserted their prior ownership claims, while Celia attempted to find party things from the scarce items that remained.

Valued as highly as ownership was hierarchical status, which the children associated with grown-up roles. Yet status was never explicitly mentioned in the first Act. Either because Annie was older or because she was the author of the play theme, it was presupposed that she held a superior position. Beth referred to Annie as "mother" before there was any explicit discussion of pretend roles (2:25). When Celia arrived, however, the distribution of power shifted. Beth aligned herself with Annie in the position of Celia's superior. Much to Celia's chagrin, the play became a story about two mothers and a daughter, two big sisters and a little one, two queens and a princess, two ladies who would marry the prince and one who would not. Celia tried repeatedly to modify this arrangement. She was willing to accept Annie's and Beth's superiority, but she was determined to play the role of big sister (a role she coveted as the youngest child in her actual family). Her persistence paid off by the end of the play. In the rush to complete the final scenes, she was named "big sister princess" (18:15,16,17), though Beth made sure to remind her that "we're still older" (18:18).

TRADITIONS, CUSTOMS, HISTORY

Despite the protracted negotiations in Act I over the possession and use of various props, there was one prop over which Annie and Beth did not argue: a long piece of glossy pink fabric sewn to fit the corners of a mattress. The two girls took for granted that this prop was to be used as a shared "coat": each sewn corner to be worn by a different player as a hood. Wearing the pink bedspread in this fashion was something most of the girls in the class had experienced at one time or another. It had become a tradition in the classroom *peer culture* (Corsaro & Eder, 1990). Annie and Beth were aware of this tradition, but not Celia.

Shortly after her arrival, Celia picked up the bedspread and announced, "I want this" (9:12). Beth replied, "This is all the coats" (9:15) and Annie explained, "Yeah, we put it on and act like it's a coat" (9:16). Realising that Celia did not understand the intended definition of the bedspread, Annie and Beth patiently articulated this key element of the play frame. However, when Celia again attempted to claim the bedspread four scenes later (13:12), the two older girls were much less patient. Beth chided, "You can't have that pink one, that's . . .;" and Annie joined in, "the coat!" (13:13–14). Annie and Beth could no longer tolerate Celia's disrespect for the tradition of the coat. Eventually, Celia came to appreciate this essential piece of classroom lore. While watching Annie unfold the bedspread, she proposed, "Pretend this is very long, so we have a[n at]tached coat" (15:26). Annie and Beth had nothing to say in response, because this was precisely how they had intended to use the prop all along.

Other elements of the play frame were not brought in from the culture of the classroom but were established during the course of the play itself. Actions performed by Annie and Beth in Act I served as precedents, or customs, to be honoured by Celia in Acts II–IV. When Celia first entered,

Annie advised, "You need some money so you can pay for the Royal Ball" (7:8) and Beth offered, "You want some tea before bedtime? (7:9). Annie and Beth knew that they would have to familiarise Celia with the play frame so that the play could continue. By offering her money and tea, they attempted to convey a definition of the situation without stepping out of character themselves. Embedded in their in-frame offerings to Celia was the out-of-frame message: This is the way we do things in our play world. With these actions, too, they competed for the superior role of Celia's provider.

For Beth, who had hitherto held a subordinate position, the opportunity to instruct Celia about the established ways of the play was especially appealing. She reviewed the arrangements that she and Annie had made about using the telephone (7:1,4) and explained the main play activity: "This is what I'm wearing for dinner—um, not for dinner, for the Royal Ball. You have to find your stuff" (8:1). Whenever Celia requested a costume, Beth reiterated this explanation until—partly out of frustration and partly in stressing her own superiority—she exclaimed "How come we have to tell you so much?" (15:7). With her relative position raised by the presence of a younger player in the latter three Acts, Beth played a more active part in framing the play (16% of her discourse units) than she did during the first Act (4%) when she was the younger of two players.

Tradition and customs were located within an imaginary social historical context, the proportions of which grew as the play progressed. In the first Act, the story of two women preparing for the ball was expanded to include an imaginary third when Annie enacted a telephone call to a friend, whom she arranged to meet "a half hour after morning" (2:1,4). She extended this notion of a future occasion both in space and time by using binoculars to see the ball "so far away" (2:5) and by suggesting that "the royal ball keeps going and going" (2:14).

In Acts II–IV, the domestic lives of three common women were transformed into the stately careers of two queens and a princess. All action stopped in Scene 14 as the three girls stood around the mirror imagining themselves to be royalty. Ordinary names were exchanged for such titles as "Queen Pink Roseabell ... queen of all pink roses in the whole land and world" (14:59). In Scenes 16 and 17, the once common "house" was transformed into a "queendom" (17:11,12), a "speaker" was found for announcing the queens' arrival at the ball (17:8), and plans were made for meeting the prince: "Pretend I saw a kingdom," proposed Celia, "so I went up to him and I did this [curtsied]" (16:1). Action again gave way to imaginative talk as Celia's proposal inspired Annie to narrate events that would lead to the royal wedding. Finally, in Scene 18, the historical moment unfolded. Celebrating the imaginary world, the girls enacted their procession to the ball, announced their arrival and took turns speaking the part of the prince who formally crowned them queens.

RULES

It is generally recognised that group norms are ubiquitous in the foundation and regulation of peer interactions beginning at age two (Hartup, 1970, p. 373) and increasing during subsequent years in frequency and in emotional intensity. Not surprisingly, as a dramatic composition and as a social activity, the royal ball play proceeded according to rules. Of the 718 discourse units in the play, 47 (7%) concerned rules. Roughly half of these were explicit rule-declarations, marked by some form of the phrase "have to". In the remaining half, players alluded to rules indirectly. Rules were invoked to regulate shared elements of the play frame (21 units), the possession of props (16 units), the privileges related to status (four units), and the players' not-play discourse as actual peers (six units).

Players made rules about the play frame in order to safeguard the aesthetic integrity of the play. At times, they were concerned with preserving the realism of their performance and therefore invoked interpretations of the adult world. For example, Annie and Beth each commented on the proper use of telephones before enacting a conversation. "You have to press this [button] first if you want it to get a dial", Annie explained (3:29). "You have to ring-a-ling it. . . . People just don't pick up the phone", Beth insisted (5:10,16). Later, Annie referred to adult norms when deciding whether or not she and Beth could both be the mothers of Celia. "You're really her step-mother," Annie said to Beth, "but she calls you 'Mommy' because . . . for real, true life nobody has two moms" (7:15,23).

At other times, the players showed concern for the play's internal consistency by incorporating new props into the existing play theme. For example, upon finding a bag of toy money, Annie announced, "We have to get some money to pay to go in . . . to get into the royal ball" (1:13, 7:28). Similarly, upon discovering a notebook, Beth claimed, "Here's my nighty-night book that I always read. Because I'm gonna take it. I have to read it." Also, upon finding a horn-shaped basket (cornucopia), Beth proposed, "This was the speaker when I was [announced] queen. We have to get all the [necessary] stuff [for] when they said we were queens, right?" (17:8,9).

A similar concern was evident when players objected to inconsistencies in the definition of the situation. For example, when Annie tried to hasten the plot by announcing before bedtime: "The royal ball is starting". Beth responded excitedly, "We have to sleep . . . We're not playing it yet . . . We're not playing it now" (9:23–30). Interchanges like this have been discussed by Forbes and his colleagues in terms of "dramatic ratios"

(Forbes, Katz & Paul, 1986; Forbes & Yablick, 1984; Katz, Forbes, Yablick & Kelly, 1983). Following Burke (1969), Forbes et al. identified five basic elements of children's pretending;—actions, scenes, agents, agency, and purpose. They observed that, during the course of a play sequence, new elements are often evaluated or justified in relation to those that have already been established. A dramatistic analysis can be applied to the above exchange: The *action* of going to sleep seemed necessary to Beth, because the current *scene* was already set as the day before the ball. Forbes et al. suggested that such "dramatistic ratios" are principles by which children achieve coherence and wholeness in social pretend play.

The royal ball players used similar principles to settle disputes. Disagreements frequently arose around the issues of possessions and status. The players invoked rules to resolve such disagreements. With respect to possessions, the primary injunctions was the "finder's rule", which held that an object belonged to the player who found it first. A corollary to this rule was the requirement that players request permission before attempting to use an owner's prop. This distinction between owning and using was particularly intriguing to Beth, who invoked it on several occasions and sometimes admonished others to be careful with her things. Bakeman and Brownlee (1982) suggested that the finder's rule, or the rule of prior possession, emerges spontaneously in peer interaction. They noted that, in the transition from the toddler to the preschool years, prior possession replaces dominance as the main principle by which children settle disputes over play materials. In the Royal Ball play, an even higher principle sometimes overruled the finder's rule; the principle of "fairness", which insured that all players had an adequate share of anything that was divisible. Together, the finder's rule and the fairness principle seemed to be an acceptable regulator of play proprietorship.

The few rules that players invoked to regulate status concerned privileges associated with age and office. Celia referred to pretend age, for example, in defending her right to be independent. "I'm not sleeping with you," she said to Annie, "I'm sleeping by myself. I'm eight years old" (10:12). Despite this, Celia was the designated "little one" and was therefore denied certain advantages. When Beth asked Celia to stay up past bedtime, Annie argued, "No, it's nighty-night and little girls um . . . they don't . . . She should go to sleep now" (11:21,23). Beth replied by invoking her own rights as a mother. "Well, I can ask her. I can ask her," she said (11:22,24). Annie again referred to Celia's lesser status when planning their meeting with the prince. "Let's pretend he called you Little One," Annie proposed, "and you went . . . he said: 'Hey Little One, you're very pretty, but I don't want to marry you'. And then he said [to me]: 'Hey, *you're* pretty. I can marry you'. And then Beth came up, and he said: 'Hey you're pretty too. I can marry . . . I'l marry you too'" (16:5).

In addition to rules about play arrangements, the girls sometimes referred to rules about not-play discourse. These concerned the proper use of language and the proper conduct of communication. For example, recognising that names and titles could not be owned, Beth declared that she could choose the same name as Annie (11:6). Indeed, all three girls chose the name of Gloria and Beth explained, "When you say 'Good night Gloria', Celia, it means both of us" (11:48). Annie added—showing off her linguistic knowledge and smiling, as she interrupted the "serious" pretend with the "playful" real, (Note the inversion where pretend is real and reality has to be marked with a smile!)—"When I say 'Good night Gloria' it means just one of you; but if I say 'Good night Glorias' it means both of you" (11:49). Annie similarly displayed her linguistic skill when she corrected Beth for confusing the words "early" and "late" (11:17).

Whereas words and names were often enjoyed playfully, the proper conduct of communication was taken quite seriously. Players insisted on having their turns to speak without being interrupted. "I need to tell what my name is", Annie said when royal titles were being chosen (14:40). "Wait, I was talking" she admonished when Beth interrupted her (14:50). A few turns later, Beth imitated, "Wait a second, I have something to say" (14:53,66). Behaviours that disrupted the flow of the play discourse, such as whining and thrashing, were scorned: "That's not grown-up" (16:30).

CONSENSUS AND RESPECT

The repeated struggles over possessions and status were counterbalanced by efforts to justify claims and achieve mutual agreement. An indication of this effort was the number of times that players sought confirmation: 13 discourse units were introduced by the phrase "how about"; 24 units included the tag questions "ok?", "alright?", "right?" and "remember?".

Players went to considerable lengths to keep one another involved in the ongoing play. This was particularly evident in the excerpt from Scene 12 that is provided in the Appendix (see pages 171–173). The interchange began when Celia inadvertently proposed that all three players be of equal status at the ball. Annie and Beth each tried to modify this proposal, suggesting that Celia would not marry the prince because she was too little. Celia objected to this designation of "little one". Annie and Beth might have ignored Celia's objection, but instead they made concessions. An elaborate discussion ensued in which it was decided that Celia could be big, as long as Annie and Beth were bigger. This satisfied Celia for the time being. In short, the royal ball players respected one another's individual personalities and were sensitive to the frailty of the pretend play world. They took care to meet the one necessary condition for shared pretending—i.e., they worked to establish consensus. This is the primary reason that, despite their many disputes, their play lasted for nearly an hour.

INTERACTIONAL USES OF PRETEND

Players not only modified the play frame in order to achieve consensus, they also sometimes manipulated the frame in order to establish favourable conditions for acquiring or protecting possessions and status. Such uses of pretend have been described by Garvey (1975) and by Ervin-Tripp (1977) as complex, indirect forms of request. In the royal ball play, however, such frame manipulations were also used to avoid requests. Consider the following interchange (2:5–9):

> B: *(pointing to a vest on A's chair)* Annie, since I found this first, can I use this?
> A: If you want this, you can use it at the royal ball.
> B: Just for the royal ball.
> A: You can use it for the royal ball, the second royal ball. 'Cause at the first one I wear it, and the second one you wear it and the next one I wear it. We take turns. But this time I wear it.

Although Annie first acknowledged Beth's reference to the finder's rule, she quickly changed her mind. She ensured her possession of the coveted vest by proposing a series of imaginary balls and inventing the principle of sharing through turn-taking. Whether or not Annie sincerely thought they would play the game more than once, she successfully dodged Beth's request without actually denying it. Thus she precluded any further attempt on Beth's part to gain control of the vest.

Beth attempted a similar manipulation of the play frame in order to safeguard her possession of the telephone. However, as can be seen in the following, this attempt was less successful: (5:6–7)

> B: Oh, since I got this first, let's pretend this was my telephone. I used it for real except it was my telephone and you used it for pretend.
> A: I could use it for real life too.

Again invoking the finder's rule, Beth differentiated between possessing and using the telephone. She further proposed that, as the telephone's rightful owner, only she was able to use it "for real", whereas Annie would have to use it "for pretend". Annie rejected Beth's proposal of a secondary pretend reality where the telephone was "really" hers and in its place referred to the "real life" reality where telephones are shared. Finally, Beth gave in and saved face by pretending to grant Annie permission to use the telephone: "Ok, ok, but Annie, let's pretend ... remember this telephone is mine, but you could only use it" (5:8).

Beth was more successful at using the pretend-reality distinction in later scenes. In Scene 7, when Annie first argued that no one in "real life" has two mothers, Beth responded: "Well, let's just do it for pretend, ok?" (7:18). At first Annie ignored Beth's proposal, but Beth repeatedly urged, "So, we're both moms, ok?" (7:20,22). Annie finally agreed, though wishing her own opinion to be recognised, added: "Ok, but for real, true life nobody has two moms" (7:23).

Having stressed the pretend over the real in Scene 7, Beth emphasised the real over the pretend in Scene 16. When Celia protested against being belittled, Beth remarked: "Anyways, we're already . . . anyways for true life, we're bigger" (16:8). She had appealed to the creative licence that comes with pretending in the former scene but invoked the constraints of reality in the latter. Just as Annie had earlier, Beth skillfully manipulated pretence and reality to her own advantage.

Finally, the excerpt provided in the Appendix is another example of frame manipulation. Here, the status associated with marrying the prince, which both Annie and Beth claimed, was contrasted with the status of "little one", which was assigned to Celia. When Celia protested, Annie and Beth cleverly relativised the meaning of "little one" by proposing pretend ages. The proposal satisfied Celia's desire to be big and the older players' desires to be bigger. The Appendix (12:54) illustrates that reaching consensus in pretend play and manipulating the play frame for personal gain may be two sides of the same coin. This is probably not too different from "real, true life", where the line between manipulation and free consensus depends more on one's point of view than on given, objective conditions.

DISCUSSION

The three young players depicted in the previous pages showed excellent interpersonal competence and know-how. Most conspicuous was their ability to construct a dramatic sequence of considerable length with a clear beginning and meaningful end. The players understood that they were expected to play together in the dramatic play corner. The oldest player chose a theme that was familiar, both from the Cinderella tale and from having played it before. Also, as was mentioned earlier, a familiar prop suggested the idea of the royal robe. But this was all that could be considered prearranged. Apart from these few givens, the vast variety of interactions and incidental happenings were free from external impositions and, in this decisive sense, spontaneous. With all its implicit know-how, its personal meaning, and its objective existence as an expressive statement, the play was a joint product of the participants, a vital part of their lives and of the society into which they were growing. Leaving aside the affective and strictly personal components, our interest focuses on the know-how displayed in the making of a pretend story, especially as it pertains to the societal content of that story. That the story had a *social-historical* content can hardly be denied. While the play itself encompassed only two days, the children spoke of future royal weddings in distant places. Intensely aware of generations, they were delighted to point out in Scene 12 (see Appendix, 12: 70–72) that ages increase with each subsequent birthday while relative age ranks are conserved. Fascinated with ceremony, in Scene 14 they chose titles of great consequence (queens of the whole land). These specific references to history were made in the context of a play sequence that was itself portrayed as an historical event. Preparations were made for a grand occasion and various incidental happenings were skillfully oriented towards that future goal. Having overcome all kinds of interactional obstacles and having finally prepared for the crowning moment, the players grew excited and the tempo of the play increased perceptibly. There was clear urgency to bring the play to meaningful closure, to present it as a well-formed *gestalt* that met the children's emotional and aesthetic expectations. There is an intrinsic relation between history and story; and the three players were indeed good story tellers.

When Celia joined them midway, Annie and Beth did not interrupt their performance to inform her of the play theme. Rather, they introduced her to the pretend world by presenting the results of past incidents— their claims of ownership and status—as *customs* in that world. Celia, although peeved at her diminished role, accepted these customs nonetheless and later on actively contributed to them by suggesting ways of doing things (e.g., a protocol for meeting the prince, 16:1; also Appendix 12:47).

General *presuppositions* and accepted *values*, reasonably inferred from the actions of the girls, were described earlier. They are mentioned here only to underline the social-historical character of the pretend play story. History in its various cultural settings is always surrounded by more or less conscious values and presuppositions (also called ideologies). Their presence in the play was expected. Yet the use the girls made of these pretend suppositions for personal interactional advantage was striking. This was not the simple deceit attributed to the "Machiavellian" social intelligence of primates (Byrne & Whiten, 1988), nor even the intentional deceit observed in very young children (Chandler, Fritz, & Hala, 1989). In fact, it should not be called deceit at all. Genuine pretend play and conscious deceit exclude one another. Rather, the players' use of pretence for interactional gain was akin to Marxian false consciousness, where imaginary constructs are accepted as natural facts and are upheld in the service of social privilege.

Rules and *norms* were in evidence throughout the play, particularly when status and ownership roles were at stake. Rules were cited for justification in the free exchange of ideas, where agreement can never be taken for granted. The frequent requests for confirmation, "ok?", indicated the children's desire for mutual *respect*. They were not satisfied until the rules they invoked were mutually accepted. The coordination of imaginary meanings allows for no less than consensus.

Finally, there were the *roles* the children played—roles that were clearly societal types, different from interpersonal roles. It was Western tradition, handed down in fairy tales and conveyed in the present culture, not personal affect or attachment that determined these roles. There was no need for the players to define roles before the play started, although the arrival of Celia gave Beth the opportunity to spell out a superior role for herself. We shall never know how the play would have proceeded if Celia had not joined midway. In any case it is clear that the children jointly constructed their roles as well as other societal features in a spontaneous, non-selfconscious manner.

Presuppositions, values, rules, norms, history, tradition, roles, status, respect; these are not haphazard characteristics fortuitously found in the play of these three girls. These are nothing else but the constitutive features of the societal-historial dimension, i.e., that which makes particular societies and cultures possible in the first place. Sociologists concerned with universal aspects of societies have referred to the symbolic structure encompassed by these features as *Legenswelt* (Habermas, 1981, vol. 2, p. 304), the lifeworld of humans; as *figurations* (Elias, 1978), the fluctuating patterns of interdependent individuals forming power balances of many kinds; as *l'imaginaire radical* (Castoriadis, 1987), the radical imaginary underlying human institutions.

Assume for the moment that, in playing together, the three girls did indeed construct a *Lebenswelt*, a collective figuration, and in this manner expressed *l'imaginaire radical*. The assumption would make good evolutionary sense, seeing that humanisation loosened the force of instinctual regulations and adapted humans to form societies and cultures, which go well beyond the face-to-face social groups found in many higher animals. Would it be reasonable to propose that, the prerequisite capacity to form mental objects having evolved, humans have an innate propensity to mentally construct a societal framework?

These ideas occurred to one of us (Furth, 1987) after he had first realised that Piaget's cognitive theory of development could not explain the departure from sensorimotor success without positing an extra-cognitive attachment of sorts that makes children want to construct symbols as objects-of-knowledge. Freud's theory of libidinal attachment along with repression and the formation of the unconscious seemed entirely appropriate to supply the motivational component for Piaget's cognitive object. In a text of 1924 (cited at the beginning of this chapter) Piaget himself suggested that libidinal desires provide the motivation for the child's first knowledge formation. But since there is so much controversy surrounding Freud, and we are not in the business of defending Freud (or Piaget, for that matter), we are content to suppose for now that some sort of pleasure-producing mechanism is associated with Piaget's object production. In plain language, for children to produce mental objects is fun. This is sufficient motivation for children between ages two and seven to do so with an urgency and intensity unmatched at any other period.

But what exactly is this mental object that children are so keen to produce, towards the construction of which an innate propensity urges them and rewards them with pleasure? Is pleasure an adequate goal of evolution? We were doubtful but did not know where else to look. At this point we asked ourselves, in what situations are children most clearly observed producing mental objects? The answer was obvious: in symbolic play. This is very different from sensorimotor play or frolicking where smiling and other external features indicate the not-serious nature of the child's activity. Symbolic play engages 2- to 7-year-old children more seriously than perhaps any other activity. From the children's viewpoint, they are doing something important and utterly real. But what *are* they doing? Merely producing pleasure? This is possible but, in biological or evolutionary terms, is not a satisfactory answer. Pleasure may be a by-product of an action competently performed, but as an end in itself it lacks biological coherence. To overcome this problem Furth (1987) spoke of pleasure in interpersonal relations and from this position he thought it feasible to reach out to further and ultimately societal relations.

However, the notion of a continuum between interindividual relations and societal relations is untenable. There is a qualitative difference between these two social relations, just as there is between action logic and object logic, between a sensorimotor and a mental, representational world. Piaget (1962, p. 241) points out that children around age two, having already developed competencies in the world of present actions and social relations, must start almost from zero as they begin to construct a world of mental objects. Now, in what sense is the mental world of objects different from the sensorimotor world of actions? Piaget, for his own reasons, focused on the epistemological difference between action-knowledge and action-disconnected knowledge. But corresponding to this difference in logical form, there should be something like a difference in substance or content.

It seemed reasonable, therefore, to postulate that the most general content of object knowledge is society, where society refers to the lifeworld of a collectivity (Furth, 1992a). From a developmental perspective, this means that children around age two are beginning to become aware of living in a societal world. They express this emerging awareness in different kinds of imaginary products. This is the psychological-developmental context in which social pretend play flourishes. From age three onwards it is found abundantly in all cultures that encourage this type of activity. A recent volume (Stambak & Sinclair, 1990) reports on the pretend play of 3-year-old children in Italy and France. The authors recognise the important contribution that Piaget made in describing the developmental roots of the mental object and representational symbols (in which pretend play is included). They write (p. 11):

"In contrast to practical [sensorimotor] intelligence, thought works with signifiers or symbols which permit a gradual detachment of perceptions and actions from the here and now. As schemes of actions are already organized into systems during the sensorimotor period, symbols (in the wide sense of mental representation) likewise are organized into systems, notably into collective systems, such as language. ...."

We would like to reword the last phrase so as to underline the major theoretical claim of this paper. We agree that children begin to form symbols around age two and that these symbols are organised into systems—what Piaget & Garcia (1991) would later call meanings organised into systems of inferences and implications. Yet we find Stambak and Sinclair's focus on language to be inadequate, especially when the authors group language with such formal systems as numbers, graphs, maps. If their statement that symbols are organised into "collective systems, such as *language*" had been written "collective systems, such as *stories*", we would have applauded, because every story implies the social-historical dimension.

Various authors have recently referred to the narrative nature of the human mind. Thus Bruner (1990, p. 68) spoke of children "making narrative sense of the world around them". However, what they have failed to emphasise is the truism that every narrative presupposes a societal framework. It would be hard to imagine a story bereft of such a frame-work. We observed in the play of three girls the enactment of a story that had a variety of societal features. On a descriptive level this is all that is meant by a societal framework. In fact, however, our constructivist proposal goes beyond this description. We are postulating that societal institutions come to the child not merely from outside, as an exogenous learning. To be sure, this kind of learning begins from birth, insofar as everything connected with infant care is deeply influenced and moulded by cultural-societal forces. To this extent, then, the child is a passive participant and imitator of society. But beginning with the developmental emergence of the mental object and the signifying symbol (i.e., the symbol signifies the object) the child's position *vis-a-vis* society changes dramatically. This is the phase of endogenous societal learning or development in the strict sense, even as exogenous learning, commonly called socialisation, proceeds apace.

We suggest that children's imaginative constructions are the place where this endogenous societal learning takes place (Furth, 1992b). This has nothing to do with innate mechanisms or ideas. On the contrary, an accumulated wealth of sensorimotor experiences is required before the psychology of children can restructure these experiences on a mental plane. This mental restructuring, we propose, is also, or better, *primarily* a social restructuring such that face-to-face interactions are now experienced within an unseen human collectivity reaching from the past into the future. The child's understanding and feeling for the human collectivity seems to us to be the basic substantive change that is consolidated during the pre-school years. In comparison with this understanding and feeling, all the other vaunted human achievements, such as language, rational logic, morals or creativity are secondary and derivative; they make no sense without a prior human society. Encompassed within that collectivity is the concept of self, alongside what Goffman (1983) calls the interaction order of co-presence.

The societal features and the interactional use of pretend frames observed in the play of 4- to 5-year-old children show competencies that stand in sharp contrast to the ignorance and inconsistencies reported for much older children in the studies reviewed at the beginning of this chapter. This is of course due to two decisive differences: First, in the one case they talked about society reflectively, here they acted out their knowing; second, and equally important, in the one case they talked about the world of grown-ups, here they constructed their own pretend society. Connected with these two differences, the younger children had the added advantage of being societally "nice", which derives etymologically from *nescius* (ignorant). In their societal role as children, they were not supposed to be constrained by the cares of daily life and were free to be creative according to their competencies. In this way they could be playful about their pretend society, unconcerned about its practical feasibility or effectiveness, but at the same time totally serious about the framing and the interactions they acted out within that frame. In fact, even in the older children's responses to questions about the grown-up world, imaginative elaborations and playful images abounded from age five up to age nine. The emerging result was "a *childish* sort of societal reality where play cannot easily be distinguished from real" (Furth, 1980, p. 79).

Children at play relate with peers in a reciprocal social situation conducive to development. No doubt the social competencies that could be observed in the royal ball play were the product of countless imaginary activities that preceded it, even as this play may have contributed to the future social growth of its participants. The play itself, while not atypical, was certainly exceptional, supported by the particular school and the milieu in which the children grew up. Unfortunately, reliable data on pretend play in various cultures are not available, but we are quite aware that within the U.S.A. alone there are probably notable differences in the quantity and quality of children's play related to the opportunities afforded by adults. Even within the same culture and class, there are likely to be individual differences, sex differences, etc. For example, we know of a person who as a little boy during the war years lived on an isolated post. He was nearly four years old before he encountered another child.

It is therefore important to grasp the precise point at which, according to our perspective, the psychology of the child and society meet. We referred to it as the mental object, the "object" of Piaget (as well as of Freud). This object is a mental construction of the child and is experienced as an imaginary event, a story, a fantasy, an image; other more technical and hence easily misunderstood terms are representation, symbol, imagination. Our claim is that these mental constructions, all referring to the object, have an inherently societal character, such that *the mental object itself is a societal object.* Consequently societal understanding cannot be said to be the direct result of social pretend play, even though social pretend play may be a privileged opportunity to expand it. If it were found that certain children or entire cultures did not engage in social pretend play, this would not disconfirm our societal theory.

In fact, we would like to consider ours as evolutionary theory. Evolution has predisposed humans to construct societies. Societies are first and foremost constituted by shared mental values, norms, images, by the shared subjectivity of each society's lifeworld. Our psychological competencies are therefore biologically adapted for the co-construction of a lifeworld. For this the prerequisite cognitive and motivational know-hows must first be developed. By age two most children have reached this threshold and begin to use their newly developed and developing psychological powers to do precisely what will eventually constitute societies and persons.

Piaget in 1924 (cited at the beginning of this chapter) recognised that children's symbolic play is based on fiction, but he added: "It is much more". Unfortunately he did not continue to specify this "more". When eight years later he published his book on the moral judgement of the child, it had as a subtitle: "Children invent the social contract". Later on for whatever reason he dropped the subtitle. He was satisfied to have shown that, as in the case of logical operations, the morality of mutual respect cannot but have an endogenous origin, based on children's own developmental achievements. Our aim here has been to make concrete Piaget's "more" of 1924 and to elaborate on his *excursus* into moral judgement. We claim that children invent a societal lifeworld, motivated by pleasure in the object-as-society. This new societal theory recasts age-old questions about the relation between the individual and society, and about the role of logic in that relation. From this perspective, these concepts stand in a dialectical-constructive relation to each other. It is the merit of Piaget's theory to have provided this constructivist approach and to have pointed in the direction of resolving these issues through empirical evidence from the thinking and playing of developing children.

REFERENCES

Bakeman, R., & Brownlee, J. R. (1982). Social rules governing object conflicts in toddlers and preschoolers. In K. Rubin, & H. Ross (Eds.), *Peer relationships and social skills in childhood* (pp. 99–111), New York: Springer.
Berti, A. E., & Bombi, A. S. (1988). *The child's construction of economics*. Cambridge: Cambridge University Press.
Bruner, J. S. (1972). Nature and uses of immaturity. *American Psychologist, 27*, 687–708.
Bruner, J. S. (1990). *Acts of meaning*. Cambridge, Mass. Harvard University Press.
Burke, K. (1969). *A grammar of motives*. Berkeley: University of California Press.
Byrne, R., & Whiten, A. (Eds.), (1988). *Machiavellian intelligence: Social expertise and the evolution of intelligence in monkeys, apes and humans*. Oxford: Oxford University Press.
Castoriadis, C. (1987). *The imaginary institution of society*. Cambridge, Mass.: M.I.T. Press.
Chandler, M., Fritz, A., & Hala, S. (1989) Small scale deceit as a marker of 2-, 3-, and 4-year olds early theory of mind. *Child Development, 60*, 1263–1277.
Cobb, E. (1977). *The ecology of imagination in childhood*. New York: Columbia University Press.
Corsaro, W. A. (1985). *Friendship and peer culture in the early years*. Norwood, N.J.: Ablex.
Corsaro, W. A., & Eder, D. (1990). Children's peer cultures. *Annual Review of Sociology, 16*, 197–220.
Elias, N. (1978). *What is sociology?* New York: Columbia University Press.
Ervin-Tripp, S. (1977). Wait for me roller-skate! In S. Ervin-Tripp, & C. Mitchell-Kernan (Eds.), *Child Discourse*. New York: Academic Press.
Fein, G. G. (1989). Mind, meaning, and affect: Proposals for a theory of pretense. *Developmental Review, 9*, 344–363.
Fenson, L., & Ramsay, D. (1980). Decentration and integration of the child's play in the second year. *Child Development, 51*, 171–178.
Forbes, D., Katz, M. M., & Paul, B. (1986). "Frame talk": A dramatistic analysis of children's fantasy play. In E. Mueller, & C. Cooper (Eds.), *Process and outcome in peer relationships* (pp. 249–265). New York: Academic Press.
Forbes, D., & Yablick, G. (1984). The organization of dramatic content in children's fantasy play. In F. Kessel, & A. Goncu (Eds.), Analyzing children's play dialogues (pp. 23–35). San Francisco: Jossey-Bass.
Franklin, M. B. (1983). Play as the creation of imaginary situations: The role of language. In S. Wapner, & B. Kaplan (Eds.), *Toward a holistic developmental psychology* (pp. 197–220). Hillsdale, N.J.: Lawrence Erlbaum Associates Inc.

Freud, S. (1959). *Creative writers and day dreaming.* Standard Edition 9, 141–154. London: Hogarth.

Furth, H. G. (1978a). Children's societal understanding and the process of equilibration. In W. Damon (Ed.) *Social cognition* (pp. 101–122). San Francisco: Jossey-Bass.

Furth, H. G. (1978b). Young children's understanding of society. In H. McGurk (Ed.), *Issues in childhood social development* (pp. 228–256). London: Methuen.

Furth, H. G. (1980). *The world of grown-ups: Children's conceptions of society.* New York: Elsevier.

Furth, H. G. (1987). *Knowledge as desire: An essay on Freud and Piaget.* New York: Columbia University Press.

Furth, H. G. (1992a). The developmental origin of human societies. In H. Beilin, and P. B. Pufall (Eds.), *Piaget's theory: Prospects and possibilities* (pp. 252–265). Hillsdale, N.J.: Lawrence Erlbaum Associates Inc.

Furth, H. G. (1992b). Psychoanalysis and social thought: The endogenous origin of society. *Political Psychology*, *13*, 91–104.

Furth, H. G., Baur, M., & Smith, J. E. (1976). Children's conception of social institutions: A Piagetian framework. *Human Development*, *19*, 351–374.

Furth, H. G., & McConville, K-L (1981). Adolescent understanding of compromise in political and social arenas. *Merrill-Palmer Quarterly*, *27*, 413–427.

Garvey, C. (1975). Request and responses in children's speech. *Journal of Child Language*. *2*, 41–63.

Garvey, C. (1977). *Play.* Cambridge, Mass.: Harvard University Press.

Garvey, C., & Kramer, T. (1989). The language of social pretend play. *Developmental Review*, *9*, 364–382.

Goffman, E. (1974). *Frame analysis: An essay on the organization of experience.* Cambridge, Mass.: Harvard University Press.

Goffman, E. (1983). The interaction order. *American Sociological Review*, *48*, 1–17.

Habermas, J. L. (1981). *Theorie des kommunikativen Handelns.* Frankfurt: Suhrkamp.

Haight, W. L., & Miller, P. J. (1991). *The social nature of early pretend play: Middle-class mothers' participation in everyday pretending.* Unpublished manuscript.

Hartup, W. W. (1970). Peer interaction and social organization. In P. H. Mussen (Ed.), *Manual of child psychology, vol. 2* (pp. 361–456). New York: Wiley.

Howes, C., Unger, O., & Seidner, L., (1989). Social pretend play in toddlers: Parallels with social play and with solitary pretend. *Child Development*, *60*, 77–84.

Jahoda, G. (1984). The development of thinking about socio-economic systems. In H. Tajfel (Ed.), *The social dimension* (pp. 69–88). Cambridge, U.K.: Cambridge University Press.

Kane, S. R., & Furth, H. G. (in press). Children constructing social reality: A frame analysis of social pretend play. *Human Development.*

Katz, M. M., Forbes, D., Yablick, G., & Kelly, V. (1983). Disagreements during play: Clues to children's constructions of reality. In K. Blanchard (Ed.), *The Many Faces of Play: Association for the anthropological study of play, vol. 9* (pp. 104–114). Champaign, Ill.: Human Kinetics Publications.

Miller, P., & Garvey, C. (1984). Mother-baby role play: Its origins in social support. In I. Bretherton (Ed.), *Symbolic play: The development of social understanding* (pp. 101–130). New York: Academic Press.

Mueller, E., & Lucas, T. (1975). A developmental analysis of peer interaction among toddlers. In M. Lewis, & L. Rosenblum (Eds.), *Friendship and peer relations: vol. IV, The origins of behavior* (pp. 223–257). New York: J. Wiley & Sons.

Nicholich, L. M. (1977). Beyond sensorimotor intelligence: Assessment of symbolic maturity through analysis of pretend play. *Merrill-Palmer Quarterly*, *23*, 89–99.

Piaget, J. (1924). Les traits principaux de la logique de l'enfant. *Journal de Psychologie*, *21*, 48–101.

Piaget, J. (1962). *Play, dreams and imitation in childhood.* New York: Norton.
Piaget, J. (1985) *The equilibration of cognitive structures.* Chicago: University of Chicago Press.
Piaget, J., & Garcia, R. (1991). *Toward a logic of meanings.* Hillsdale, N.J.: Lawrence Erlbaum Associates Inc.
Rosenberg, S. W. (1988). *Reason, ideology and politics.* Hillsdale, N.J.: Lawrence Erlbaum Associates Inc.
Rubin, K. H. (1980). Fantasy play: Its role in the development of social skills and social cognition. In K. H. Rubin (Ed.), *Children's play* (pp. 69–84). San Francisco: Jossey-Bass.
Stambak, M., & Sinclair, H. (1990). *Les jeux de fiction entre enfants de 3 ans.* Paris: P.U.F.
Sutton-Smith, B. (1979). *Play and learning.* New York: Gardner.
Sylva, K. (1977). Play and learning. In B. Tizard, & E. Harvey (Eds.), *The biology of play* (pp. 59–73). London: Heineman.
Vandenberg, B. (1983). Mere child's play. In K. Blanchard (Ed.), *The many faces of play: Association for the anthropological study of play, vol. 9* (pp. 115–120). Champaign, Ill.: Human Kinetics Publications.
Vandenberg, B. (1986). The realities of play. In D. Morrison (Ed.), *Organizing early experience: Imagination and cognition in childhood* (pp. 198–204). Amityville, New York: Baywood.
Vygotsky, L. S. (1976). Play and its role in the mental development of the child. In J. S. Bruner, H. Jolly, & K. Sylva (Eds.), *Play: Its role in development and evolution* (pp. 537–554). New York: Basic Books.

APPENDIX

The Royal Ball Play: Act III, Scene 12, Units 47–72

UNIT	ANNIE	BETH	CELIA
12:47			Pretend we were the prettiest girls at the party.
12:48	And . . . and she (*sic*) married me. And Beth was one of our sisters. And she . . . she (*C*) was one of our sisters.		
12:49		How about this. Pretend he married two of us and you (*C*) were the sister. Ok? You were the sister of us— ok?—of both of us, 'cause you were the littler one.	

UNIT	*ANNIE*	*BETH*	*CELIA*
12:50			No, I don't want to be a little one.
12:51		No, you're both . . . you're big. Um, lets pretend. . . .	
12:52	But we were a little bit bigger.		
12:53		You're twenty.	
12:54			Yeah.
12:55		And . . . and, uh . . . both of us are twenty-one.	
12:56			Ok, so that means. . . .
12:57	So, we're one month older than you.		
12:58			Yeah.
12:59		Yeah. We're one month older than you.	
12:60			I'll show you how big you are on the calendar.
12:61	I want to put some make-up on.		
12:62		It's not up there yet. Twenty isn't up there yet.	
12:63	Why it isn't up there yet?		
12:64		Because we're not there yet.	
12:65			No, I'll show you where we are.
12:66		It's not up there yet. Ok, twenty's not there.	
12:67	You're not twenty-one yet. Until next month it's going to be our. . . .		

UNIT	ANNIE	BETH	CELIA
12:68		And one month ... and one month it's going to be our birthday, so we are going to be twenty-two and you are going to be twenty-one.	
12:69	My skirt fell off.		
12:70			And then, when you're twenty-three, I'll be twenty-two. And when you're twenty-four, I'll be twenty-three. And when you're twenty-five, I'll be twenty-four. ...
12:71	Yeah it goes on and on and on. ...		
12:72			Yeah, on and on and for. ...

7
Friendships and their Developmental Significance

Willard W. Hartup
University of Minnesota, U.S.A.

INTRODUCTION

Most children and adolescents have a "best friend" and several "good friends". Infants and toddlers have friends, too, although these relationships are not as extensively differentiated as among older children and adolescents. Mothers sometimes argue that their young children have best friends when, in fact, the children are merely regular playmates and their interaction harmonious. Nevertheless, mutually-regulated "friendships" can be observed among many young children (Howes, 1983). By 4 and 5 years of age, approximately three out of four children are involved in a close relationship with some other child, and about three out of ten have more than one (Hinde, Titmus, Easton & Tamplin, 1985; Howes, 1989).

Friendship networks remain relatively small during the preschool years, with the number of mutual friends averaging 0.88 for boys and 0.63 for girls. Unilateral relationships (i.e., unreciprocated friendship choices) supplement these mutual ones, averaging 1.68 and 0.86 for boys and girls, respectively (Hartup, Laursen, Stewart, & Eastenson, 1988). School-aged children, in contrast, average five best friends, a number that declines only slightly among adolescents (Hallinan, 1980). About 80% of today's teenagers have at least one best friend and several good friends, and fewer than

Support in the completion of this manuscript was provided by the Rodney S. Wallace Endowment, College of Education, University of Minnesota.

10% have no contact with friends outside school (Crockett, Lossoff, & Petersen, 1984). Conversations with school-aged children and adolescents confirm that these relationships are exceedingly important to the youngsters themselves (Goodnow & Burns, 1988; Youniss & Smollar, 1986) and that, when "on their own", more time is spent by children and adolescents with friends than with family members or any other associate (Medrich, Rosen, Rubin, & Buckley, 1982; Laursen, 1989). Becoming friends and maintaining these relationships are regarded by children themselves as among the most significant achievements of childhood and adolescence.

Our interest in children's friendships, however, extends beyond their ubiquity. We need to know whether having friends, as contrasted with not having friends, predicts good developmental outcome and, if so, why. We need to know whether friendships between socially competent children differ from friendships between less competent children. We need to know whether friendship relations are as necessary to good developmental outcome as parent-child relations. Friendships furnish children with socialisation opportunities not easily obtained elsewhere, including experience in conflict management as well as experience in cooperation and sharing. But how important is it that these experiences occur with friends? At the moment, we know more about the ubiquity of children's friendships than about their developmental significance.

Children's friendships are discussed in this essay in four sections: First, conceptual and significance issues will be considered, including the "markers" of friendship (i.e., how friendships may be defined), the "conditions" of friendship (i.e., what circumstances are responsible for the formation and maintenance of friendships), the "stages" of friendship (i.e., the temporal dimensions of these relationships), and the "functions" of friendship (i.e., the contributions these relationships may make to social development). "Beginnings" will then be discussed, including the processes that appear to be implicated in becoming friends, the friendships of infants and toddlers, and behavioural manifestations in early childhood. Childhood and adolescent friendships will be examined next, with emphasis on friendship selection and "being friends". Age and sex differences will also be considered. Finally, friendship experience and its contributon to developmental outcome will be discussed, considering both what contemporary studies show us and what they don't. The theme running through the essay is essentially that friendships are developmental advantages for children and adolescents rather than developmental necessities.

CONCEPTUAL ISSUES AND SIGNIFICANCE

The Conditions of Friendship

The essentials of friendship are reciprocity[1] and commitment between individuals who see themselves more or less as equals. Children's attachments to their friends are not as exclusive or as robust as their attachments to their mothers and fathers. In addition, interaction between friends rests on a more equal power base than the interaction between children and their parents. Recognising this egalitarian structure, some writers regard friendships as "affiliative" relations rather than "attachments" (Weiss, 1986). Children make a considerable emotional investment in their friends, however, and these relationships are relatively enduring. Separation from friends sometimes elicits anxiety and a sense of loss similar to the manner in which separation from an attachment figure elicits these emotions (Park & Waters, 1988; Howes, 1989). Similarities as well as differences thus exist between the relationships that children construct with friends and the attachments they construct with their elders.

The main themes in friendship relations—affiliation and common interests—are understood by children beginning in early childhood. Among preschool and younger school-aged children, friendship expectations centre on common pursuits and concrete reciprocities ("When you have got something wrong, they help. And I give them food, so they give me food back" [Grade 2][2]). Later on, children's views about their friends centre on mutual understanding, loyalty, and trust; children also expect to spend time with their friends, share interests, and engage in self-disclosure with them. ("A good friend is someone who likes you and spends time wih you and forgives you and doesn't actually bash you up" [Grade 6]). Friends have fun with one another; they enjoy doing things with one another and care about one another. Although school-aged children and adolescents never use words like empathy or intimacy to describe their friends, these constructs also distinguish friends from other children in the child's thinking. Friends: "tell you their secrets and you tell them yours", "will listen to you and understand you", "don't drop you as soon as something

---

[1] The term reciprocity is not used consistently in the literature. Reciprocity sometimes refers to the contingent occurrence of the same actions during social interaction (e.g., talk followed by talk). At other times, the term refers to behavioural "complements" (e.g., chase/being chased; give/take). The construct also refers to equivalancies in the "benefits" deriving from a social exchange. Contingency and equivalence seem to be the core elements in this word's meaning.

[2] The quotations from children's interviews given in the text were obtained by Goodnow and Burns (1988) and are used with permission.

goes wrong". Children recognise that conflicts may occur with their friends, but they believe that friends have a special commitment to one another in the management of conflict ("A good friend is someone you fight with, but not forever") and that conflicts may also strengthen these relationships. Overall, then, friendships are understood by children and adolescents as delicate balances of social exchange occurring within egalitarian contexts: within these relationships, self-interest is weighed against consideration for the other and conflicts are weighed against cooperation. Ordinarily, children believe that the social exchanges occurring between friends are mutually beneficial.

Children's friendship expectations have been studied extensively (Peevers & Secord, 1973; Bigelow & LaGaipa, 1975; Selman, 1980; Furman & Bierman, 1984; Goodnow & Burns, 1988). Considerable agreement exists in these accounts: with age, increases occur in the number of psychological constructs used, the flexibility and precision with which they are used in children's talk about their friends, the complexity and organisation of children's information and ideas about friends, the level of analysis used in interpreting the behaviour of other children, and recognition that certain attributes (e.g., intimacy and loyalty) are characteristic of these relationships.

Most writers assume that these age differences in children's notions about their friends derive from more general changes in cognitive and language development. Some investigators, however, argue that these changes are elaborations of the child's understanding of a single construct—social reciprocity (Youniss, 1980). Others believe that they reflect structural transformations in the child's understanding of social relations (Selman, 1980). And still others argue that these age differences represent cumulative representations of basically unrelated "themes" or expectations, e.g., common interests, commitment, and intimacy (Berndt, 1981). These theoretical differences have not been resolved, although the evidence shows clearly that children's notions about friendship relations become more and more differentiated as they grow older (Berndt & Perry, 1986).

The Markers of Friendship

Children's friendships can be identified in four ways: (1) by asking someone to identify the child's friends; (2) by asking someone to assess the degree of "liking" or attraction that exists between two children; (3) by assessing the extent to which two children seek and maintain proximity with one another over time; and (4) by measuring the reciprocities and coordinated actions existing in the social interaction between two children.

Best Friends.   Asking someone to identify the child's friends is the most common method used to single out these relationships. One may simply ask children to nominate their best friends from among their classmates or their acquaintances, assuming that children understand and use the word "friend" consistently and in the same way that other people do. Although systematic studies do not exist, the available evidence indicates that children use the word more or less consistently by the fourth year—earlier in many cases. One may also ask teachers or parents to identify children's friends, thus assuming that these respondents know enough about children's feelings towards one another to be able to make valid assessments.

Mutual Liking.   Children's friendships can also be identified by asking children to name other children who are "especially liked". This strategy assumes that close relationships between children rest on strong, affectively-toned attraction as well as a sense that children feel supported and cared for by one another. The validity of this method depends on children's knowing what it means to "like" someone. According to the evidence, usage is reliable by the time children are 6 or 7 years of age, although questions can be raised about the consistency with which younger children nominate one another as "liked" (Hymel, 1983). One other difficulty with mutual liking as a means of identifying children's friendships is that this method does not make it easy to distinguish "best friends" from "friends", a distinction that children themselves regard as significant (Goodnow & Burns, 1988). Once again, teachers or other individuals who know the children can also be used as respondents in assessing mutual liking (McCandless & Marshall, 1957).

Proximity.   "Moving sociometrics", through which close relationships are singled out by observing proximity-maintenance, were invented long ago (Hyde & York, 1948). Used originally to identify interpersonal relationships in a mental hospital, these techniques were later adapted for use with children (McCandless & Marshall, 1957) and have proved useful for identifying strong associations existing among very young children (Hinde, et al., 1985; Hartup, et al., 1988; Howes, 1989; Ladd, Price, & Hart, 1990) as well as adolescents (Wong & Csikzentmihalyi, 1991). In this instance, measurement assumes that friends are more motivated to spend time together than nonfriends and, conversely, that children who spend time together usually like one another.

Behavioural Reciprocities.   Coordinations and reciprocities in social interaction are sometimes employed as methods for identifying children's friendships (Howes, 1983). Actually, more attention has been given to these complementarities as relationship concomitants than as relationship indicators. Behavioural reciprocities clearly differentiate friends from nonfriends (see p. 191) but self-reports, mutual liking, and proximity-seeking are easier ways to identify these relationships.

Concordances among these Markers. Concordances among these methods are substantial: First, among preschool-aged children, significant agreement exists between best friends identified by means of sociometric nominations and best friends identified through observational measurement of proximity-seeking. In one investigation (Howes, 1989), agreement between these indicators was 72% among the 4154 dyads studied, and most of the disagreements occurred because a behaviourally-identified friend received a unilateral rather than a mutual sociometric nomination. Other studies show somewhat lower concordances between these two identification methods but, always, the average amount of social interaction is considerably higher with preferred companions than with disliked ones (Chapman, Smith, Foot, & Pritchard, 1979; Hymel, Hayvren, & Lollis, 1982).

Children who are considered to be best friends by outside observers also stand out in terms of proximity-seeking: among preschool children, teacher nominations and observational methods were in agreement for 85% of the available dyads, with nearly all of the disagreements involving unilateral nominations (Howes, 1989). In an earlier study (Howes, 1983), 97% of the friends identified by behavioural criteria were also identified by teachers, and 100% of the friendships identified by the teachers were also identified by the behavioural criteria. Mother-nominations (when the children were both enrolled in the same nursery school) agreed 53% for 42-month olds with proximity-based methods for identifying friends and 69% for 50-month olds (Hinde, et al., 1985).

Numerous studies show that friendships identified by asking children whom they "like" or "like to play with" are also concordant with observed proximity-seeking. Biehler (1954) reported that 80% of preschool-aged children's most preferred companions, as determined by observations, were named as either first or second choices on a picture sociometric test requiring the children to name the classmates whom they liked best. Other investigators have also shown that children spend more time with their best liked companions than with other classmates (Hartup, et al., 1988). Finally, self-reports and teacher-reports are in good agreement concerning which children have friends and who they are. Teacher and child nominations agreed for 78% of the dyads studied in one instance (Howes, 1989).

Contextual variations must be taken into account in examining the concordances among these friendship markers for school-aged children. Sociometric choices are not strongly related to proximity-seeking in the classroom or playground (Chapman, et al., 1979), for example, since social interaction in these settings is externally constrained. Seating arrangements and classroom activities are teacher-determined, thereby attenuating these concordances; games and sports activities reduce the extent to which social attraction accounts for proximity between children in the playground. In contrast, time-use studies show that, when outside school and on their own, school-aged children spend most of their time with their friends rather than nonfriends (Medrich, et al., 1982).

The Stages of Friendship

Close relationships have beginnings, middles, and ends. Relationship dynamics vary accordingly. Children's friendships differ from one another in their temporal course, and this needs to be taken into consideration in studying them. Some relationships progress more-or-less directly from acquaintanceship to termination without much consolidation in between. Others undergo extensive "build-up" and last for long periods of time. And age differences are evident: preschool-aged children's friendships, for example, are not as stable as older children's (Hartup, 1983).

These variations are well-recognised but seldom studied. We know that children whose friendships are destined to end within a short time tend to talk more frequently about disloyalty and lack of intimacy than children whose friendships are stable (Berndt, Hawkins, & Hoyle, 1986). We also know that children with emotional difficulties are more likely to have unstable friendships than children without difficulties (Rutter & Garmezy, 1983). But, otherwise, relatively little can be said about temporal variations in children's friendships and their significance.

Research attention is currently centred on five relationship "stages": acquaintance, build-up, continuation and consolidation, deterioration, and termination (Levinger, 1983; Levinger & Levinger, 1986). Although some relationships do not move through every one of these stages, those relationships that we call friendships encompass most of them.

Propinquity.   Close relationships begin with propinquity (i.e., physical proximity). For this reason, every demographic force that brings two children together is relevant to their becoming friends. That is, the conditions that bring two families to the same neighbourhood or two children to the same school or classroom have as much to do with the beginnings of friendship as who the children are (Sancilio, 1989).

Propinquity alone is not a sufficient condition for the establishment of friendship relations. Whether two children become friends depends on the benefits each child perceives as deriving from interaction with the other, especially in relation to what the relationship is believed to "cost". Most individuals (children not excepted) assume that these benefits will be greater in exchanges with someone who is similar to themselves than with someone who is not (Byrne, 1971). Direct experience with one another also contributes to expectations that continued social interaction will be mutually rewarding.

First Encounters. Although a considerable amount is known about the attributes that attract children to one another (see Hartup, 1983), relatively little is known about their first encounters. The available evidence suggests that these encounters are largely devoted to establishing common ground (or the lack thereof). Social interaction during first encounters is mostly driven by the activities or tasks in which the children are engaged. Social interdependencies are likely to be confined to these tasks, and the empirical evidence confirms this (Furman & Childs, 1981). On first meeting, children are more likely to be concerned with who gets the first turn with an attractive toy than with "being friends". At this stage, relationships are relatively superficial, emotionally-speaking.

Build-up. In time, some relationships achieve a momentum of their own, i.e., their existence does not depend so much on environmental monitoring or the activities in which the individuals engage. Among adults, this transition is marked by a shift from an "I-centred" to a "we-centred" orientation (Kelley, 1979); other increases in mutuality also occur. Among children who are "hitting it off", communication becomes increasingly connected, conflicts are confronted and managed successfully, similarities between themselves are stressed, and self-disclosure is initiated (Gottman, 1983). Relationships are not especially stable during this stage; seeking common ground remains a necessity. Should children not maintain their common interests, it is necessary to re-engage in information exchange much like the information exchanges that take place during first encounters.

Continuation. The transition from "build-up" to "continuation" is marked by increasing stability in the interactions between individuals. Stability, itself, emerges mainly on the basis of commitment—a condition that rests, in turn, on each individual's investment in the relationship (Levinger, 1983).

Virtually nothing is known about the conditions that strengthen children's commitments to one another, but several studies demonstrate that commitment becomes significant in children's thinking about friendship relations by 10 to 11 years of age (Bigelow & LaGaipa, 1975; Bigelow, 1977). One should not rule out the possibility that commitment is important to younger children, but information is too sketchy to say much about these dynamics in early childhood.

One interesting convergence suggests that a causal connection does indeed exist between commitment and stability in children's friendships. Between 10 and 11 years, two transitions are evident:

1. For the first time, significant numbers of children mention commitment in interviews about their friendship expectations ("A friend is a person that sticks by you when all the troubles come" [Goodnow & Burns, 1988]).
2. An increase (to two-thirds) occurs in the number of these relationships that last for at least a year (Berndt et al., 1986).

Friendships would surely be more stable among younger children were commitments more salient among them. But, as intriguing as these notions are, more needs to be learned about commitment and friendship relations, especially the conditions that foster commitment and weaken it, and its relation to the stability of these relationships.

Deterioration.   Children may cease to "hit it off" at any time and the circumstances are not always clear-cut. Breakdown is sometimes marked by disagreements, similar to the manner in which disagreements sometimes accompany marital distress (Gottman, 1979). At other times, breakdown is marked only by alienation; overt contention and disagreement are notably absent. Sometimes one child will be dissatisfied while the other remains happy with the relationship. Clearly, no single dynamic signals deterioration in children's friendships.

Since commitment emerges for the first time in children's thinking about these relationships in middle childhood (see p. 178), one would not expect commitment violations to be important in friendship breakdown among younger children; contemporary studies bear this out (Bigelow, 1977; Rizzo, 1989). Conflicts themselves can be distress signals among both younger and older children but, as mentioned, alienation between children often occurs in the absence of argument; children simply drift apart (and sometimes regret it) but are not able to explain exactly why. Observations conducted in one first-grade classroom confirmed that friendships frequently terminate simply because children cease to interact; neither emotional outbursts nor arguments forecast their demise, nor were overt declarations made (Rizzo, 1989). Similar ethnographic work, however, has not been conducted with older children.

Endings.   Friendships terminate when common ground dissolves and children cease to be behaviourally interdependent. Deterioration does not lead inevitably to termination. Relationships can be renewed, providing the children can discover a basis for restoring their commitment to one another. Nevertheless, friendships (unlike parent-child relationships) cannot withstand betrayal and disloyalty for very long nor can they weather incessant disagreement.

Ordinarily, termination means that children reduce the time they spend together; conflicts seldom occur following breakup simply because the children avoid one another rather than interact. Actually, friendship endings have not been studied, so relatively little can be said about the transition from deterioration to endings or about the relation between endings with old friends and beginnings with new ones.

Friendship Functions

Mutual attraction ensures continuing interaction between the children involved. Four other functions can be identified that friendships serve:

1. these relationships are contexts in which basic social skills are acquired or elaborated (e.g., social communication, cooperation, and group entry skills);
2. they are information sources for acquiring self-knowledge, knowledge about others, and knowledge about the world;
3. they are emotional and cognitive resources (both for "having fun" and adapting to stress); and
4. they are forerunners of subsequent relationships (modelling the mutual regulation and intimacy that most close relationships require).

One must remember that these contributions to the child's development derive from an egalitarian context: friendships are symmetrically or horizontally structured in contrast to adult-child relationships, which are asymmetrically or vertically structured (Youniss, 1980). Friends are similar to one another in developmental status; friends engage one another mostly in play and "socialising". Friendship residuals among individual children undoubtedly reflect these egalitarian dimensions.

One must remember, too, that friendship functions may vary with age. Or, rather, some functions may vary with age while others remain constant (Price & Ladd, 1986). Mutual attraction, for example, supports proximity-seeking and continued social interaction between companions among both children and adolescents (Hartup et al., 1988; Laursen, 1989). Social interaction, however, consists mostly of play among young children and "socialising" among older ones (Whiting & Whiting, 1975; Medrich et al., 1982). Play and socialising have certain similarities (e.g., both are fun), but these activities are also different. Socialising involves camaraderie, intimacy, caring, and other support manifestations that play does not. Developmental considerations, then, need to be taken into account in speculating about the functions of friendship.

Friendships and Social Competence. Considerable evidence shows that friendships are cooperative socialisation contexts (Hartup, 1989). Preschool-aged friends engage in more frequent positive exchanges (as well as neutral ones) than unselected partners or children who don't like one another (Masters & Furman, 1981). Mutual attraction also goes along with sustained social exchanges, complementarities in social interaction, and mutually-directed affect (Howes, 1983; 1989). Conflicts between friends are less intense and resolved more frequently by mutual disengagement than conflicts between nonfriends (Hartup, et al., 1988); competition is less intense (Charlesworth & LaFreniere, 1983). Older children, too, cooperate more readily with friends than nonfriends, are more interactive, smile and laugh more, play closer attention to equity rules in their conversations, and direct their conversations toward mutual rather than egocentric ends (Newcomb & Brady, 1982). Conflict and competition are experienced differently, too, by school-aged friends and nonfriends, although these differences vary greatly according to context (Hartup, in press a).

Longitudinal evidence corroborates the notion that children's relationships with their friends support cooperation and reciprocity between individuals. One investigator (Howes, 1983) assessed infants (5–14 months), toddlers 16–23 months), and preschool-aged children (35–49 months) on six occasions during the course of a school year. "Maintained friends" (consistent mutual attraction verified by observations as well as teacher nominations) were contrasted with "sporadic" friends (who were friends only once during the year or inconsistently) and "nonfriends" (children who were never friends at any time). Social overtures (successful ones), elaborated exchanges, reciprocal play, positive emotional exchanges, and vocalising increased significantly over time among maintained friends; only vocalising increased among sporadic friends and none of the observed behaviours increased among the nonfriends. Socialising between mutual friends thus became more complex during the year but remained constant among the other dyads. Other longitudinal evidence shows that, among preschool-aged children, social behaviour with a stable friend is generally more competent than with an unstable one: children are more successful in group entry, more complementary and reciprocal in their social play, more cooperative, and more likely to enage in pretend play. After losing friends, competence is diminished (Howes, 1989).

Among school-aged children, talk about intimacy also differentiates stable and unstable friends. Across the transition to adolescence, intimacy considerations differentiate friendship relations more sharply than anything else. Comments about sharing thoughts and feelings increase, along with comments about self-disclosure (Berndt & Perry, 1986). Both self-disclosure and intimate knowledge are endorsed as friendship expectations more and more commonly between the ages of 11 and 17 (Sharabany, Gershoni, & Hofman, 1981). Frankness and spontaneity, knowing and sensitivity, attachment, exclusiveness, and giving and sharing are the specific dimensions of intimacy that increase most with age.

Overall, then, friendships support cooperation, reciprocity, and effective conflict management, beginning in early childhood and extending through adolescence. Intimacy considerations become increasingly salient during middle childhood and, along with commitment, are the social skills most extensively utilised by adolescents in these contexts.

Friendships as Information Sources. Children teach one another in many situations and are generally effective in this capacity.[3] Peer teaching occurs in three main varieties (Damon & Phelps, 1989): peer tutoring, cooperative learning, and peer collaboration. Peer tutoring refers to the didactic transmission of information from one child to another, ordinarily from an "expert" to a "novice". Peer tutoring is sometimes employed in schools, but also occurs when children are on their own. Cooperative learning refers to schemes in which children are asked to combine their contributions in problem-solving and to share rewards. Peer collaboration, in contrast, refers to situations in which novices work together on tasks that neither is able to do separately. Empirical studies indicate that each of these methods works, although some are content specific. Collaboration, for example, works best in mastering abstract, basic concepts (e.g., proportionality) whereas tutoring works best with mechanics and specific skills (Damon & Phelps, 1989).

Quite possibly, friends interact differently in these situations from nonfriends. Mutual friends know one another better than nonfriends; they are more accurate than "unilateral associates" in assessing the characteristics they have in common as well as more knowledgeable about their differences (Ladd & Emerson, 1984). Close relationships require that the individual "... know the other's needs and goals and how the individual impinges on those, know the responses the other is likely to exhibit in reaction to the individual's own behavior, and, then, possess the capability of performing

---

[3] The instructional methods they use are remarkably similar to those employed by adults in teaching children (Ludeke & Hartup, 1983).

the responses necessary to bring about the desired effect" (Berscheid, 1985, p. 71). Given these considerations, friends should be uncommonly good teachers and collaborators, better than nonfriends in most circumstances.

Empirical studies relating to these hypotheses are scant. Tutoring effects have never been studied in relation to the attraction existing between tutor and tutee. Earlier studies suggest that on-task behaviour actually declines when a young child is observed by a friend; in contrast, on-task behaviour is sustained when the observer is a nonfriend (Hartup, 1964). But whether friends are better tutors (and whether children like to be tutored better by friends than by nonfriends) is not known. Similarly, we know almost nothing about friendship relations and cooperative learning. Cooperative experiences promote solidarity and social attraction within classrooms (Johnson, Johnson, Johnson, & Anderson, 1976) but no one knows whether cooperative outcomes are better among groups of friends than among groups of nonfriends.

Peer collaboration, however, has been examined among both friends and nonfriends. Newcomb and Brady (1982) observed children who were asked to explore a many-faceted "creativity box" with either a friend or a nonfriend. More extensive exploration occurred among children with their friends; conversation was also more vigorous and connected. Most important, the children who explored the box with a friend remembered more about it afterwards. Other evidence shows that when children were observed while attempting to resolve conflicts about social ethics, friends gave more explanations to one another than nonfriends, as well as criticised their companions more freely (Nelson & Aboud, 1985). Once again, outcomes also differed: friends changed to more mature solutions through these discussions to a greater extent than did nonfriends, although the total number of changes did not differ.

Friends and nonfriends also differ in group collaboration. Social interaction is more democratic and cooperative as well as more efficient in some tasks, e.g., making up stories (Scofield, 1960). This efficiency may not last long, though, since friends feel freer to stop working with one another than nonfriends (Shaw & Shaw, 1962).

While the empirical documentation is relatively weak, existing studies thus suggest that friendships are unique contexts for transmitting information from one child to another. Since friends may be more effective as teachers or collaborators in some situations than others, these functions need to be explored more extensively.

Friends as Resources.   Friendships are cognitive and emotional resources furnishing the child with maximum capacity for problem-solving as well as security for striking out into new territory, meeting new people, and tackling new problems. According to these hypotheses, friendships extend children's problem-solving capabilities as well as provide buffering from stress.

Logically, friendships should facilitate reaching goals and meeting challenges simply because two children working as a well-meshed "team" work more efficiently than two children who are strangers. Friends share motives; children and their friends also work out verbal and motor "scripts" that enable them to combine their talents and achieve their goals more extensively than nonfriends. New studies show clearly that child-child collaboration is effective in mastering certain tasks (Azmitia, 1988) but the evidence is scanty concerning the hypothesis that friends cooperate better than nonfriends in obtaining desired resources. One investigation (Charlesworth & LaFreniere, 1983), though, demonstrates that small groups of friends actually gained access to a scarce resource (movie cartoons) more readily and with fewer conflicts than small groups of nonfriends.

As emotional resources, friendships support both "having fun" and stress-reduction. Once again, the evidence is not extensive. Foot, Chapman and Smith (1977) observed children while they watched a comedy film. The duration and frequency of laughing, smiling, looking and talking were greater between friends than between strangers, as well as response matching (a measure of behavioural concordance between the children). Strangers may not be the best dyads to compare to friends (the comparison confounds familiarity with liking) but these results nevertheless suggest that friendships support "having fun".

Friends furnish one another, too, with a sense of security in strange situations. In one investigation (Ipsa, 1981), preschool-aged children were observed, together with either a classmate or another child enrolled in a different classroom, in the presence of a strange adult. With familiar companions, the children displayed little distress at the departure of the adult, whereas children with unfamiliar companions were upset. Schwartz (1972) also observed more positive affect, greater mobility, and more frequent talk in a strange situation between preschool children who were considered by their teachers to be friends than between children who were unacquainted. Once again, the studies confound friendship and familiarity, but the results are suggestive.

The most important issue to be explored in this area has not been touched: whether stable friendships buffer children and adolescents from the adverse effects of negative events occurring in everyday life, e.g., family conflict, terminal illness, unemployment, or school failure. One investigation (Wallerstein & Kelly, 1981) suggests that friendships may indeed ameliorate the stress associated with divorce. School-aged boys turned readily to friends, seemingly to distance themselves from the troubled household. Girls, however, entered into friendships only when their mothers were especially supportive. Similar results were obtained by Elder (1974), who studied the records of children reared in the United States during the Great Depression. When their fathers lost their jobs, boys continued with their friends more-or-less as before; girls, on the other hand, stayed home, experienced strain in their relations with age-mates, and evidenced greater concern about having friends than before the family economic situation deteriorated. Considering the centrality of stress management in child health and social relations, additional work in this area is badly needed.

Friendships and Subsequent Relationships. Sullivan (1953, pp. 245–246) has stated that:

> ... when he finally finds a chum—somewhere between eight-and-a-half and ten—you will discover something very different in the relationship—namely, that your child begins to develop a real sensitivity to what matters to another person ... preadolescence is marked by the coming of the integrating tendencies which, when they are completely developed, we call love, or, to say it another way, by the manifestation of the need for interpersonal intimacy.

These words express one of the best-known notions about friendships, namely, that children acquire dispositions within them that generalise to other relationships with their contemporaries. In this sense, children's friendships are thought to be templates used in constructing subsequent relationships. To be sure, new relationships are never exact copies of old ones; relationships always reflect the idiosyncracies of one's partners (Hinde, 1979). This theory suggests, however, that the organisation of behaviour within relationships generalises from old ones to new ones. Only the most indirect evidence supports this claim. Friendship experience is correlated with an altruistic outlook and other manifestations of inter-personal sensitivity (Mannarino, 1976). Children with many friends are generally effective in child-child relations and are well-liked (Ladd, Price, & Hart, 1990). On the other side of the coin, children who are involved in bully/victim relationships (as either bullies or victims) are likely to be involved in other bully/victim relationships subsequently (Olweus, 1980). Clearly, continuities exist from relationship to relationship, but continuities from one friendship to another have not been studied.

BEGINNINGS

Becoming Friends[4]

"Exchange theories" (and their variants) are based on the argument that close relationships emerge only to the extent that interaction between individuals is mutually satisfying (Kelley, 1979). We don't know exactly how children evaluate what is "received" from the many social exchanges in which they are involved, why they are so strongly motivated to make comparisons between themselves and others, and why they are so concerned with "fairness" (see Hinde, 1979). Nevertheless, exchange theory is a viable explanation for the emergence and maintenance of the relationships that children construct with their friends.

Most of the basic information needed by children about exchange outcomes can be divided into two classes: affirmations and conflicts. Affirmations (or agreements) provide children with a sense of what is correct and workable in an exchange, and provide them with a basis for estimating the likelihood that a continuing relationship will "work" or "pay off". Especially when their occurrence coincides with anxiety-reduction, affirmations establish other children as emotional and cognitive resources (see p. 188). Affirmations are also the events suggesting to the child that exchanges with similar individuals are likely to be more gratifying than exchanges with dissimilar ones.

Conflicts (or disagreements) create doubts about what might be correct and workable, thereby motivating change in thinking and acting. Conflicts are instrumental in establishing friendships since they illuminate the "fit" between individuals, i.e., by demonstrating when the skills, interests, and goals of two children are not concordant, as well as by marking relationship boundaries, i.e., those behavioural "limits" that can be exceeded only by risking separation. Stated another way: conflicts assist children, in reverse, in recognising the common ground that exists between them.

A continuous dialectic between affirmation and disaffirmation is needed in order to construct and maintain relationships. Affirmations, alone, carry little information about exchange possibilities except in contrast with disaffirmations. Similarly, disaffirmations establish common ground only through contrasts with affirmations. Disagreements and agreements are therefore "tandem essentials" in friendship formation and maintenance. Beyond suggesting that agreement/disagreement ratios must be favour-able, exchange theory does not specify the "climate of agreement" needed

---

[4] This section derives from a manuscript appearing elsewhere (Hartup, in press a) and is used with permission.

for friendships to emerge and endure. Available studies suggest that these ratios must exceed unity: Gottman (1983), for example, observed children interacting with their friends with agreement/disagreement ratios that averaged somewhat less than 2:1.

Overall, exchange theory furnishes a good general account of the manner in which agreements and disagreements are involved in "becoming friends". Disagreement/agreement ratios need to be better specified, equilibration in social exchanges better understood, and contextual variations need to be taken into account. Agreements and disagreements need clarification, especially, as "tandem essentials" in mutual attraction.

The Friendships of Infants and Toddlers

Observations in child care centres show considerable differentiation in the social interaction occurring among infants and toddlers. Sociometric "stars" are evident: certain infants are approached more consistently than others, and some are more consistently avoided. Sought-after babies are likely to be more active in initiating contacts with other babies as well as to react contingently to their overtures. Least sought-after babies are likely to be asocial; both the number and complexity of their social interactions are likely to depend on whether they themselves initiated them (Lee, 1973). Social responsiveness, in this sense, is closely akin to generalised reciprocity, and sociometric stars make overtures to which other children readily respond, as well as responding to other children contingently and more-or-less equivalently.

When reciprocity and complementarity are mutual, social attraction will be too: a "climate of agreement" is established and children become friends. One investigator (Howes, 1983) empirically established this occurrence. Observing infants, toddlers, and preschool children, the investigator distinguished dyads from one another according to three criteria:

1. their social overtures needed to result in interaction at least half the time;
2. complementarities needed to occur in their play; and
3. positively-toned affective exchanges needed to be evident (e.g., smiling and laughing).

Sheer amount of social interaction was not used as a criterion, although dyads meeting the other criteria turned out to be more interactive than those that didn't. The most interesting results, though, were these: most of the dyads displaying successful social overtures, complementary play, and shared affect were considered by the children's teachers to be "friends". Other investigators have also reported that special relationships are mirrored in the social interaction occurring among infants and toddlers, and that their actions vary according to the identity of their companions (Ross & Lollis, 1989). The commodities exchanged between infant friends differ from those exchanged by older ones. Babies who are stable friends exchange objects more frequently than toddlers or preschool-aged friends. Concomitantly, preschool children and their friends spend more time in reciprocal and complementary play than infants and toddlers, and vocalise more to them (Howes, 1983). Seemingly, then, the child's development does not change the basis for mutual attraction (i.e., reciprocity in social relations), merely the commodities exchanged (i.e., from objects to complementarities in play).

Conflict and aggression are not closely connected to friendship relations among very young children. Relationships based mainly on enmity are difficult to find, mainly because children who don't like one another don't interact. Generally, toddlers fight most with classmates who are also their friends, although not all toddlers fight with their friends. Consequently, one sees "fighting friends" from time to time, although many toddlers are friends without the accompanying conflict (Ross, Conant, & Cheyne, 1987).

CHILDREN AND ADOLESCENTS

Similarities between Friends

Age. Children and their friends are concordant in age, reflecting the egalitarian nature of these relationships. Age concordances between friends are not great within single classrooms but are considerable within entire schools. This situation extends from early childhood through adolescence (Kandel, 1978b).

Sex. Children and their friends are same-sex. Opposite-sex friendships are relatively rare, even among preschoolers. Among school-aged children, opposite-sex relationships are ordinarily seen as romantic or sexual, and frequently invite teasing and joking (Thorne, 1986; Goodnow & Burns, 1988). Romantic relationships become increasingly evident during adolescence, but most teenagers continue to choose members of their own sex as best friends. Only one in twenty friendships among adolescents is opposite-sex (Duck, 1975). Gender concordances decline slightly among older adolescents from high school through adulthood (Epstein, 1983).

Race. Racial concordances between friends are also evident, increasing from early childhood through adolescence. Among American children, own-race choices increase during middle childhood; choices of own-race play or work companions then stabilise but own-race friendship choices continue to increase through adolescence (Asher, Singleton, & Taylor, 1988). Similar concordances (including the age differences) exist among British children: friendship choices are own-race more often than chance among primary grade children, increasingly progressively among older children, and especially among adolescents (Jelinek & Brittan, 1975).

Behavioural Similarities. Behavioural concordances among friends and nonfriends are not especially well-studied in early and middle childhood. Existing evidence suggests that these similarities are not as great as the similarities between friends in age, sex, and race (Hartup, in press b). Better studies exist for young adolescents, although behavioural similarities between friends are not especially great at this time, either. The most striking concordances occur in three areas: school attitudes, including educational aspirations and attitudes about achievement; attitudes about certain normative behaviours in contemporary teen culture, e.g., drinking and drug-taking (Kandel, 1978b); and sexual experience—among girls only (Billy, Rodgers, & Udry, 1984).

Determinants. Similarities between friends occur for two main reasons:

1. similar children and adolescents choose one another as friends, and
2. friends socialise one another in similar directions.

Unfortunately, selection and socialisation effects are not easy to disentangle empirically. One investigator (Kandel, 1978a) succeeded, however, by studying continuity and change among adolescents in drug use, educational attitudes, and delinquent involvement across one school year. Both selection and socialisation effects were evident, in equal amounts. Gender and race concordances, of course, represent selection effects only.

Behaviour with Friends

Friendship formation in early and middle childhood is more elaborate than among infants and toddlers, although first indications of social attraction continue to include sustained social exchanges, complementarities in these exchanges, and mutually-regulated affect. Gottman (1983) examined conversations between children (strangers) on three successive occasions and also obtained estimates from mothers of how well the children were "hitting it off" after two months. Results revealed that the clarity and connectedness of communication during the children's first encounters was the best predictor of hitting it off; information exchange, conflict resolution, and common play activities were also correlated with this outcome. Communication clarity in subsequent sessions was also closely related to hitting it off, and self-disclosure assumed significance. Regression analyses showed that these variables accounted for more than 80% of the variance in the children's becoming friends, an unusually large amount.

Once friendships are established, cooperation and reciprocity become markers of these relationships. Competition and conflict are related to friendship functioning according to context, i.e., friends differ from nonfriends in conflict management according to the setting in which social interaction occurs. On playgrounds and in other "open" situations, friends disagree less often per unit time than nonfriends, but have more total disagreements because friends spend more time with one another than nonfriends. Conflicts are less heated between friends than between non-friends, mutual disengagements are used more commonly as resolution strategies, and outcomes are more equal. Friends remain together more frequently than nonfriends in open situations, too, once the conflict is over (Hartup, et al., 1988). In "closed" situations, however, (i.e., when the children must interact with one another, not changing partners or activities) friends actually disagree more often per unit time (Hartup, in press a). Conflicts in closed situations are also more intense between friends than between nonfriends (Gottman, 1983; Nelson & Aboud, 1985). Friends thus seem to make more vigorous efforts than nonfriends to reduce the damage resulting from their disagreements in open situations and to ensure continued interaction. In closed situations, they apparently feel "freer" to disagree.

This interaction between friendship and context in conflict management can only be inferred currently by comparing the results of different studies. Setting and friendship variations have not been examined simultaneously within a single investigation, and this omission needs to be corrected. Age differences must also be looked at: certain studies, for example, suggest that adolescents generate more conflicts with friends than with nonfriends in open situations (Laursen, 1989) but fewer conflicts in open ones (Berndt et al., 1986), exactly the opposite of the case with children.

With increasing age, children's friendships become suffused with expectations of loyalty, trust, self-disclosure, and intimacy (see p. 177). Children themselves confirm these generalisations, primarily in interviews and questionnaires. Observational methods are difficult to use for capturing intimate nuances among older children and adolescents.

Sex Differences

Sex differences are evident in the interaction that occurs between children and their friends, reflecting general differences between boys and girls in social orientation and behaviour (Huston, 1983). Few investigators have examined sex differences in social interaction among friends and non-friends separately. Since most observational studies centre on events occurring between children who spend time together, one can assume that the resulting sex differences characterise friends, but this may not always be the case. Friendships themselves differ between boys and girls. Among school-aged children, for example, girls' relationships are usually more "intensive" and less "extensive" than boys'. Using factor analytic methods, Waldrop and Halverson (1975) found that intensiveness (i.e., the extent to which the child's mother discusses best friends and their importance) loaded highly on a peer-orientation factor among girls but not boys. At the same time, extensiveness (i.e., emphasis on group activities and games) loaded on peer-orientation only among boys.

Friendship networks vary in exclusiveness, too. Eder and Hallinan (1978) obtained sociometric choices from five classrooms, determined the number of triads in each classroom that included an exclusive, reciprocated friendship, and divided this number by the total number of same-sex triads existing in the class. Exclusive friendship dyads were more common among girls' triads than boys', while non-reciprocated choices were more common among boys'. Girls' choices also grew more exclusive during the school year whereas boys' choices either became non-exclusive or didn't change. What are the origins of these sex differences? We are uncertain. Play interests may be partly responsible: boys' activities commonly involve numerous individuals whereas girls' activities are likely to be dyadic. One can also argue, however, that the extensiveness in boys' friendship networks supports strivings for autonomy and mastery, while the intensiveness in girls' networks supports needs for closeness and intimacy in social relations.

Whatever their determinants, these sex differences are widely recognised among adolescents. Girls spend more time with their friends, on average, than boys do (Wong & Csikzentmihalyi, 1991). Both boys and girls characterise girls' friendships as more intimate than boys' (Bukowski & Kramer, 1986). Intimacy is more commonly mentioned in girls' talk about their friendships than in boys' talk, and ratings of their same-sex friendships are, in general, more intimate (Sharabany et al., 1981). Girls also report the occurrence of self-disclosure between themselves and their friends more frequently than boys do (Rivenbark, 1971). Finally, male adolescents are more likely than females, on average, to believe that their conflicts don't affect their close relationships. Conversely, females talk more often about the long-term implications of disagreements with their friends (Laursen, 1989).

Mean differences, however, may not tell the entire story with respect to sex differences. Boys' friendships, for example, are more variable than girls' with respect to intimacy. Youniss and Smollar (1986) found that most adolescent girls describe their friendships in terms of shared activities, intimacy, and mutual understanding, and 40% of the adolescent boys in this investigation also described their friendships in this way. Only 30% of the boys characterised their friendships as communicatively guarded and lacking in mutual understanding.

FRIENDSHIP EXPERIENCE AND DEVELOPMENTAL OUTCOME

Children who are disliked by other children are at risk generally, mostly of mental health difficulties in adolescence and early adulthood and of early school leaving. Being disliked is a common experience among aggressive children, but early aggressiveness is more closely related to later criminality than is social rejection. Shyness is sometimes accompanied by peer rejection, but only among older children (Hartup, in press b).

Being disliked and being without friends, however, are not the same. Indeed, some children who are disliked by other children have best friends, most commonly children who are socially rejected themselves (Cairns, Cairns, Neckerman, Gest, & Garieppy, 1988). Since friendship experience may have its own social functions, one cannot assume that it will be related to the same developmental outcomes as peer rejection. Relatively few investigators have sought to verify the developmental significance of friendship experience. A small number of correlational studies establish the relation between having friends, on the one hand, and social competence, on the other. These investigations show that:

1. Preschool-aged children with emotional difficulties are friendless more frequently than better-adapted children, and are less likely to maintain the friendships they have. Even so, many young children with emotional difficulties also have friends (Howes, 1983).
2. Among school-aged children referred to child guidance clinics, 30% to 75% (depending on age) are reported by parents as having peer difficulties (Achenbach & Edelbrock, 1981). Referred children have fewer friends as well as less contact with them than nonreferred children, and their friendships are less stable over time (Rutter & Garmezy, 1983).
3. Referred children understand the reciprocities and intimacies in friendships less maturely than non-referred children (Selman, 1980).

Other studies show that, among unselected children and adolescents, friendship experience is correlated with various indicators of social skill:

1. Among preschoolers, children with mutual friends evidence more mature affective perspective taking than children who only have unilateral (i.e., unreciprocated) relationships (Jones & Bowling, 1988).
2. Preschoolers with mutual friends enter groups more easily than children with no mutual friends, engage in more cooperative pretend play, have fewer difficulties with other children, and are more sociable (Howes, 1989).
3. Among preadolescents, those with stable chums are more altruistic than those without them, as measured by concern for others and defaults in a prisoner's dilemma game (Mannarino, 1976).
4. Children with friends display greater altruism than children without friends, as assessed by both teacher ratings and observations (McGuire & Weisz, 1982).
5. Finally, the transition to adolescence is marked by increasing positive correlations between social competence, sociability, and self-esteem, on the one hand, and the intimacy, satisfaction, and companionability of the individual's friendships, on the other. Negative correlations between hostility and anxiety/depression, respectively, and friendship intimacy also increase (Buhrmester, 1990).

Although this evidence is impressive, the results cannot be used to specify causal direction: close relationships may support good adjustment and its development but, alternatively, well-adjusted children may simply be better at establishing friendships than poorly-adjusted ones. Causality can be better argued from regression models used with longitudinal data. Thus far, two short-term studies have been conducted, both yielding results supporting the thesis that friendship experience contributes to socialisation outcome.

In one investigation (Ladd, et al., 1990), the playground behaviour of preschool children was observed on three occasions during the school year in order to assess friendship relations. Friendship variables included number of frequent play companions (i.e., playmates present in more than 30% of a child's observations) and network affinity (i.e., the proportion of frequent companions who also indicated they liked the subject). Social adjustment was measured in terms of sociometric status and teacher ratings. Results indicated, first, that the number of frequent companions was significantly correlated with the adjustment measures in each measurement interval separately but, also, that the correlations between network affinity and these measures increased over time. Most interestingly, the results indicated that the number of frequent companions at the beginning of the year predicted social ratings at the end of the year, but social ratings at the beginning did not predict companion scores at the end.

In a second investigation, Ladd (1990) obtained repeated measures of friendship relations, sociometric status, and school adjustment (perceptions, anxiety/avoidance, and performance) among kindergarten children. Personal attributes (e.g., mental age and prior school experience) predicted early school performance to some extent, but regression analyses also showed that children with many friends at school entrance developed more favourable school perceptions in the early months than children with fewer friends. Those who maintained these relationships also liked school better as the year went by. Making new friends in the classroom also predicted gains in school performance over the year whereas being disliked by other children forecast unfavourable school perceptions, school avoidance, and progressively poorer school performance. Contrasting analyses, estimating the regression of friendship status on school adjustment, showed relatively weak results: e.g., favourable school perceptions predicted friendship maintenance over the year but, otherwise, school adjustment did not forecast friendship experience. Friendship relations thus predicted school adjustment in these data better than the reverse.

Taken together, the results suggest that early adaptation to school derives partly from personal attributes (e.g., mental age) but also from friendship experience (Ladd, 1990, p. 1097):

... children's classroom peer relationships tended to add to the prediction of school adjustment, above and beyond that which could be accounted for by their personal attributes and experiences. Furthermore, features of children's classroom peer relationships forecasted both their adjustment during the early weeks of kindergarten and changes in their adjustment during the school year. The fact that changes in children's school adjustment were predicted by these variables lends support to the hypothesis that children's personal attributes, their prior experiences, and their relationships with classmates affect their adaptational progress ...

While the processes through which friendship relations contribute to social competence are not illuminated by these results, the contention that these relationships contribute importantly and directly to socialisation is supported. Most important, several different dimensions in friendship relations turn out to be significant: i.e., having friends in one's classroom to begin with, keeping them, and making new ones.

Prospective studies are time-consuming and laborious, but without them the developmental significance of children's friendships cannot be established. Currently, one wishes for longer-term studies and studies that extend beyond the school milieu. One also wishes for studies in which family relations are included in the regression model as well as child-child relations, since qualitative differences in early relationships between mothers and children are related to making friends later and, possibly, to what those friendships are like (Elicker, Englund, & Sroufe, in press). Even so, the weight of the current evidence suggests that friendship relations have considerable developmental significance.

Whether friends are "necessities" in child and adolescent development remains uncertain. Should friends not be available, other relationships may be elastic enough to serve the friendship functions enumerated earlier. Children with friends may be better off than children without friends but, if necessary, other relationships may be substituted for friendships. Stated another way: friendships may be optimal settings for learning about egalitarian relationships and the social exchanges necessary to them, but children may be able to exploit other relationships to learn these same things. Nature seldom leaves us with only one means to an adaptational end; numerous means are usually available. These redundancies, of course, assure successful adaptation when primary adaptational mechanisms cannot be used. Consequently, we argue that friendships are best viewed as developmental advantages rather than developmental necessities, and we read the current evidence concerning friendships and their developmental significance in this light (Hartup & Sancilio, 1986).

CONCLUSION

Children understand that reciprocity and equality are the basic conditions of friendship. These conditions are understood by young children in relatively concrete terms and by older children in more psychological ones. Emotional investment in these relationships is taken for granted, especially among older children and adolescents: caring and social support are expected to be exchanged with one's friends. Commitment and trust eventually become important conditions undergirding these relationships, and intimacy becomes a major issue during adolescence. Whether these expectations are manifestations of a single, over-riding concern with equity or separate social considerations remains to be established.

Beginning in early childhood, children reliably identify certain children as best friends, whether they are asked to classify their associates as friends or as individuals who are liked. Parents and teachers identify these same children as friends, and children spend more time with those classmates whom they designate as friends than with other children. Liking one another and spending time together are the most obvious markers of these relationships.

Friendship relations can be divided into a series of "stages" ranging from first encounters through deterioration and endings. Wide variation exists from friendship to friendship in these time-related elements. Common ground is especially significant in establishing relationships; commitment is especially important to their continuation and maintenance. Children's relationships with one another deteriorate for many different reasons, although commitment violations are salient beginning in pre-adolescence. Conflicts sometimes signal friendship endings, but not always. Endings are as likely to be accompanied by alienation as argument. Children's friendships serve proximally as mechanisms for ensuring interaction with agemates. More distally, friendships serve as contexts for acquiring social skill, sources of information about both the social and non-social world, cognitive and emotional resources, and precursors of other relationships. Empirical evidence concerning these functions is scattered, diverse, and mostly circumstantial (as evidence about distal function inevitably is). Better understanding of friendship functions is among the greatest needs in this area.

A "climate of agreement" seems to be required for friendships to begin. Close relationships, however, are always constructed on the basis of a dialectic between agreements and disagreements, as these are involved in establishing common ground between individuals and reciprocity in their social interaction. Infants and toddlers display both reciprocities and complementarities with one another, and these characteristics (along with shared affect) distinguish friends from nonfriends. Reciprocity continues to be the basis for mutual attraction through the preschool years, although the commodities exchanged between friends undergo considerable change.

Friends are concordant in age, sex, and race. Behavioural concordances are not as strong, although school-aged children and their friends evidence moderate similarity in educational and normative attitudes. Based on current evidence, behavioural similarities both contribute to friendship selection and result from these relationships. Conflict as well as cooperation differentiates the social interaction of friends and nonfriends from early childhood through adolescence. Contextual variations are evident, however, especially in manifestations of conflict and competition. Children's own accounts of their friendship expectations increasingly emphasise commitment, but behavioural manifestations of these developments are not well documented.

Boys interact differently with their friends from girls, although sex differences have rarely been examined among friends and nonfriends separately. Girls' relationships appear to be more intensive and less extensive than boys', and to encompass greater concerns with intimacy. Boys may be more variable with their friends than girls, however, suggesting caution in making simple statements about sex differences in friendship relations.

Correlational studies show that children with friends are more socially competent than children who do not have friends, and that troubled children have difficulty in friendship relations. Causal models, tested with longitudinal data, suggest that friendship experience forecasts developmental outcome in conjunction with personal attributes and other experiences. Making friends, keeping them, and making new ones are all relevant. The current evidence suggests, however, that we can better argue that friendships are developmental advantages than argue that these relationships are developmental necessities.

REFERENCES

Achenbach, T. M., & Edelbrock, C. S. (1981). Behavioral problems and competence reported by parents of normal and disturbed children aged 4 through 16. *Monographs of the Society for Research in Child Development, 46* (1, No. 188).

Asher, S. R., Singleton, L. C., & Taylor, A. R. (1988). *Acceptance versus friendship: A longitudinal study of racial integration.* Manuscript submitted for publication.

Azmitia, M. (1988). Peer interaction and problem-solving: When are two heads better than one? *Child Development, 59,* 87–96.

Berndt, T. J. (1981). Relations between social cognition, nonsocial cognition, and social behavior: The case of friendship. In J. H. Flavell, & L. Ross (Eds.), *Social cognitive development* (pp. 176–199). Cambridge, U.K.: Cambridge University Press.

Berndt, T. J., Hawkins, J. A., & Hoyle, S. G. (1986). Changes in friendship during a school year: Effects on children's and adolescents' impressions of friendship and sharing with friends. *Child Development, 57,* 1284–1297.

Berndt, T. J., & Perry, T. B. (1986) Children's perceptions of friendships as supportive relationships. *Developmental Psychology, 22,* 640–648.

Berscheid, E. (1985). Interpersonal modes of knowing. In E. W. Eisner (Ed.), Learning the ways of knowing. *The 85th yearbook of the national society for the study of education* (pp. 60–76). Chicago: University of Chicago Press.

Biehler, R. F. (1954). Companion choice behavior in the kindergarten. *Child Development, 25,* 45–50.

Bigelow, B. J. (1977). Children's friendship expectations: A cognitive developmental study. *Child Development, 48,* 246–253.

Bigelow, B. J., & LaGaipa, J. J. (1975). Children's written descriptions of friendship: A multidimensional analysis. *Developmental Psychology, 11,* 857–858.

Billy, J. O. G., Rodgers, J. L., & Udry, J. R. (1984). Adolescent sexual behavior and friendship choice. *Social Forces, 62,* 653–678.

Buhrmester, D. (1990). Intimacy of friendship, interpersonal competence, and adjustment during preadolescence and adolescence. *Child Development, 61,* 1101–1111.

Bukowski, W. M., & Kramer, T. L. (1986). Judgments of the features of friendship among early adolescent boys and girls. *Journal of Early Adolescence, 6,* 331–338.

Byrne, D. (1971). *The attraction paradigm.* New York: Academic Press.

Cairns, R. B., Cairns, B. D., Neckerman, H. J., Gest, S., & Garieppy, J.-L. (1988). Peer networks and aggressive behavior: Peer support or peer rejection? *Developmental Psychology, 24,* 815–823.

Chapman, A. J., Smith, J. R., Foot, H. C., & Pritchard, E. (1979). Behavioural and sociometric indices of friendship in children. In M. Cook, & G. D. Wilson (Eds.), *Love and attraction* (pp. 127–130). Oxford, U.K.: Pergamon.

Charlesworth, W. R., & LaFreniere, P. (1983). Dominance, friendship, and resource utilization in preschool children's groups. *Ethology and Sociobiology, 4,* 175–186.

Crockett, L., Losoff, M., & Petersen, A. C. (1984). Perceptions of the peer group and friendship in early adolescence. *Journal of Early Adolescence, 4,* 155–181.

Damon, W., & Phelps, E. (1989). Strategic uses of peer learning in children's education. In T. J. Berndt, & G. W. Ladd (Eds.) *Peer relationships in child development* (pp. 135–157). New York: Wiley.

Duck, S. W. (1975). Personality similarity and friendship choices by adolescents. *European Journal of Social Psychology, 5,* 351–365.

Eder, D., & Hallinan, M. T. (1978). Sex differences in children's friendships. *American Sociological Review, 43,* 237–250.

Elder, G. (1974). *Children of the Great Depression.* Chicago: University of Chicago Press.

Elicker, J., Englund, M., & Sroufe, L. A. (in press). Predicting peer competence and peer relationships in childhood from early parent-child relationships. In R. D. Parke, & G. W. Ladd (Eds.), *Family-peer relationships: Modes of linkage.* Hillsdale, N.J.: Lawrence Erlbaum Associates Inc.

Epstein, J. L. (1983). Selection of friends in differently organized schools and classrooms. In J. L. Epstein, & N. Karweit (Eds.), *Friends in school: Patterns of selection and influence in secondary schools* (pp. 73–92). New York: Wiley.

Foot, H. C., Chapman, A. J., & Smith, J. R. (1977). Friendship and social responsiveness in boys and girls. *Journal of Personality and Social Psychology, 35,* 401–411.

Furman, W., & Bierman, K. L. (1984) Children's conceptions of friendship: A multidimensional study of developmental changes. *Developmental Psychology, 20,* 925–931.

Furman, W., & Childs, M. K. (1981, April). *A temporal perspective on children's friendships.* Paper presented at the biennial meetings of the Society for Research in Child Development, Boston.

Goodnow, J. J., & Burns, A. (1988). *Home and school: Child's eye view.* Sydney: Allen & Unwin.

Gottman, J. M. (1979). *Marital interaction: Experimental investigations.* New York: Academic Press.

Gottman, J. M. (1983). How children become friends. *Monographs of the Society for Research in Child Development, 48,* (No. 201).

Hallinan, M. T. (1980). Patterns of cliquing among youth. In H. C. Foot, A. J. Chapman, & J. R. Smith (Eds.), *Friendship and peer relations in children* (pp. 321–342). New York: Wiley.

Hartup, W. W. (1964). Friendship status and the effectiveness of peers as reinforcing agents. *Journal of Experimental Child Psychology, 1,* 154–162.

Hartup, W. W. (1983). Peer relations. In E. M. Hetherington (Ed.), & P. H. Mussen (Series Ed.), *Handbook of child psychology, Vol. 4, Socialization, social development, and personality* (pp. 103–196). New York: Wiley.

Hartup, W. W. (1989). Behavioral manifestations of children's friendships. In T. J. Berndt, & G. W. Ladd (Eds.), *Peer relationships in child development* (pp. 46–70). New York: Wiley.

Hartup, W. W. (in press, a). Conflict and friendship relations. In C. U. Shantz, & W. W. Hartup (Eds.), *Conflict in child and adolescent development.* Cambridge, U.K.: Cambridge University Press.

Hartup, W. W. (in press, b). Peer relations in early and middle childhood. In V. B. van Hasselt, & M. Hersen (Eds.), *Handbook of social development: A lifespan perspective.* New York: Plenum.

Hartup, W. W., Laursen, B., Stewart, M. A., & Eastenson, A. (1988). Conflict and the friendship relations of young children. *Child Development, 59,* 1590–1600.

Hartup, W. W., & Sancilio, M. F. (1986). Children's friendships. In E. Schopler, & G. Mesibov (Eds.), *Social behavior in autism* (pp. 61–79). New York: Plenum.

Hinde, R. A. (1979). *Towards understanding relationships.* New York: Academic Press.

Hinde, R. A., Titmus, G., Easton, D., & Tamplin, A. (1985). Incidence of "friendship" and behavior with strong associates versus non-associates in preschoolers. *Child Development, 56,* 234–245.

Howes, C. (1983). Patterns of friendship. *Child Development, 54,* 1041–1053.

Howes, C. (1989). Peer interaction of young children. (1989). *Monographs of the Society for Research in Child Development, 53* (Serial No. 217).

Huston, A. C. (1983). Sex-typing. In E. M. Hetherington (Ed.), & P. H. Mussen (Series Ed.), *Handbook of child psychology, Vol. 4, Socialization, personality, and social development* (pp. 387–467). New York: Wiley.

Hyde, R. W., & York, R. H. (1948). A technique for investigating interpersonal relationships in a mental hospital. *Journal of Abnormal and Social Psychology, 43*, 287–299.

Hymel, S. (1983). Preschool children's peer relations: Issues in sociometric assessment. *Merrill-Palmer Quarterly, 29*, 237–260.

Hymel, S., Hayvren, M., & Lollis, S. (1982, May). *Social behavior and sociometric preferences: Do children really play with peers they like?* Paper presented at the annual meeting of the Canadian Psychological Association, Montreal.

Ipsa, J. (1981). Peer support among Soviet day care toddlers. *International Journal of Behavioral Development, 4*, 255–269.

Jelinek, M. M., & Brittan, E. M. (1975). Multiracial education: I. Inter-ethnic friendship patterns. *Educational Research, 18*, 44–53.

Johnson, D. W., Johnson, R. T., Johnson, J., & Anderson, D. (1976). Effects of cooperative versus individualized instruction on student prosocial behavior, attitudes toward learning, and achievement. *Journal of Educational Psychology, 68*, 446–452.

Jones, D. C., & Bowling, B. (1988, March). *Preschool friends and affective knowledge: A comparison of mutual and unilateral friends.* Paper presented at the Conference on Human Development, Charleston, S.C.

Kandel, D. B. (1978a). Homophily, selection, and socialization in adolescent friendships. *American Journal of Sociology, 84*, 427–436.

Kandel, D. B. (1978b). Similarity in real-life adolescent friendship pairs. *Journal of Personality and Social Psychology, 36*, 306–312.

Kelley, H. H. (1979). Personal relationships: Their structures and processes. Hillsdale, N.J.: Lawrence Erlbaum Associates Inc.

Ladd, G. W. (1990). Having friends, keeping friends, making friends, and being liked by peers in the classroom: Predictors of children's early school adjustment? *Child Development, 61*, 1081–1100.

Ladd, G. W., & Emerson, E. S. (1984). Shared knowledge in children's friendships. *Developmental Psychology, 20*, 932–940.

Ladd, G. W., Price, J. M., & Hart, C. H. (1990). Preschoolers' behavioral orientations and patterns of peer contact: Predictive of peer status? In S. R. Asher, & J. D. Coie (Eds.), *Peer rejection in childhood* (pp. 90–115). Cambridge, U.K.: Cambridge University Press.

Laursen, B. (1989). *Interpersonal conflict during adolescence.* Unpublished doctoral dissertation, University of Minnesota.

Lee, L. C. (1973, July). *Social encounters of infants: The beginnings of popularity.* Paper presented at the biennial meeting of the International Society for the Study of Behavioural Development, Ann Arbor, Mich.

Levinger, G. (1983). Development and change. In H. H. Kelley, E. Berscheid, A. Christensen, J. H. Harvey, T. L. Huston, G. Levinger, E. McClintock, L. A. Peplau, & D. R. Peterson (Eds.), *Close relationships* (pp. 315–359). New York: W. H. Freeman.

Levinger, G., & Levinger, A. C. (1986). The temporal course of close relationships: Some thoughts about the development of children's ties. In W. W. Hartup, & Z. Rubin (Eds.), *Relationships and development* (pp. 111–133). Hillsdale, N.J.: Lawrence Erlbaum Associates Inc.

Ludeke, R. J., & Hartup, W. W. (1983). Teaching behaviors of nine- and eleven-year-old girls in mixed-age and same-age dyads. *Journal of Educational Psychology, 75*, 908–914.

Mannarino, A. P. (1976). Friendship patterns and altruistic behavior in preadolescent males. *Developmental Psychology, 12*, 555–556.

Marshall, H. R., & McCandless (1957). A study in prediction of social behavior of preschool children. *Child Development, 28*, 149–159.

Masters, J. C., & Furman, W. (1981). Popularity, individual friendship selections, and specific peer interaction among children. *Developmental Psychology, 17,* 344–350.

McCandless, B. R., & Marshall, H. R. (1957). A picture sociometric technique for preschool children and its relation to teacher judgments of friendship. *Child Development, 28,* 139–148.

McGuire, K. D., & Weisz, J. R. (1982). Social cognition and behavior correlates of preadolescent chumship. *Child Development, 53,* 1478–1484.

Medrich, E. A., Rosen, J., Rubin, V., & Buckley, S. (1982). *The serious business of growing up.* Berkeley, Cal.: University of California Press.

Nelson, J., & Aboud, F. E. (1985). The resolution of social conflict between friends. *Child Development, 56,* 1009–1017.

Newcomb, A. F., & Brady, J. E. (1982). Mutuality in boys' friendship selections. *Child Development, 53,* 392–395.

Olweus, D. (1980). Bullying among school boys. In R. Barnen (Ed.), *Children and violence.* Stockholm: Akademic Litteratur.

Park, K. A., & Waters, E. (1988). *Security of attachment and preschool friendships.* Unpublished manuscript, State University of New York, Stony Brook.

Peevers, B. H., & Secord, P. F. (1973). Developmental changes in attribution of descriptive concepts to persons. *Journal of Personality and Social Psychology, 27,* 120–128.

Price, J. M., & Ladd, G. W. (1986). Assessment of children's friendships: Implications for social competence and social adjustment. In R. J. Prinz (Ed.), *Advances in behavioral assessment of children and families, Vol. 2* (pp. 121–149). Greenwich, C.T.: J.A.I. Press.

Rivenbark, W. H. (1971). Self-disclosure patterns among adolescents. *Psychological Reports, 28,* 35–42.

Rizzo, T. A. (1989). *Friendship development among children in school.* Norwood, N.J.: Ablex.

Ross, H. S., Conant, C., & Cheyne, J. A. (1987). *Reciprocity in the relationships of kibbutz toddlers.* Poster presented at the biennial meetings of the Society for Research in Child Development, Baltimore.

Ross, H. S., & Lollis, S. P. (1989). A social relations analysis of toddler peer relationships. *Child Development, 60,* 1082–1091.

Rutter, M., & Garmezy, N. (1983). Developmental psychopathology. In E. M. Hetherington (Ed.), P. H. Mussen (Series Ed.), *Handbook of child psychology, Vol. 4, Socialization, social development, and personality* (pp. 775–911). New York: Wiley.

Sancilio, M. F. (1989). *Making friends: The development of dyadic social relationships among previously unacquainted adolescent boys.* Unpublished doctoral dissertation, University of Minnesota.

Schwartz, J. C. (1972). Effects of peer familiarity on the behavior of preschoolers in a novel situation. *Journal of Personality and Social Psychology, 24,* 276–284.

Scofield, R. W. (1960). Task productivity of groups of friends and nonfriends. *Psychological Reports, 6,* 459–460.

Selman, R. L. (1980). *The growth of interpersonal understanding.* New York: Academic Press.

Sharabany, R., Gershoni, R., & Hofman, J. E. (1981). Girlfriend, boyfriend: Age and sex differences in intimate friendship. *Developmental Psychology, 17,* 800–808.

Shaw, M. E., & Shaw, L. M. (1962). Some effects of sociometric grouping upon learning in a second grade classroom. *Journal of Social Psychology, 57,* 453–458.

Thorne, B. (1986). Girls and boys together . . . but mostly apart: Gender arrangements in elementary schools. In W. W. Hartup, & Z. Rubin (Eds.), *Relationships and development* (pp. 167–184). Hillsdale, N.J.: Lawrence Erlbaum Associates Inc.

Waldrop, M. F., & Halverson, C. F. (1975). Intensive and extensive peer behavior: Longitudinal and cross-sectional analyses. *Child Development, 46,* 19–26.

Wallerstein, J. S., & Kelly, J. B. (1981). *Surviving the breakup: How children and parents cope with divorce.* New York: Basic Books.

Weiss, R. S. (1986). Continuities and transformations in social relationships from childhood to adulthood. In W. W. Hartup, & Z. Rubin (Eds.), *Relationships and development* (pp. 95–110). Hillsdale, N.J.: Lawrence Erlbaum Associates Inc.

Whiting, B. B., & Whiting, J. W. M. (1975). *Children of six cultures.* Cambridge, Mass.: Harvard University Press.

Wong, M. M., & Csikzentmihalyi, M. (1991). Affiliation motivation and daily experience: Some issues on gender differences. *Journal of Personality and Social Psychology, 60,* 154–164.

Youniss, J. (1980). *Parents and peers in social development: A Piaget-Sullivan perspective.* Chicago: University of Chicago Press.

Youniss, J., & Smollar, J. (1986). *Adolescent relations with mothers, fathers and friends.* Chicago: University of Chicago Press.

8 Cultural Artefacts in Social Development: The Case of Computers

Charles Crook
Durham University, Durham, U.K.

INTRODUCTION

In comparison with other essays in this volume, the concerns of the present chapter may seem rather particular. However, by reflecting here on children's engagement wih new technology, I hope it may be possible not only to review this rather particular phenomenon but also to review broader issues of theory and method that arise within psychological research on social development. In part, then, the present topic of computers is a vehicle: one that may lead us towards a distinctive perspective on the study of social development. This perspective will be articulated in later sections of the chapter.

Before going further, it may be useful to anticipate both the flavour of the conclusions I shall reach and a little more of that theoretical perspective upon which this review converges.

Understanding how advanced technologies impinge on children's development is surely an urgent challenge for psychology. Yet, the literature reviewed here creates a sense of only modest progress. Part of the problem may lie in a traditional style of research that pursues the effects of unitary "variables" acting on isolated social actors. My argument is that the case of computers and social development illustrates a pressing need to construct an analysis that does not decouple the individual from the contexts in which development is taking place. Thus, cultural artefacts such as computers must be viewed as features of the environment that serve to organise, promote and constrain various kinds of social experience. In this way, *starting* our research from the organising role of cultural context, we are likely to discover a more complex texture to social experience and thereby develop a richer vocabulary for expressing social development in relation to technological artefacts.

Having declared that the following review will lead us to themes of broader significance, it may be unnecessary to establish at the outset that computers are such singular artefacts within early social experience that they justify privileged discussion. However, I am inclined to believe that the technology actually does deserve special status in this respect. Thus, while the number of childhood "things" that could be explored as social objects is very great—skateboards, novelty turtles and so on—most of them support only transitory pastimes and are of modest significance in comparison with a powerful and evolving technology of information. Simply clarifying that this pervasive technology *can* impact on early social experience in important ways remains one important purpose of the present chapter.

In the following three sections of this paper, I shall take up three senses in which experience with computers can be seen to have social developmental significance. First, there are "indirect" effects: engagement with computers has a potential to narrow the sheer scope of interpersonal experience. Second, because they are themselves objects for reflective understanding, computers have significance in socio-cognitive development. Third, this technology is implicated in the mediation of novel communication activities within which children may participate. These three themes do not compose an easily-integrated whole: in fact, they have rarely been discussed together. The first two are perhaps the most familiar. Yet I shall argue that the third may prove the most significant and the most provocative in the longer term.

INDIRECT EFFECTS: THE SCOPE OF INTERPERSONAL EXPERIENCE

The concept of "indirect" effects is borrowed from a distinction common within the literature of television research (e.g., Maccoby, 1964; Robinson, 1977). The point is merely that, by virtue of their demand on attention, computers (like television viewing) will displace other activities. There is some particular concern that they may displace activities with a significant interpersonal dimension; experiences that would otherwise be more available to the socially developing individual. The possibility that computer engagement may encourage in young people a certain reclusiveness has been raised by numerous commentators (e.g., Boden, 1977; Bontinck, 1986; Simons, 1985).

There appear to be no large scale reports on recreational uses of computers that reveal just which other activities they can displace.

However, whatever future research might show, there is already a popular concern that using computers provokes more than simply a benign reordering of leisure time priorities. This concern arises from certain distinctive characteristics of the activity: properties that could be especially threatening to the social texture of experience.

There are three relevant observations about computers that provide popular starting points from which to articulate this concern. The particular arguments emerging from each of these perspectives will be considered in the remainder of this section. The three observations are as follows: First, the circumstances associated with computer use appear to be inherently solitary in nature. Second, there is often an apparently obsessive character to engagement with this technology. Third, the technology furnishes a mediated form of communication, the potency of which may serve to cultivate the formation of private worlds. These three properties combine to suggest a worrying prognosis for young people attracted by computers: distraction from, and even distortion of, the social dimension of early experience. This prognosis does deserve attention.

These observations regarding the indirect effects of computer use will be discussed here under three headings. In looking at each theme it will emerge that at successive turns the argument becomes more sophisticated. In terms of the distinction between direct and indirect effects mentioned earlier, we are gradually led away from "mere" issues of time allocation towards questioning whether the *content* of computer-based activity is in real tension with a fulfilling social development.

To anticipate the direction of this argument: experience with new technology is first identified as experience that tends to be solitary—thus, computer interaction is, by its very nature, somewhat isolating. However, the capacity for becoming particularly absorbed in the activity leads to the idea that it can furnish a satisfactory *substitute* for social experience. Finally, the possibility is encountered that real engagement in this activity leads to shifts in how an individual thinks about the social plane of experience. In short: themes of distraction, preoccupation, and then distortion.

Computer Activity as an Isolating Experience

Our first question regarding the impact of computers concerns how far this technology offers a class of activities that tend to get done *alone*. There are two levels at which computer activities might be isolating in this sense. The first level concerns the kind of behavioural interaction that the very design of this technology naturally affords: the structure of moment-to-moment interactions with a computer may simply not be compatible with shared engagement. The second level concerns the purposes for which the technology is used: does it tend to encourage activities in which the goals of one individual can become coordinated with those of others?

In respect of the first "low" level consideration: the very design of computers invites from the user a particularly narrow focus of attention: events are located on a small screen. Moreover, the medium has equally localised demands defining the point of user input: a small keyboard or pointing device. All of this naturally suggests a posture comparable to that associated with watching television. However, the similarity is limited in one respect. In terms of our present interest in "indirect" effects, watching the television fares well as something that can easily be a shared experience; computer use may be different in that the very structure of the activity seems to exclude socially-organised involvement.

While the interface to this technology may well tend to encourage solitary engagement; what users *do* with it could still have a significant social dimension. Of course, this idea requires us to clarify just what sorts of things computers are used for at different points within development. The picture is probably changing very fast and, unfortunately, it is not being very carefully monitored by social scientists. There are two areas that have each received some research attention: computers used in education and computers used for game playing.

The extensive penetration of this technology into classrooms has been well documented (e.g., Jones & Scrimshaw, 1988). The question here must be whether its educational applications tend to foster the solitary or the social learner. This is an important issue: not only because cognitive development is argued to be grounded in social exchange (cf. Rogoff, 1990; Schaffer, this volume) but also because classroom life is an important general source of interpersonal experience during the early years (Kutnick, 1989).

At first sight, the dominant paradigms for practice in educational computing tends to suggest that it is the solitary condition of learning that is ascendant. Many applications of computers within education can be aligned with one of two metaphors: a conception of computer-as-teacher and a conception of computer-as-pupil. They both tend to marginalise the social dimension of learning.

In the former case the technology is programmed with some sort of intelligence that simulates tuition. The instructional flavour of "intelligent tutoring systems" (or, less glamorous, drill and skill programmes) is didactic. One purpose is to displace the communicative role of the teacher (or, more positively, to free them for other activities). This is not, then, a tradition whereby contact with computers supports strongly social experience in learning. In the case of computer-as-pupil, the learner/computer relationship is reversed: the learner's challenge is to exercise creatively some body of principled understanding such that they can thereby make the technology *do* something. The pedagogic model is more discovery-oriented and, for many practitioners, more appealing. However, the interactions at the core of this approach are between learner and technology: there is no basic accommodation of a socially-organised experience. This is not to say that, in actual practice, development of this resource could not be socially supported. The point is merely that for educational computing to be a positive force within the social experience of learning, then, in the present climate, there has to be a will to create those conditions of support.

This summary might suggest a rather gloomy relationship between technology and social development; at least as it is realised in the dominant context of schooling. Indeed, the future may well be gloomy if we ignore patterns of practice within educational computing as they are currently evolving: for there are many signs that information technology in schools need not be decoupled from the social quality of learning. Whereas I hope that the remarks in this section serve to identify an issue of concern, in a later section I shall return to the setting of education in order to make more optimistic points: namely, that the technology can be fashioned to play a quite liberating role in communicative processes within education—if we choose that route. Now we turn to other settings in which an isolating experience might be cultivated.

The falling cost of microcomputers has found them a place in domestic and leisure environments as well as in classrooms. The start of this consumer interest may be traced to around 1980. In Britain, for example, this was the year in which the first mass produced microcomputer appeared (the Sinclair ZX80). It is hard to be sure how far computer ownership extends into children's home lives 10 years on: one recent survey in Britain suggests that around 45% of secondary age children have access to a computer at home and that 80% of them will claim to make some use of it (Shotton, 1989). What they actually do is less certain. Computer-based games are the most familiar commercial product and studies suggest that these may occupy at least half of the time young computer owners spend with the technology at home (e.g., Braun, Goupil, Giroux, & Chagnon, 1986). This phenomenon is less well-studied than the case of educational applications but it is possible to make some tentative remarks about this activity in terms of its socially "isolating" influence.

Research attention has been concentrated on the more broadly defined "video game" culture. In particular, ethnographers have found the arcade environment an accessible setting for field work. Considering just indirect effects (rather than, say, the influence of themes portrayed in these games), there is one body of opinion that argues the game arcade culture is less impoverished socially than appears at first sight.

Brooks (1983) spent two years talking to over 900 adolescents frequent-
ing the arcades of northern California. He noted that for more than 50% of
them, less than half of their time in these environments was actualy spent
playing the games. Rather than being isolating experiences, the games
could furnish contexts for animated discussions both during and after the
activity. Egli and Meyers (1984) present a similar picture from an interview
study of 150 Californian teenagers. Isolated and compulsive players, they
conclude, are in the minority.

On the other hand, Braun et al. (1986) present a less positive picture
from questioning over 800 16-year-olds in Canada. A school-based survey
revealed that where a computer was being used at home, about half of this
time was spent alone. They also report a survey of 940 types of arcade
game: they found that none of them could be defined as intrinsically
cooperative in the sense of allowing progress in the game to arise from
helping one's partner. Most of the games invited merely a sequential
pattern of competition. Finally, they noted that half of the youngsters they
observed in arcades were playing alone.

Impact within the home is less easily assessed. One modest study of
20 families does suggest that computer game playing can be a better
disciplined and more socially-based experience than popular conceptions
allow. Mitchell (1983) reports that across the four month period following
a purchase, none of the families had developed reservations about the
activity. Involvement dropped off somewhat across this period but there
was a strong pattern of that involvement being organised as a shared or
joint experience.

Evidently, the picture emerging from these limited observations of
recreational computing is still unclear. Perhaps the significant point is that
the activity need not be intrinsically asocial. These observations, along
with the still relatively modest market for game products, suggest the game
playing possibility of computers does not displace early social experiences
much more than does, say, train spotting, skateboarding, or other absorbing
distractions. Whether computer games are less wholesome or improving
than these comparable activities can be debated elsewhere: at least one
distinguished commentator has made an interesting case for cognitive
benefits associated with mastering electronic game technology (Greenfield,
1987).

Games do remain just one variety of computer experience, albeit a
significant one. However, there is further research literature that addresses
a different preoccupation: the enthusiasm for programming computers. I
have chosen to take this up in the following section as the presentation of
this issue has more normally been organised around the particular theme of
computers as "compulsive" experiences.

The Compulsive Quality of Computer Use

Isolating users is one distinctive feature of the medium; another is the obsessive nature of the involvement it encourages. If one well-known fact about computers is that they induce phobic responses among many potential users (Meier, 1985), another equally well-known fact is that, for others, the technology can be totally engaging. This is sometimes raised as a worry in respect of game playing, although the observations made earlier suggest that games may still be a localised and modest problem. The other domain of usage that has been described as "compulsive" is computer programming itself—although there is a vague arena of activities that are neither games nor (strictly) programming but which also elicit compulsive involvement. Taken as a whole, such activities have been somewhat concealed from research observers. However, even if they also prove to be a minority interest at the present time, there is cause to evaluate the situation now on the assumption that this is an area that may increasingly capture youthful interest.

One basis for popular concern regarding obsessive (and socially isolating) programming is traceable to various reports of precocious programmers who were conspicuous during the 1970s in east coast American schools and colleges. Notable and most accessible of these observations were Tracey Kidder's narrative of life within a software development team (Kidder, 1981); Stephen Levy's participant observation of "hackers" (Levy, 1984), and Sherry Turkle's theoreticaly sophisticated account of children and adolescents encountering computer culture in 1970s Boston (Turkle, 1980; 1982; 1984). Arguably at the fountain head of this literature was a critical commentary on computer culture by Weizenbaum (1976), himself a distinguished computer scientist. Weizenbaum conjured up (from his own teaching experience) a compelling image of "hollow-eyed youths" absorbed in computer programming to the exclusion of most other human activity. The detailed narratives of the other observers mentioned earlier served, for many, to establish the reality of this vivid image.

How extensive is the hacker and hobbyist community today and how far does its membership exemplify an obsessive level of involvement? More particularly, in what ways might this engagement serve to distort individual social development in ways that some commentators seem to fear?

A useful window into this culture is provided by Shotton's (1989) study of 75 dedicated home enthusiasts in Britain, although these were all adults. She compared them with two control groups: one of matched individuals not owning a computer and a second of computer owners, but not fervent users. Study of the so-called "dependent" adults revealed that they were different from their peers in ways that implied less satisfactory relationships with other people. However, Shotton is at pains to stress that such differences reached back into early childhood. In particular, the dependent group reported poor social contacts during early schooling and distant relationships within families, especially with fathers. It is therefore argued that these are individuals who were experiencing social problems in childhood prior to engagements with technology. Indeed, there is some implication that an enthusiasm for concrete "activity" arose from discoveries that their visible successes in this domain could be effective in eliciting parental interest or approval.

Shotton's account is a sympathetic one: she sees these dependent individuals as simply finding a kind of "release" from imperfect social experiences, a release that is no different from the less high profile solutions that others might find in collecting coins, watching birds, or whatever. Their common pattern of social unease predates the emergence of a computer "solution".

Students of social development may feel uneasy with this analysis. The study is certainly a valuable resource and does help fix a slippery topic. However, it is hard to escape a feeling that engagement with computers is not like other hobbies that people find to displace disappointing social experiences. Determining more about the actual status of this particular "solution" is important. We doubtless feel that a network of supportive interpersonal relations is an important resource for children to cultivate. In which case, we must be concerned with the impact of this, or any other, distraction: is it a benign preoccupation or does it impede more constructive solutions to unfulfilled social experience during development? Shotton's subjects may have found an activity that is especially potent in displacing social experience.

Perhaps the feature of computing that does distinguish it from other hobbyist distractions is sheer interactivity. It is this that can make it a compelling substitute for social engagement. In other words, the experience offers a responsiveness that may mimic something of what people are seeking within interpersonal encounters. Far from direct commerce with our material and social world, we are offered *mediated* experience of an advanced kind. The seductive nature of this experience is taken up in the next section.

Computer Activity and the Immediacy of Experience

This worry about mediated experience is one species of a fundamental concern that has a long history: it was expressed by Rousseau in his plea for innocence and, perhaps, by Plato in his sceptical expectations for the impact of literacy upon human understanding. Access to computer interactions (like access to literate forms) involves a loss in the immediacy of experience. Acting within the representational systems of computer "worlds" entails a highly mediated form of exchange. Of course, the evolution of mediated interactions with the physical and social world is at the heart of our cultural history. Thus, this is not the first occasion for contemplating the threat (in this case from computers) of an invitation to "retreat" into potentially private worlds.

Writing at a time of manifest development work on "virtual realities", it would be complacent to dismiss the significance for social experience of increasingly mediated encounters. However, our grasp of the prospects arising out of this climate remain informed only by speculative extrapolation. A lively example is found in one psychologist's elaboration of the likelihood of an "intimate machine" (Frude, 1983). Here we are offered the possibility of individuals entering into relationships with technology that have all the hallmarks of that intimacy we associate with human social life. This will not be so far-fetched to those who are familiar with Weizenbaum's (1976) account of the strikingly intimate reactions of people using the programme ELIZA—a simulation of the most modest of psychotherapeutic conversations.

The point concerning the strongly mediated nature of computer encounters is raised here partly to highlight the potency of this technology for substituting social experience. However, our concern might go beyond its status as a potent alternative to social relations; the character of experience with this "displacement" activity may be such as to exaggerate basic difficulties of social integration.

The point would be that contact with information technology may cultivate a distinctive style of thinking about other people and our relations with them. For example, Olson has championed the view that contact with the written word has strongly influenced the general way we reason and problem solve (e.g., Olson, 1986). He has also extrapolated this argument to accomodate the impacts of learning how to control information technology (Olson, 1985). Briefly, he suggests that the precision of expression demanded by computers cultivates an attitude to human communication that gives priority to the "very words" and their literal meanings. The significance of this claim for social development would lie in the possibility of a breakdown of social skill among those intensively involved with controlling computers. The examples in Kidder (1981) and Shotton (1989)—many of them furnished by frustrated wives and family—suggest that there can be an insensitivity to the nuances of communication that *might* arise from over-exposure to the formalisms of programming.

There is another manner in which it is suggested that the very character of our social behaviour may be influenced via such cognitive impacts. Our understandings of how computer technology works and our expectations of it may spill over to influence our implicit theory of how other people "work". Numerous commentators have voiced this concern that over-exposure to computer interaction may lead enthusiasts to a confusion in their thinking about people on the one hand and technology on the other (e.g., Boden, 1981; Brod, 1984; Papert, 1980; Turkle, 1984). These worries, if justified, are particularly urgent problems for social development research. Their force concerns not simply children encountering a "distraction" from social experience or even a "numbing" of social experience; in this case we are contemplating emerging changes in our very models of the psychological nature of other people. I shall take up this issue in the next section, which is concerned with computers as objects of reflection in this sense.

COMPUTERS AS OBJECTS OF THOUGHT

It is well known that people are anthropomorphic in their encounters with computers (e.g., Sheibe & Erwin, 1979). Although this is a feature of our interaction with many other mechanisms, the richness of the anthropo-morphic vocabulary in this case suggests a more significant overlap between our understanding of human activity and our understanding of the activity of a non-human artefact.

Turkle's research (e.g., Turkle, 1984) aroused an early interest in the idea that young children may be especially curious about the relevance of psychological language to computer functions. In fact, she distinguishes three stages in the development of early interest in this technology: a preschool and early school year period where experience with technology stimulates metaphysical questioning; a period following this where mastery is the issue and, finally, during adolescence a period when attention is focused on questions concerning personal identity and its relation to technology. It is claims regarding the first and the third period that are of most relevance to our interest in social development.

Turkle believes that computers have a peculiar status for young children: they are evocative objects, objects that invite reflection. In a sense, they bring philosophy into everyday life by revealing a mysterious ambiguity in the distinction between physical and psychological phenomena. So Turkle is able to describe children grappling with such questions as whether computers "think", or dealing with the curiosity of witnessing recursion—computers "in a loop". She concludes that young children do master well enough the ambiguity of psychological status and that it tends to be by reference to the issue of whether emotional characteristics are manifest. However, the point is not simply whether or not the problem gets resolved but what the impact of the reflection has been. Turkle suggests that, if emotional criteria are the key to resolving the ambiguities, then perhaps we should be wary of children developing notions whereby thinking and feeling are too easily dichotomised, such that a rather shallow and sentimental perspective on "feelings" might develop. The force of this account is that contact with new technology is a formative experience for children who are coming to terms with psychological language. The account certainly complements other claims that young children can—and do—reflect on such metaphysical problems (Matthews, 1980). Moreover, if children's thinking about people is being influenced in this manner, this influence is important to understand: for there is a modern (cognitive) movement within the study of social development that has highlighted the significance of children's implicit theories of mind (e.g., Astington, Harris, & Olson, 1989). This movement reminds us that social experience is a source of cognitive reflection during development. Thus, children's contact with it should be examined with proper attention to the influence of developing *understandings* about that domain.

Unfortunately, apart from Turkle's reports, there is little to indicate just how far children's social understandings are being coloured by their contacts with new technology. The accounts of Turkle's conversations with young people are vivid and the theoretical framework is a stimulating one, but they are almost all we have to base a judgement on. However, there is one recent study that does offer some support for Turkle's perspective—as well as suggesting some caution.

Hughes, Brackenridge and Macleod (1987) report findings from talking to 100 7- and 10-year-old children regarding their ideas about computers. One finding that is worth mentioning (because it often arises in computer survey literature) was a widespread enthusiasm for this technology among their sample. More relevant to an assessment of Turkle's work is their observation that children were inclined to attribute animistic qualities to computers. These children were questioned twice (in 1983 and 1985), between which times their classroom contact with the technology was greatly extended. It is therefore interesting to note that the children's inclination to talk animistically increased between the times of the two interviews. It seems that exposure to the technology may have resulted in them becoming more easy with such animistic ideas and more interested in puzzling over them. On the other hand, the authors inject a note of caution by admitting to a feeling that it may have been the act of questioning that was important in provoking such puzzlement, rather than there being a strong spontaneous curiosity regarding the material and psychological. This stands as a real possibility running through much of the work on this topic, grounded as it is in conversational encounters.

Taken together, these accounts suggest that children can and do reflect upon psychological terms as they relate to the domain of computing. It is also likely that the extension of new technology into their lives (especially within school) will serve to stimulate their thinking further. Where that thinking might lead them remains unclear.

One view is that tending to ascribe psychological states to mechanisms will provoke significant restructuring in children's developing theories of mind and psychological states. Interacting with this technology may increasingly invite thinking about the computer in terms of its intentions, moods, whimsy, friendliness and so on. In which case, the overlap in children's vocabulary for characterising interactions in the two cases may blur their appreciation of some differences between minds and machines. This in turn may influence the sensitivity with which they manage social interaction. But this prediction is not self-evident. The same observations can lead others to anticipate quite the opposite trend: Olson (1985) suggests that the demands of computers for precision of meaning (and their ignorance of nuance) will highlight for children the very difference between these mechanisms and human nature.

We must conclude that these encounters with new technology are certainly potent in respect of themes within socio-cognitive development. How their impact will be felt remains controversial. Sheer exposure is certainly one factor that seems implicated in determining this impact. But another factor may be the uses to which technology comes to be put by children. Many of Turkle's children (and most of her adolescent respondents) were caught up in the specialist interest of computer programming. Perhaps the experience of controlling the technology at this level makes users particularly prone to evolving ontologies with a mechanistic flavour. If so, we should note that it may not be *programming* computers that children are now drawn to as the technology becomes increasingly accessible. Any prognosis for the impact of computer experience on children's social thinking may need to recognise changes in what they are doing with the technology. I will conclude this section with a general observation about such changes. This will lead conveniently into the last of the three themes around which the research literature has been organised.

One direction of development for new technology has been towards increasingly sophisticated interfaces between computers and their users. There are some observers (e.g., Boden, 1981) who fear that extending the accessibility of computer technology in this way is merely a greater threat to healthy social development—in terms of its potential for fostering yet more social recluses. However, recent advances such as direct manipulation interfaces have not simply seduced a larger constituency of users, they have altered the profile of what computers get used *for*. This new range of applications may be less provocative in leading youthful users to decouple from social life in the way that has previously been discussed.

Thus, today, young children may expect to use computers for such disparate activities as drawing, design, publishing, and making music.

Moreover, sophisticated interfaces may cause the "feel" of exercising these tool-like functions to be very different within each example: this is certainly not the focused (and often self-fulfilling) world of programming captured in the accounts of Turkle and others.

These technical developments provoke interest in the quality of experience that arises during interactions with computers; they suggest a model of computing that conjures up the metaphor of "convivial tools" rather than that of singular computational activities (cf. Norman, 1986). Perhaps as a consequence of this we should feel uneasy with talk about "the" computer (and its effects). This is partly because versatile interfaces make using a computer a less circumscribed experience. But another reason arises from a further technical trend: towards increasing connectivity. Networking can also make talk of "the" computer seem inappropriate. Indeed, one pillar of computer industry takes as its slogan the notion that "the network *is* the computer".

What is implied is a need to respect the separate activities into which computers enter: then to enquire how the technology is mediating a user's interaction with the world in each instance. The example of networking and the activities mediated in that case is a particularly powerful one for the present argument. It illustrates a dimension of new technology that has interesting social developmental significance. This topic will be briefly reviewed next, in the last of these three sections that describe research orientations to the present topic.

COMPUTERS FOR COMMUNICATION

There are two distinct senses in which children's encounters with computers can have a communicative dimension (Crook, 1987). In the first, the communication arises in face-to-face discourse that is organised *around* computers. In the second, the communication occurs across boundaries of geographical and temporal separations and is organised *through* computers.

Children Communicating Around Technology

In my earlier remarks, I suggested that dominant theoretical perspectives guiding the use of computers for learning tended to marginalise the social quality of educational experience. However, such perspectives informing the design of curriculum materials may not always be respected in actual classroom practice.

The pattern for actually using computers in schools tends to be a social one: pupils are organised into small groups. Often the justification for this is quite straightforward: too many pupils seeking too few computers. However, whether by design or whether by accident of under-resourcing, many teachers have discovered the potency of computer-based work for stimulating socially-organised problem solving. Certainly in the primary education sector in Britain, it is unusual to see a classroom computer being used by a solitary child.

As would be hoped, the educational and psychological research community recognised these trends and there have been some studies of social interactions supported by these arrangements for learning (e.g., Crook, 1987; Eraut & Hoyles, 1989; Hawkins, Sheingold, Gearhart, & Berger, 1982; Light & Blaye, 1989; Trowbridge, 1987). The pattern of findings gives cause for optimism: work organised in this way is frequently found to be stimulating for the participants and, in some cases, is associated with more significant gains in understanding.

Thus, computers facilitate collaborative work and such collaborative work is effective. So far, the literature takes us only to this point. What is required (and this point will be expanded towards the end of this paper) is an analysis that gives more detailed consideration to the actual patterns of social interaction that are supported by working at this particular medium. An example of a research tradition that does explore social *processes* underlying cognitive change (while not focusing on computer-based work) is the work of Doise and his colleagues (e.g., Doise & Mugny, 1984). For these authors, the demands of peer conflict and its negotiation are emphasised. For others, concepts of "co-construction" may prove more compelling (e.g., Forman & Cazden, 1985). Whatever the theoretical preference, there is a real need for researchers to study the setting of computer-based learning with more attention to the processes of social interaction that it supports.

What is the likely significance of these classroom computer arrangements for social development as it is broadly understood? For most of us, schooling is the forum in which we discover some perspective on the nature of intellectual endeavour itself. Developing in children a model of problem solving that foregrounds processes of social coordination would represent a fairly radical departure from the prevailing ethos of formal education. The deployment of technology to support such experiences is a real possibility—one that might lead towards a stronger sense of knowledge itself as something that is negotiated within social discourse (Edwards & Mercer, 1987). Such developments might further challenge the increasingly uncomfortable distinction between social and cognitive development as it is made in the research literature of psychology.

However, this is just one route that computer-based education might take. Our earlier taxonomy of educational computing in terms of computer-as-teacher and computer-as-pupil reminds us that there are other, less social, models of the relationship between learning and technology. So far, there are positive evaluations of those practices that deploy the potential of computers for a socially grounded experience of learning. The great opportunity is to examine this circumscribed arena for learning in terms of the social processes that constitute cognitive change. Again, this is an invitation about which more will be said later in this paper.

Children Communicating Through Technology

This is a second sense in which new technology bears upon children's opportunities for communications in education. Even 10 years ago, there was little indication that microcomputers would become so instrumental in supporting communication. Yet in the workplace (Collins, 1986), within research communities (Newell & Sproull, 1982) and, now, in education, the idea of interacting "through" computer networks is commonplace.

Such computer-mediated communication does include a hobbyist community. In fact, Shotton identifies this enthusiasm as one category of her (adult) computer "dependents". A (barely visible) culture of computer bulletin boards and electronic mail is certainly active (Meeks, 1987); however, it shows some difficulty in gaining any more momentum than, say CB radio—a medium with which it shares some characteristics. Perhaps the point is that communication mediated in this way develops most energy when it is directed by some purposeful concern shared among the participants (until recently this concern has invariably been computers themselves). While recreational contexts have created only modest achievements in this respect, educational contexts have provided rich and purposeful environments to explore communication mediated in this way.

There are two levels at which this configuration of the technology exerts an influence on social processes in school: the networking of computers at the level of local premises (the school) and networks that offer exchanges of national and international scope. Curiously, the former, local, level of organisation has created only scarce examples of innovation in early education (Newman, 1988; Crook, in press). By contrast, in further and higher education, local communications networks may be having quite radical impacts on the social organisation of learning (Crook, 1988; Harasim, 1990).

On the other hand the promise arising from accessing larger scale networks has generated more attention. Numerous impressive initiatives of this kind have been documented. To make a simple statement of its potential: this form of communication opens up exchanges between children who are growing and learning in, perhaps, very different cultural contexts (e.g., Levin, Reil, Rowe, & Boruta, 1985). It can also create real audiences for their work and a real possibility of intellectual coordination with peers in the pursuit of joint projects (e.g., Turnbull & Beaver, 1989; Reil, 1989; Reil & Levin, 1990). These initiatives are beginning to furnish intriguing theoretical discussions, stimulated by the problems of sustaining powerful interactions among young participants (e.g., Belyaeva & Cole, 1989).

The idea that children's social development could be enriched by meaningful and intimate contact with peers in other cultures is one straightforward claim for the relevance of this activity to social development. But the key point is, again, to draw attention to how computer-based initiatives of this kind blur the distinction in our thinking between the social versus the cognitive. Here we are describing a technology that is locating knowledge and learning within a context of social experience while locating aspects of social development within a context of reasoning and problem solving.

Like other assessments made here, the link suggested earlier between social development and technology may be real but it may be slow to be exploited. I am inclined to the view that this technology *will* play an increasingly prominent role in many contexts of development—including a role that shapes social experience in significant ways. Whether or not this view prevails, there may still be found within the "case" of computers and social development a broader challenge to reflect on theory and method as it exists within social developmental research. I will take up this possibility in the next section.

A FRAMEWORK FOR CULTURAL ARTEFACTS WITHIN SOCIAL DEVELOPMENT

What impression is created by this overview of computers and their relationship to social development? It seems we have a reasonable map of a territory to be explored. Our own explorations here have already suggested some compelling questions. These include how far computers moderate the scope of early interpersonal experience, and how far contact with this technology influences children's developing understanding of psychological concepts. Yet, there could also be a feeling that after ten years of—albeit modest—research investment, we have only a rather poor grasp of the prospects. In fact, current levels of research interest suggest to some that the scientific community is missing an opportunity similar to the one missed during the early years of television (Chen, 1984).

My own view is that tackling the topic defined by this paper invites a particular theoretical framework and a particular empirical attitude. Unfortunately, this attitude is one that is not often found within the mainstream of social developmental research. The possible form of a productive research agenda will be developed within the remainder of this paper. I shall attempt to create a glimpse of an approach that might enrich our understanding of the present topic and, if it were more widely endorsed, other issues of social development as well.

The theoretical framework that we might do well to appropriate is that associated with *cultural* approaches to psychological development (e.g., Cole, 1990; Laboratory of Comparative Human Cognition, 1983, Stigler, Shweder, & Herdt, 1990). Note that this approach is not to be equated with cross-cultural psychology (although it draws upon insights from such comparative study). Nor does this approach simply refer to studies of social cognition that explore children's reflective understanding of cultural institutions themselves. Cultural psychology offers a more self-contained and integrated theoretical tradition than cross-cultural psychology and its reach extends beyond the concerns of social cognition. For the "cultural" approach, the issue of "mediational means" is central. Cultural psychology confronts the fact that human development occurs in an environment fashioned by the creative activity of very many previous generations. It invites us to pay special attention to this feature of the human condition: to recognise that development takes place in a medium of culture. It, therefore, dwells upon our engagement with the various technologies (and the various social rituals) that have evolved to mediate our interactions with the material environment and with each other.

In claiming a special interest in technological artefacts, this approach evidently sounds relevant to our present concerns. However, cultural psychology is not just "about" cultural artefacts and practices: it is an approach that moves them into the very foreground of any psychological analysis. It proposes that all human action must be understood in terms of its embedding in the *context* of culture. This context is manifest in the structure of the material environment, in the availability of various technologies and in the forms taken by various conventionalised social interactions. The implications of this perspective are radical. In particular, it questions a favoured style of psychological research: one that isolates unitary sources of causal influence whose effects we may then attempt to understand by a partitioning of variance estimates. It questions the (related) strategy of de-contextualising human action in order to derive abstract principles of psychological functioning—"context" within that strategy becoming only a catalogue of independent variables subsequently to be reinstated and probed. What is proposed instead is well captured in Cole's discussion of the suitable analytic unit for a cultural consideration of psychological functioning: "an individual engaged in goal-directed activity under conventionalised constraints" (Cole, 1985, p. 158). In other words, we must orient towards the person-in-a-context as the proper level of analysis.

Cultural psychology is not the only tradition to reflect a "mutualist" (Still & Costall, 1987) commitment not to decouple persons and contexts.

In particular, the importance of context in development is also stressed by ecological approaches (Barker, 1968; Bronfenbrenner, 1979; Oppenheimer, 1989; Valsiner & Benigni, 1986; White & Siegel, 1984) and these have exerted rather more influence than cultural theory within the psychology of *social* development. Sherman and Oppenheimer (1989) illustrate a compatibility between these two traditions in how they can systematise material from social developmental research.

The influence of these perspectives within cognitive psychology is visible in current claims that cognition is best understood as "situated" (e.g., Suchman, 1987) or embedded "in practice" (Lave, 1988; Rogoff & Lave, 1984). Similarly, the cultural approach has been very influential within the psychology of cognitive *development*. Thus, there is now a flourishing body of research viewing cognitive development in terms of children's participation in culturally organised "cognitive practices" (e.g., Heath, 1983; Laboratory of Comparative Human Cognition, 1983; Rogoff, 1990). Yet the study of *social* development—our present concern—does not seem to have been as closely affected by the cultural approach.

This is well enough illustrated by the research reviewed here on children and computers. It is persistently posing questions of the form "what are the effects of …" (…exposure to programming, compulsive game playing, working in groups, etc.). It tends to frame questions of social development in terms of various processes of "facilitation". Where does this lead? Typically it encourages an understanding in terms of structural changes within individual social actors. The currency of much social developmental theorising is "social skill", "motivational structures", "social cognitions" and so on. Even conceptions of "relationships" are liable to be formulated as the abstract psychological attributes of individuals. Our habit is to start research from a point of interest in these social attributes: designing experiments that explore their properties. Here I am suggesting that, instead, we start our inquiry from a position of interest in the contexts within which social experience is constituted.

What would a respect for context imply for the present case of children growing up around computers? In a sense, what is required is an approach that is prepared to put "things" at the *centre* of any analysis. If this strategy is hard to locate within psychological traditions, it might be expected that anthropology would furnish models of research practice of this kind. To some extent it does. Certainly Whiting and Edwards (1988) exemplify an anthropological orientation on social development that respects the issue of setting or context. However, this work does not illustrate any strategy for taking cultural artefacts—things—as focal in this way. Such a specific orientation can be traced within anthropology but it turns out to be more about the rather particular issue of *commodities* and their associated rituals of exchange (e.g., Appadurai, 1988; Douglas & Isherwood, 1978).

Nor does an ecological approach offer us good empirical models of what we are after, although this approach does furnish a useful technical term— the notion of "affordance" and, more recently, the notion of "social affordance" (e.g., Valenti & Good, 1991). This conveniently points us in two directions: to the subject but also to the material world supporting the subject's behaviour. In the case of some artefact, we may ask "what actions does its presence *afford?*". A rather isolated example of posing this question can be found in certain studies of television and social behaviour where the presence of this technology has been conceptualised as a force that constrains or promotes certain patterns of family interaction (e.g. Maccoby, 1951; Rosenblatt & Cunningham, 1976).

Thus, there is a need to acknowledge that social experience is grounded within settings, and organised around artefacts that constrain, support and facilitate the possibilities of social exchange. It would be irresponsible not to give some examples of what this perspective might imply for the particular case of children and computers. I shall conclude by sketching four concrete examples: cases drawn from research with which I am personally involved and that define problems inviting an approach of the kind presented here.

The first example arises if we inquire how classroom computers can re-organise the interactions among pupils and teachers. One issue is captured in the idea that a *reversal of competence* can arise in this situation. That is, we sometimes detect a capacity for energetic and interested young minds to become confident with this technology in advance of their (sometimes) cautious and suspicious teachers. There may be something subversive in this; certainly, in the longer term, it may at least facilitate a different kind of social dynamic between teacher and pupil. What is implied is that we now give some attention to teacher/pupil discourse in classroom settings where new technology is taken as a focal point.

My next two examples are also especially relevant to classroom settings and concern collaborative work around technology. Here the computer is re-organising the interaction among peers. Research concerned with peer exchange around classroom computers has been mentioned earlier in this chapter and it may seem to be illustrative of the context-sensitive approach advocated here. But in some respects it still falls short. Often it seems preoccupied with a different purpose: relating undifferentiated organisational variables to cognitive outcome measures. Or it takes the discourse sustained under group working arrangements as primarily a window into private worlds of cognitive structures—these distractions have been more fully discussed elsewhere (Crook, in press).

In place of this we need accounts of social interaction around computers that clarify how the "thing" itself is entering into the total dynamic. A model drawn from the literature on adult social behaviour might be

Bannon's (1986) analysis of interaction around new technology in the workplace. Thus, my second example for social developmental consideration concerns *parallel collaboration* and is inspired by Bannon's observation of social interaction among individuals working alongside each other on computer-based tasks. Insofar as computer rooms are adopted within educational institutions, we must appreciate that (like libraries) their structure supports (or denies) certain possibilities for social engagement in relation to shared purposes. For example, my own university department includes a computer room where a great deal of loose, parallel, unsupervised collaborative talk about work is supported—not a phenomenon so visible in any other arena that the institution provides. If this setting is widely reproduced within the primary and secondary school system, then we have a challenge to map out and evaluate a novel social pattern in children's developing experience with the activity of learning.

My third example also relates to the context of peer interaction but concerns *keyboard management*: something arising in the more intimate conditions of younger children working together at the same computer. Two features of children's interactions supported in this setting have been striking in my own observations (e.g., Crook, 1987). First, the demands of some educational software seem to impose a rather rigid turn-taking approach among young children working together. Second, the explicitness (correct/incorrect) of feedback from some programmes cultivates conversations about the activity that dwell upon relative competence and achievement. We may be inclined to reflect upon such exchanges in terms of their significance for our interest in cognitive development. But, ultimately these are events whose potency resides in their nature as *social* encounters— and they are encounters that are structured by the mediation of the computer.

The same applies to my final example, which concerns occasions of *guided participation* as they may occur between a child and an adult acting jointly on a task. A setting commonly observed by developmental psychologists has been book reading (e.g., Heath, 1982; Ninio & Bruner, 1978). It is surely not fanciful to anticipate the growth of joint parent/child interactions mediated by computer activities. In which case they are likely to be as rich a forum for examining early social experience as have other more familiar joint cognitive engagements. The challenge here will also be to highlight the manner in which this technology serves to define the shape of the social experience. Again we set off from an awareness of the organising role that a computer might take in a social setting.

CONCLUSIONS

In the early 1980s there was a flurry of psychological interest in young children's use of new technology. Much of that interest related to psychological development within the social domain. Of particular concern was the potential of computers to instil mechanistic models of human nature and their potential for disengaging children from a full social life. Neither of these themes is as anxiously pursued at the start of the 1990s. Across a decade that has been marked by the significant extension of this technology into children's lives, our concerns may have shifted, so that there seems less anxiety that children are appropriating blinkered, mechanistic ontologies. Perhaps, in part, this reflects an underlying awareness that some professional psychologists working in the artificial intelligence tradition have themselves come to doubt the significance of the computational metaphor (e.g., Dreyfus & Dreyfus, 1986). It also reflects a shift in the kind of things that computers are used for—in particular, a shift away from the preoccupying and often self-fulfilling activity of computer programming itself.

A shift in patterns of usage is also implicated in an easing of popular concern regarding the potential of new technology for creating private worlds. What is striking about computers in the hands of young people today is the sheer range of possible functions for which they can be mobilised, although even in the early literature that gave rise to these worries of alienation, there were indications that any unitary syndrome of isolated engagement was a simplification. For example, Levy (1984) highlights pockets of activity within the early hacker communities where computers were deployed to support the various advocacy groups emerging at that time. Such social coordination is one function that persists and it has been discussed earlier; now the technology has become yet more versatile in respect of the shared activity for which it plays a mediational role.

It may be that the research community has recognised this diversification; concluding that what may have seemed a challenging social-developmental topic is now less so. Certainly, levels of empirical inquiry have not kept pace with a growing intrusion of the technology into children's everyday lives. What has been argued in the present paper is that this "intrusion" does merit a new growth in research interest.

In particular, I have suggested that we adopt a cultural perspective in thinking about the present topic. Cultural psychology orients us to the settings in which social experience is constituted. This approach includes implications for the study of social development: thus, I have argued that our research enterprise should concern itself more with how contexts serve to organise social behaviour during development. Empirical work needs to be more inspired by a sensitivity to ways in which cultural artefacts shape the possibilities within social interaction. In respect of a concern for computers in development, progress may wait upon a simple shift in our orientation to the phenomena: we must discover a real curiosity about the character of social encounters that this technology affords.

ACKNOWLEDGEMENTS

I am grateful to Jim Good, David Middleton and Rhona Nicol for their valuable comments during the preparation of this paper.

REFERENCES

Appadurai, A. (1988). *The social life of things*. Cambridge: Cambridge University Press.

Astington, J. W., Harris, P. L., & Olson, D. R. (1988). *Developing theories of mind*. Cambridge: Cambridge University Press.

Bannon, L. J. (1986). Helping users help each other. In D. A. Norman, & S. Draper (Eds.), *User centred system design* (pp. 339–410). Hillsdale, N.J.: Lawrence Erlbaum Associates Inc.

Barker, R. G. (1968). *Ecological psychology: concepts and methods for studying the environments of human behaviour*. Stanford, Cal.: Stanford University Press.

Belyaeva, A., & Cole, M. (1989). Computer-mediated joint activity in the service of human development: An overview. *Quarterly Newsletter of the Laboratory of Comparative Human Cognition, 11*, 45–56.

Boden, M. (1977). *Artificial intelligence and natural man*. Brighton, U.K.: Harvester Press.

Boden, M. (1981). *Minds and mechanisms*. Brighton, U.K.: Harvester Press.

Bontinck, I. (1986). The impact of electronic media on adolescents, their everyday experience, their learning orientations and leisure time activities. *Communications, 12*, 21–30.

Braun, C. M., Goupil, G., Giroux, J., & Chagnon, Y. (1986). Adolescents and microcomputers: Sex differences, proxemics, task and stimulus variables. *Journal of Psychology, 120*, 529–542.

Brod, C. (1984). *Technostress: The human cost of the computer revolution*. Reading, Mass.: Addison-Wesley.

Bronfenbrenner, U. (1979). *The ecology of development*. Cambridge, Mass.: Harvard University Press.

Brooks, B. (1983). A survey of youth between 10 and 18 who frequent video game arcades. In S. Baughman, & P. Clagett (Eds.), *Video games and human development*. Cambridge, Mass.: Gutman Library, Harvard School of Education.

Chen, M. (1984). Computers in the lives of our children: Looking back on a generation of television research. In R. Rice, (Ed.), *The new media*. Beverley Hills: Sage.

Cole, M. (1985). The zone of proximal development: Where culture and cognition create each other. In J. V. Wertsch (Ed.) *Culture, communication and cognition: Vygotskyian perspectives*. Cambridge: Cambridge University Press.

Cole, M. (1990). *Cultural psychology: A once and future discipline*. CHIP 131. Center for human information processing, U.C.S.D., San Diego.

Collins, E. G. (1986). A company without offices. *Harvard Business Review, 1*, 127–136.

Crook, C. K. (1987). A social context for classroom computers. In J. Rutkowska, & C. Crook (Eds.), *Computers cognition and development* (pp. 35–54). Chichester: Wiley.

Crook, C. K. (1988). Electronic media for communications in an undergraduate teaching department. In D. Smith, (Ed.), *New technologies and professional communications in education* (pp. 119–124). London: National Council for Educational Technology.

Crook, C. K. (1991). Computers in the zone of proximal development: Implications for evaluation. *Computers and Education, 17*, 81–92.

Crook, C. K. (in press). Educational practice within computer networks. In C. O'Malley (Ed.) *Computer-supported collaborative learning*. Springer.

Doise, W., & Mugny, G. (1984). *The social development of the intellect*. Oxford: Pergamon Press.

Douglas, M., & Isherwood, B. (1978). *The world of goods*. London: Penguin.

Dreyfus, H. L., & Dreyfus, S. E. (1986). *Minds over machines*. Oxford: Basil Blackwell.

Edwards, D., & Mercer, N. M. (1987). *Common knowledge*. London: Methuen.

Egli, E. A., & Meyers, L. S. (1984). The role of video game playing in adolescent life: Is there reason to be concerned? *Bulletin of the Psychonomic Society*, *22*, 309–312.

Eraut, M., & Hoyles, C. (1989). Groupwork with computers. *Journal of Computer-assisted Learning*, *5*, 12–24.

Forman, E., & Cazden, C. B. (1985). Exploring Vygotskian perspectives in education: The cognitive value of peer interaction. In J. V. Wertsch (Ed.) *Culture, communication and cognition: Vygotskian perspectives*. Cambridge: Cambridge University Press.

Frude, N. (1983). *The intimate machine*. New York: NAL.

Greenfield, P. (1987). Electronic technologies, education and cognitive development. In D. Berger, K. Pezdek, & W. Banks (Eds), *Applications of cognitive psychology: Problem solving, education and computing*. Hillsdale, N.J.: Lawrence Erlbaum Associates Inc.

Harasim, L. (1990). *On line education: Perspectives on a new environment*. New York: Praeger.

Hawkins, J., Sheingold, K., Gearhart, M., & Berger, C. (1982). Microcomputers in schools: Impact on the social life of elementary classrooms. *Journal of Applied Developmental Psychology*, *3*, 361–373.

Heath, S. B. (1982). What no bedtime story means: Narrative skills at home and school. *Language in Society*, *11*, 49–76.

Heath, S. B. (1983). *Ways with words: Language, life and work in communities and classrooms*. Cambridge: Cambridge University Press.

Hughes, M., Brackenbridge, A., & Macleod, H. (1987). Children's ideas about computers. In J. C. Rutkowska, & C. K. Crook (Eds.). *Computers, cognition and development* (pp. 9–34). Chichester, U.K.: Wiley.

Jones, A., & Scrimshaw, P. (1988). *Computers in education 5–13*. Milton Keynes: Open University Press.

Kidder, T. (1981). *The soul of a new machine*. Boston: Little Brown.

Kutnick, P. (1989). *Relationships in the primary school classroom*. London: Chapman.

Laboratory of Comparative Human Cognition. (1983). Culture and cognitive development. In W. Kessen (Ed.), *Handbook of child psychology* (Vol. 1), New York: Wiley.

Lave, J. (1988). *Cognition in practice: Mind, mathematics and culture in everyday life*. Cambridge: Cambridge University Press.

Levin, J. A., Reil, M. M., Rowe, R. D., & Boruta, M. J. (1985). Maktuk meets Jacuzzi: Computer networks and elementary school writers. 8. In S. W. Freedman (Ed.), *The acquisition of written language* (pp. 160–171). Norwood N.J.: Ablex Publishing Corporation.

Levy, S. (1984). *Hackers: Heroes of the computer revolution*. New York: Anchor Press.

Light, P., & Blaye, A. (1989). Computer-based learning: The social dimension. In H. Foot, M. Morgan, & R. Shute (Eds.) *Children helping children*. Chichester, Sussex: Wiley.

Maccoby, E. E. (1951). Television: Its impact on school children. *Public Opinion Quarterly*, *15*, 421–444.

Maccoby, E. E. (1964). The effects of mass media. In M. Hoffman, & L. Hoffman (Eds.), *Review of child development research*. New York: Russell Sage Foundation.

Matthews, G. (1980). *Philosophy and the young child*. Cambridge, Mass.: Harvard University Press.

Meeks, B. (1987). Computers for communication. In J. Rutkowska, & C. Crook (Eds), *Computers, cognition and development* (pp. 55–68). Chichester, U.K.: Wiley.

Meier, S. T. (1985). Computer aversion. *Computers in Human Behaviour*, *1*, 171–179.

Mitchell, E. (1983). The effects of home video games on children and families. In S. Baughman, & P. Clagett (Eds) *Video games and human development*. Cambridge, Mass.: Gutman Library, Harvard School of Education.

Newell, A., & Sproull, R. F. (1982). Computer networks. Prospects for scientists. *Science*, *215*, 843–852.

Newman, D. (1988). Sixth graders and shared data: Designing a LAN environment to support collaborative work. *Proceedings of the Conference on Computer Supported Cooperative Work*. New York: ACM.

Ninio, A., & Bruner, J. S. (1978). The achievements and antecedents of labelling. *Journal of Child Language*, *5*, 1–15.

Norman, D. A. (1986). Cognitive engineering. In D. A. Norman, & S. Draper (Eds), *User centred system design* (pp. 31–62). Hillsdale, N.J.: Lawrence Erlbaum Associates Inc.

Olson, D. R. (1985). Computers as tools of the intellect. *Educational Researcher*, *14*, 5–8.

Olson, D. R. (1986). Intelligence and literacy: The relationships between intelligence and the techniques of representation and communication. In R. Sternberg, (Ed.), *Practical intelligence*. Cambridge: Cambridge University Press.

Oppenheimer, L. (1989). The nature of social action; social competence versus social conformism. In S. H. Schneider, G. Attilli, J. Nadel, & R. P. Wessberg (Eds.), *Social competence in developmental perspective*. Dordrecht, NL: Kluwer.

Papert, S. (1980). *Mindstorms*. Brighton, U.K.: Harvester Press.

Reil, M. M. (1989). Four models of educational telecommunications: Connections to the future. *Education and Computing*, *5*, 261–274.

Reil, M. M., & Levin, J. A. (1990). Building electronic communities: Success and failure in computer networking. *Instructional Science*, *19*, 145–169.

Robinson, J. (1977). *How Americans use time*. New York: Praeger.

Rogoff, B. (1990). *Apprenticeship in thinking: Cognitive development in social context*. New York: Oxford University Press.

Rogoff, B., & Lave, J. (Eds.) (1984). *Everyday cognition*. Cambridge, Mass.: Harvard University Press.

Rosenblatt, P. C., & Cunningham, M. R. (1976). Television watching and family tensions. *Journal of Marriage and the Family*, *38*, 105–111.

Scheibe, K., & Erwin, M. (1979). The computer as altar. *Journal of Social Psychology*, *108*, 103–109.

Sherman, L. W., & Oppenheimer, L. (1989). *Affordances in preschool lesson structures and socially competent task-related behaviours: A Gibsonian ecological re-interpretation*. Paper presented to the Fifth International Conference on Event Perception and Action, Oxford, Ohio.

Shotton, M. (1989). *Computer addiction: A study of computer dependency*. London: Taylor & Francis.

Simons, G. (1985). *Silicon shock: The menace of the computer invasion*. Oxford: Basil Blackwell.

Stigler, J., Shweder, R. A., & Herdt, G. (1990). *Cultural psychology: Essays on comparative human development*. Cambridge: Cambridge University Press.

Still, A., & Costall, A. (1987). Introduction: In place of cognitivism. In A. Still, & A. Costall (Eds.), *Cognitive psychology in question*. Brighton, U.K.: Harvester Press.

Suchman, L. A. (1987). *Plans and situated actions*. Cambridge: Cambridge University Press.

Trowbridge, D. (1987). An investigation of groups working at the computer. In D. Berger, & K. Pezdek (Eds.), *Applications of cognitive psychology*. Hove, U.K.: Lawrence Erlbaum Associates Ltd.

Turkle, S. (1980). Computer as Rorschach: Subjectivity and social responsibility. In B. Sundin, (Ed.), *Is the computer a tool?* Stockholm: Almquist & Wiknell.

Turkle, S. (1982). The subjective computer: A study in the psychology of personal computation. *Social Studies of Science*, *12*, 173–206.

Turkle, S. (1984). *The second self*. New York: Simon & Shuster.

Turnbull, G., & Beaver, K. (1989). *100 schools network project*. Glasgow: Scottish Council for Educational Technology.

Valenti, S. S., & Good, J. M. M. (1991). Social affordances and interaction I: Introduction. *Ecological Psychology*, *3*, 77–98.

Valsiner, J., & Benigni, L. (1986). Naturalistic research and ecological thinking in the study of child development. *Developmental Review*, *6*, 203–223.

Weizenbaum, J. (1976). *Computer power and human reason*. San Francisco: Freeman.

White, S., & Siegel, A. (1984). Cognitive development in time and space. In B. Rogoff, & J. Lave (Eds.), *Everyday cognition*. Cambridge: Cambridge University Press.

Whiting, B. B., & Edwards, C. P. (1988). *Children of different worlds*. Cambridge, Mass.: Harvard University Press.

Author Index

233

238 AUTHOR INDEX

Killin, M., 121, 126
Klinnert, R.D., 21, 28
Knight, R., 139, 147
van Knippenberg, A., 45, 57
Kohlberg, L., 78, 93
Kohn, M.L., 138, 147
Kontos, S., 105, 110, 127
Kramer, T., 152, 170, 195, 201
Kremen, A., 93
Kreppner, K., 138, 146
Kreuzer, T., 89, 96
Kuczynski, L., 139, 147
Kutnick, P., 210, 229

Laboratory of Comparative Human
  Cognition, 223, 224, 229
Lack, D., 14, 28
Ladd, G.W., 179, 184, 186, 189,
  197, 198, 203, 204
LaFreniere, P., 34, 38, 58–59, 185,
  188
LaGaipa, J.J., 178, 182, 201
Lagerspetz, K.M.J., 36, 59
Lampman-Petraitis, C., 68, 93
Landry, S.H., 112, 127
Lapsley, D.K., 66, 78, 79, 93
Laron, Z., 73, 93
Larson, R., 68, 91, 93
Laupa, M., 80, 82, 93
Laursen, B., 80, 82, 93, 95, 175, 176,
  184, 194, 195, 203
Lave, J., 224, 229, 230
Leaper, C., 82, 93
Leckman, J.F., 128–129
Lee, L.C., 191, 203
Lees, P., 54, 59
Lenard, H.G., 16, 29
Lerner, R.M., 63, 93
Levin, J.A., 221, 229, 230
Levine, M., 63, 93
Levinger, A.C., 181, 203
Levinger, G., 181, 182, 203
Levinson, D.J., 41, 59
Levy, S., 213, 226, 229
Lewis, M., 39, 58
Liddell, C., 101, 128
Light, P., 17, 28, 220, 229

Lipsitz, J., 64, 93
Livesley, W.J., 76, 77, 79, 93
Lloyd, B.B., 38, 41, 49, 56, 57,
  59
Lockman, J.L., 109, 127
Loebl, J.H., 76, 95
Lollis, S.P., 180, 192, 204
Longfellow, C., 108, 127
Loriaux, D.L., 94, 97
Lossoff, M., 176
Low, H., 65, 94
Lucas, T., 152, 170
Ludeke, R.J., 186, 203
Lukes, S., 59
Lynch, M.E., 51, 58, 82, 92

Maccoby, E.E., 31–35, 37–39, 41,
  43, 58, 59, 79, 93, 134, 138, 147,
  208, 225, 229
Mackie, D., 120, 126
Macleod,H., 217, 229
Macrae, M., 44, 56
Magnusson, D., 65, 74, 84, 88, 94,
  96
Magzamen, S., 121, 126
Main, M., 19, 28
Maltz, D.N., 36, 59
Mannarino, A.P., 189, 197, 203
Marfo, K., 116, 117, 127
Marks, I., 20, 21, 28
Marlow, L., 82, 92
Marshall, H.R., 179, 203, 204
Marshall, W.A., 71, 94
Martin, C.L., 43, 59
Martin, J.A., 134, 138, 147
Martin, P., 13, 28
Masters, J.C., 185, 204
Matthews, G., 217, 229
Mattsson, A., 65, 94
McAnarney, E.R., 63, 93
McCandless, B.R., 179, 203, 204
McCloskey, L.A., 41, 42, 57
McCluskey-Fawcett, K.A., 82, 95
McConville, K-L., 150, 170
McDonald, L., 116, 127
McDonald, M., 44, 47, 52, 53, 56
McGillicuddy-De Lisi, A.V., 139, 147

Subject Index